Conceptual Change in Childhood

The MIT Press Series in Learning, Development, and Conceptual Change

Lila Gleitman, Susan Carey, Elissa Newport, and Elizabeth Spelke, editors

Names for Things: A Study in Human Learning, by John Macnamara, 1982

Conceptual Change in Childhood, by Susan Carey, 1985

"Gavagai!" or the Future History of the Animal Language Controversy, by David Premack, 1986

Systems That Learn: An Introduction to Learning Theory for Cognitive and Computer Scientists, by Daniel N. Osherson, Scott Weinstein, and Michael Stob, 1986

Conceptual Change in Childhood

Susan Carey

A Bradford Book
The MIT Press
Cambridge, Massachusetts
London, England

This book was set in VIP Times by Village Typographers, Inc., and printed
and bound by Halliday Lithograph, in the United States of America.

Library of Congress Cataloging in Publication Data

Carey, Susan.
　Conceptual change in childhood.

　(MIT Press series in learning, development, and
conceptual change)
　"A Bradford book."
　Bibliography: p.
　Includes index.
　1. Cognition in children.　I.　Title.　II.　Series.
BF723.C5C365　1985　　155.4′13　　85-7720
ISBN 0-262-03110-8

For my parents, William, Mary, and Joan

Contents

Series Foreword   xi

Acknowledgments   xiii

Introduction   1

Research Methods   8

Conclusions   12

Chapter 1

What Is Alive?   15

A Close Look at the Published Data:
Single-Criterion Definitions   20

Experiment 1: A Replication of
Laurendeau and Pinard   23

Experiment 2: Removing the Trap of
Conscious Criterion Building   36

Conclusions   39

Chapter 2

The Human Body   41

People's Insides   42

Bodily Functions: The Digestive
System   43

Bodily Functions: The Circulatory
System   46

Bodily Functions: The Respiratory
System   47

Conclusions: Digestion, Circulation,
Respiration   47

Contents

Bodily Functions: The Nervous
System   48

Summary: Bodily Functions   51

Gender and Gender Constancy   51

Reproduction   54

Death   60

Growth and Personal Identity   65

Conclusions   69

Chapter 3

The Biological Concept *Animal*   72

Experiment 1: Attribution of Animal
Properties   77

Experiment 2: Further Constraints
on a Model   87

Experiment 3: From Properties to
Animals   102

Experiment 4: Similarity Judgments
105

Conclusions   109

Chapter 4

**The Projection of Spleen (Omentum)
111**

Experiment: Patterns of Projection
113

Procedure   114

Results   116

Conclusions   135

Chapter 5

**Projection of Properties of Two
Objects   140**

Experiment 1: Projection of Spleens
(Omenta) from Dogs and Bees   142

Experiment 2: Projection of Golgi
from Animals and Plants   149

Conclusions   160

Contents

Chapter 6

Matters of Ontology   162

Ontologically Basic Categories
162

Animal and Plant Species as Natural
Kinds   171

Chapter 7

Conclusions   181

Summary of Results   181

Restructuring in What Sense?   186

Implications for Child Development
190

Constraints on Induction   194

Conceptual Change   197

Explanations of Development   199

Theory-like Conceptual Structures
200

Appendix   203

Notes   213

References   217

Index   223

Series Foreword

This series in learning, development, and conceptual change will include state-of-the-art reference works, seminal book-length monographs, and texts on the development of concepts and mental structures. It will span learning in all domains of knowledge, from syntax to geometry to the social world, and will be concerned with all phases of development, from infancy through adulthood.

The series intends to engage such fundamental questions as

The nature and limits of learning and maturation: the influence of the environment, of initial structures, and of maturational changes in the nervous system on human development; learnability theory; the problem of induction; domain specific constraints on development.

The nature of conceptual change: conceptual organization and conceptual change in child development, in the acquisition of expertise, and in the history of science.

Lila Gleitman
Susan Carey
Elissa Newport
Elizabeth Spelke

Acknowledgments

I would like to express my debt to Jill and Peter de Villiers. As graduate students in the early 1970s, we collaborated on the study that is reported here as Experiment 1 of chapter 3. It was this study, and many long conversations with Jill and Peter, that started me on the line of thought that has led to this book.

I have had other collaborators along the way. Two students carried out studies that are reported here. One is Carol Smith, now at the University of Massachusetts at Boston. Carol and I were co-PIs on a grant from NSF that supported both her work on transitive inferences in preschool children and the experiment reported in chapter 4. Along with Marianne Wiser, Carol and I have continued to collaborate in investigating conceptual change in childhood. I am grateful for Carol's and Marianne's contributions to my thinking. The other student whose work is presented here is Richard Carter, now at Lesley College. Richard carried out the first study in my laboratory on conceptual combination (chapter 5, Experiment 2).

Many research assistants have also made valuable contributions to this work, especially Jeanne Melamed (chapters 1 and 3), Toby Landes (chapter 4), and Nancy Somers (chapter 5).

This book was begun in 1981 when I was a Sloan Fellow at the Center for Cognitive Studies at the University of California at Berkeley and was completed in 1984 when I was a fellow at the Center for Advanced Studies in the Behavior Sciences at Stanford University, where my fellowship was supported by the Spencer Foundation. The empirical research reported in the book was supported by the National Institute of Education and the National Science Foundation. I gratefully acknowledge the support of the Centers, the Sloan and Spencer Foundations, and the NSF and NIE.

Finally, I would like to thank many colleagues who have generously read and commented on early drafts of this book. The current shape of my work owes most to my husband, Ned Block, who is also my mentor on matters philosophical. Ned, Tom Kuhn, Rochel Gelman, Frank Keil, Ellen Markman, Carol Smith, and Henry Wellman all provided comments that led me to rewrite and rethink parts of this manuscript. My editor, Anne Mark, made sure I got the details right and worked valiantly to help me to improve my prose, for which I thank her.

Introduction

No one can doubt that a major source of the differences between young children and adults is that young children know less. Young children are novices in many domains in which adults are experts. Indeed, children have been dubbed "universal novices" (Brown and De Loache 1978).

Cognitive science has mounted a major research effort toward understanding the novice-expert shift in adults. As the name implies, the study of the novice-expert shift is the study of the change that occurs as a beginner in some domain gains expertise. Many domains have been studied—most extensively, expertise at chess, in the physical sciences (especially mechanics), and in mathematical problem solving (see Chi, Glaser, and Rees 1982 for a review). Most relevant here is work in the second domain.

Chi, Glaser, and Rees describe three principal methods that have been used to characterize the differences between novices and experts in various scientific domains: diagnoses of misconceptions, analyses of perceived similarities among elements in the domain, and information-processing analyses of how problems are solved. I will briefly illustrate the use of each method, starting with the diagnosis of a misconception. Consider the problem in part A of figure 1.1. A coin is tossed; in position (a) it is on the upward part of its trajectory and in position (b) it is on the downward part of its trajectory. The subject's task is to indicate, with arrows, the forces that are acting on the coin at (a) and at (b). Novice physicists (even those who have had a year of college physics in which they have been taught the relevant part of Newtonian mechanics) draw the arrows as in part B of figure 1; experts draw the arrows as in part C (Clement 1982). The novices explain their two arrows at (a) as follows:

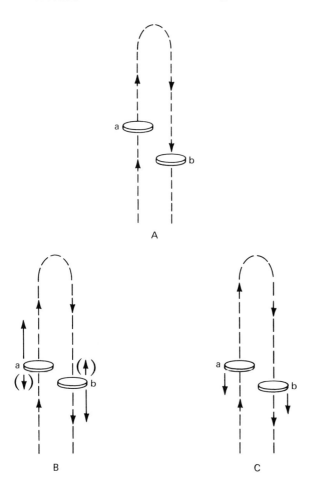

Figure 1.1
Example of problem used to diagnose intuitive mechanics

There are two forces acting on the coin in its upward trajectory—the force imparted when it was thrown up and the force of gravity. The former force is greater in the upward trajectory; that's why the coin is going up. In the downward trajectory the force of gravity is the only force, or else it is the greater of the two, which is why the coin is descending.

To an expert, in contrast, once the coin has been set in motion, the only force affecting it is gravity. Apparently, novices have a misconception about motion, one highly resistant to tuition, something like "no motion without a force causing it." This violates Newton's laws, which recognize a related conception: "no acceleration without a force causing it." By diagnosing a wide variety of misconceptions of this sort, researchers hope to characterize the naive physics that students bring to the task of learning mechanics in the classroom (see, for example, McCloskey 1983, Clement 1982).

Research by Chi and her colleagues can illustrate the use of the second method. Novices and experts were asked to group physics problems according to similarity. Novices grouped problems according to the type of object involved: problems about pulleys in one group, problems about inclined planes in another, and so on. In contrast, experts grouped problems according to their method of solution: problems solvable with Newton's laws of motion in one group, problems solvable with energy equations in another, and so on (Chi, Glaser, and Rees 1982). These two classifications were orthogonal; inclined plane problems, for example, can be of both types. Experts apparently organize their knowledge of physics in terms of abstract schemata not salient to novices. The force of this difference is brought home by studies using the third method. Larkin and her coworkers have shown that when solving mechanics problems, novices use painful means-end analyses, working with equations they hope are relevant to the problem. In contrast, experts apply correct equations in a forward direction, indicating that they have planned the whole solution before they begin (Larkin et al. 1980). The schemata in terms of which experts organize their knowledge of physics enable them to grasp the structure of problems in a way that novices cannot.

The first goal of psychologists working on the novice-expert shift is descriptive, to capture the differences between successive snapshots (the novice's conceptual system, the intermediate's, the expert's). Some students of the shift stress that these differences involve *restructuring* of knowledge as well as accumulation of new facts, new production rules, and so on. Here, "restructuring" refers to two things. First, experts represent different relations among concepts than do novices (as in the change from "no motion without a force" to "no acceleration without a force"). Second, patterns among these new relations motivate the creation of new, abstract concepts and schemata that either are not represented by novices at all or are not very accessible to them (as reflected in the changes in perceived similarity among physics problems and in the changes in the ways of attacking them). As Chi, Glaser, and Rees put it, "What is basic level for the novice is subordinate level for the expert" (for instance, with expertise the concepts that articulate Newton's laws—*force, mass, velocity, acceleration,* etc.—

become basic level and the instantiations of those concepts in particular problems, such as those involving pulleys and inclined planes, become subordinate level).

So far what I have said about the novice-expert shift suggests that the two systems share many concepts. Nodes corresponding to concepts such as *force, energy,* and so on, can be identified in both systems, and the terms for these concepts either are identical or can easily be translated from one system to the other. Only if this is so may we conceive of the novice's misconceptions as being different beliefs from the expert's about the same physical magnitudes, or as the novice's representing different relations from the expert among the same stock of concepts. Only if this is so may we credit novices with understanding when they manage to choose the correct equations, even in their bumbling way, to apply to a given problem. And only if this is so may we think of restructuring primarily as implicating a basic level–subordinate level shift, for this description presupposes that those concepts that are basic level for the novice and subordinate for the expert must be the same in both systems. In other words, the kind of restructuring explicated by Chi, Glaser, and Rees does not include conceptual change, change at the level of the individual concepts that articulate the knowledge of novices and experts.

The study of theory change in the history of science has led to a much more radical view of restructuring of knowledge (Kuhn 1962, Toulmin 1953, Feyerabend 1962). The original formulations of this radical view embraced a kind of meaning holism, in which the meaning of each concept in a theory is determined by its relations with all other concepts in the theory. On this view, any theory change necessarily involves conceptual change. This view had other consequences: that successive theories are incommensurate, cannot disagree about data, and are unfalsifiable. These early formulations have been rejected by most philosophers of science (see Suppe 1974 for extensive discussion), but a strong view of restructuring has survived, one that allows for true conceptual change among core concepts of successive theories (see Kuhn 1984). On the surviving formulation, successive theories differ in three related ways: in the domain of phenomena accounted for, in the nature of explanations deemed acceptable, and even in the individual concepts at the center of each system. Differences of these three types at times have the consequence that some terms in one theory may not even be translatable into the terms of the other (Kuhn 1984). In successive theories of mechanics, each of the core terms, such as *force, velocity, time,* and *mass,* has a fundamentally different meaning in the later compared to the earlier theory.

As an example, consider the concepts *motion* and *velocity* in Aristotelian and Galilean mechanics. For Aristotle, motion included all change over time: movement, growth, decay, and so on. He distinguished two fundamentally different types of motion: natural and violent. His physics accounted for the two in quite different ways. Natural motions included objects falling to the earth, smoke rising, flowers growing, and so on, and were explained in terms of each kind's natural place or state. Violent, or artificial, motions were those caused by an active agent, such as the movement of a person or the heat of a fire, and were explained in terms of entirely different mechanisms. In contrast, Galileo restricted his study to movement through space, saw that in fact there was no distinction to be made between natural and violent motion, and so collapsed the two, bringing both into the domain of a single mechanical theory. Galileo's system had no concept of natural place or natural state. Moreover, Aristotle did not distinguish between average velocity and instantaneous velocity—the key distinction that got Galileo's kinematics off the ground (Kuhn 1977b). These changes at the level of individual concepts are the reason that the core terms of Aristotelian mechanics and Galilean mechanics are not intertranslatable.[1] The changes between Aristotelian and Galilean mechanics did not come easily. One cannot understand the process by which they occurred without considering the changes in the whole theory—in the domain of phenomena to be explained and in the kinds of explanations considered acceptable. All three kinds of change—in domain, concepts, and explanatory structure—came together. Change of one kind cannot be understood without reference to the changes of the other kinds.

I have contrasted two different senses of "restructuring." The first, weaker sense is the one spelled out in Chi, Glaser, and Rees 1982. With expertise, new relations among concepts are represented, and new schemata come into being that allow the solution of new problems and change the solutions to old problems. The second, stronger sense includes not only these kinds of change but also changes in the individual core concepts of the successive systems. The analysis of conceptual change is extremely difficult; I will not attempt to provide criteria for telling whether a particular case of restructuring has involved this type of change. Nonetheless, consideration of clear examples such as the transition from Aristotelian to Galilean mechanics can help us decide other cases. In this transition several differentiations and coalescences occurred, which are both paradigm cases of conceptual change. Further, the ontological commitments of the theories differ. Aristotle was committed to the existence of natural places and natural states, for these played a central explanatory role in his theory. According to Galileo's theory, however, such things did not exist. These changes— differentiations, coalescences, changes in ontological commitments— are understandable only in terms of changes in domains and causal notions between the successive theories. When all of these changes are found, we should be confident that the knowledge reorganization in question is of the stronger kind, involving conceptual change.

Weak restructuring occurs as a player gains expertise in chess. Novices and experts alike share the "individual core concepts" of a chess game: its pieces, moves, rules, and ultimate goal. Moreover, acquiring expertise in chess does not require abandoning a highly developed alternative theory of chess in the way that the transition to Galilean mechanics required abandoning the highly developed alternative theory of Aristotelian mechanics. But despite the lack of conceptual change, there is no doubt that weak restructuring deserves to be called "restructuring." The expert articulates myriad intermediate goals not even known to the novice, and sees the chessboard in terms of configurations of pieces interpretable in terms of these intermediate goals. These differences yield different strategies for playing the game, different capacities for remembering games, and so on (see Chi, Glaser, and Rees 1982 for a review).

Whether a particular case of knowledge restructuring is weak or strong has consequences for empirical research. The study of restructuring in the weak sense focuses on the expert's system, finding what the novice lacks, noting that the novice does not represent particular relations and does not have certain schemata available to organize problem solving, memory, and inductive inference. The study of restructuring in the strong sense focuses both on these issues and on the alternative, but also highly structured, conceptual system of the novice.

The history of science recognizes at least two broad types of theory change. In one, which we may call "true theory change," a well-developed domain of study (e.g., mechanics) undergoes revolution, as in the transition from the impetus theory to Newtonian mechanics or from Newton's theory to Einstein's. In the other, which we may call "theory emergence," a new theoretical domain emerges from a parent domain (or domains), as the new domains of evolutionary biology, logic, psychology, and chemistry emerged in the nineteenth century. Even theory emergence involves true theory change. This is because some of the phenomena that motivate the new domain are already studied in the parent scientific traditions. As in clear cases of true theory change, three developments are intertwined: new domains of phenomena are encountered, new explanatory apparati are developed, and conceptual change sometimes occurs. Insofar as the new domain overlaps with older theories, the changes in explanatory framework and concepts constitute true theory change. That is, the phenomena in the domains that overlap are reconceptualized and are articulated in terms of new concepts.

The discussion of theory change by historians and philosophers of science raises two questions relevant to psychologists. First, does the novice-expert shift among adults involve restructuring in the stronger sense? There are certainly reasons to doubt it. Convincing examples in the history of science occur over years, even centuries, of conscious theory building by mature scientists. Nevertheless, recent work by students of the novice-expert shift begins to suggest that such restructuring does occur as individuals learn a new science. Larkin (1983) has proposed that novices think of physical causality in terms of time-based propagation of physical effects. In similar contexts experts think in terms of explanation based on state equations. Wiser and Carey (1983) documented a similar change in the historical development of thermal theories in the century between Galileo and Black. Clement (1982) and McCloskey and his colleagues (McCloskey 1983) have claimed that beginners at mechanics bring an intuitive theory of mechanical phenomena to their study of mechanics, and that this theory is identical to the pre-Galilean impetus theory of the Middle Ages. The misconception in figure 1 is one source of evidence for this claim; the novice's upward force is the impetus imparted to the coin when it is tossed. The reason that students' misconceptions are so resistant to tuition is that learning mechanics requires a theory change of the sort achieved by Galileo— indeed, an even more radical change than his, all the way from impetus theory to Newtonian mechanics. I am not endorsing McCloskey's claims here; in my view the data supporting them are not yet conclusive. Rather, I am urging that we must establish what kinds of data are necessary to evaluate such claims, for if they are true, they have profound consequences for the study of learning and for science education.

The second question for psychologists concerns knowledge acquisition during childhood. Does restructuring in either sense occur during child development? Even if it turns out that we must reconceptualize knowledge reorganization within adult learners undergoing the novice-expert shift, restructuring in the stronger sense may not characterize children's conceptual development at all. Must children's concepts of the physical, biological, and social world be viewed in terms of theory-like structures, requiring changes in concepts to be analyzed in terms of changes in theories—that is, in terms of changes in explanatory principles and changes in domains of phenomena accounted for?

This monograph is a case study of the acquisition of biological knowledge during the years 4 to 10. I argue that this period of childhood witnesses a restructuring of the child's knowledge of animals and living things, a restructuring at least of the weaker sort and very likely of the stronger sort that must be seen as full-fledged theory change, involving conceptual reorganization. The restructuring can be thought of as the emergence of a new theory (an intuitive biology) from its parent theory (an intuitive theory of animal behavior).

Research Methods

My claims about the restructuring of the child's knowledge about animals and living things are based on many different phenomena, the results from five quite different research methods. In this section I describe the five methods I have employed in this case study of knowledge reorganization in childhood.

Inductive Projection

We constantly make inferences that are not deductively valid. Taught that we humans have membranes called omenta that hold our digestive organs in place, most adults infer that all mammals have omenta. Some infer that all vertebrates do so, and others infer even more widely. Adults do not think that dolls have omenta, even though dolls appear more similar to people in many respects than do, for example, dolphins. One role of our theories (naive or otherwise) is to constrain inductive projections of this sort. Our biological theory tells us that dolphins are similar to people in the relevant respects, whereas dolls are not. Because this is so, patterns of inductive projection provide evidence about the theories held by the person making the inferences. This fact is exploited in the studies reported in chapters 4 and 5.

Four-year-olds, no less than adults, make sensible projections of newly taught biological properties. For example, when given some vague information about a previously unknown internal organ (such as that a spleen is a round, green thing found inside of people), subjects at various ages between 4 years and adulthood projected the new organ to other animals, with decreasing likelihood from mammals, through birds, insects, and worms. At all ages they attributed spleens significantly less often (usually not at all) to inanimate objects and plants. In spite of these constancies throughout development, the induction technique yielded the best single piece of evidence that the 4-year-old's knowledge is organized differently from the adult's. The relevant data came from other conditions in the same study, in which subjects were taught that dogs, or bees, have some internal organ. In these cases, 4- and 6-year-olds had markedly different patterns of projection from adults. Analysis of the developmental differences in patterns of projection is presented in chapter 4.

The patterns of induction are assessed in several ways with respect to the roles played by the concepts *animal* and *living thing* in constraining projection. First, the similarity metric underlying projection is analyzed to see whether it respects the animal-nonanimal boundary (or living thing–nonliving thing boundary). To test the limits of this respect for the animal-nonanimal boundary, objects superficially very much like people, such as a mechanical monkey, were sometimes included among those probed for attribution of the new properties. Second, subjects were sometimes taught that two animals (e.g., dogs and bees) have a given property, to see whether they would conclude that all animals must have it. Similarly, they were sometimes taught that dogs and flowers both have a given property, to see whether they would infer that all living things must have it. Finally, the role of the property projected was studied. For example, how does the fact that an internal organ is being projected change the similarity metric among objects, relative to the metric when other properties are being projected or when the subject is merely asked to assess the similarity between pairs of objects? All of these variations of the basic induction paradigm provide insight into the content and structure of the subject's knowledge of animals and living things. The results and their interpretation are given in chapters 4 and 5.

Patterns of Attribution of Biological Properties
Processes such as growth, reproduction, death, digestion, and respiration play a central role in the adult's intuitive biological theory. In the research described here, children's knowledge of internal organs and of bodily processes was probed in two different ways. First, as described in chapter 3, several studies were designed and carried out to discover how children generate answers to questions such as "Does an x breathe?" Children were asked what things in the world eat, breathe, sleep, think, have babies, have hearts, have bones, etc. In chapter 3 the patterns of attribution are analyzed for what they directly reveal about children's knowledge of biology. Four-year-olds, and to a lesser extent 7-year-olds, differ from 10-year-olds and adults in various ways that reveal the extreme poverty of the young child's knowledge of biological processes. The detailed discussion of the patterns of attribution in chapter 3 also helps in describing the information-processing model of how young children generate their judgments. It seems that 4-year-olds answer the question "Does an x breathe?" by recalling that people breathe and then projecting breathing to other objects according to their similarity to people. So too for the other properties probed. A different model accounts for how 10-year-olds and adults answer such questions. These information-processing differences in turn reflect differences in the organization of knowledge. This argument is developed in chapters 3 and 4.

The Piagetian Clinical Interview
The second method for probing the child's knowledge of bodily processes is the clinical interview. There is voluminous literature on the child's concept of death, and a smaller amount on growth, gender, the contents of the body (including the brain), digestion, and other biological processes. All of these studies tell the same story: there is a marked change between the ages of 4 and 10, such that all of these concepts have become *biological* by age 10, whereas at age 4 they are not. This story is developed in chapter 2.

A core concept in a biological theory is *living thing*. Piaget (1929) developed a clinical interview for probing developmental changes in the meaning of the word "alive." In the Piagetian interview, children are asked what the word means and then whether each of a series of objects is, or is not, alive. Each judgment is justified. The results of such interviews are well known to developmental psychologists: the young child is animistic. Various inanimate objects, such as the sun, the moon, cars, fires, stoves, clouds, rivers, the wind, televisions, rocks rolling down hills, etc., have been judged alive by young children in the throes of childhood animism (Piaget 1929, Laurendeau and Pinard 1962).

Piaget's characterization of the developmental stages in the meaning of the word "alive" presupposes the classical Empiricist view of meaning. Each stage is described in terms of the child's current criterion for life, such as movement or autonomous movement. The criterion of each stage provides necessary and sufficient conditions for being alive. In chapter 1 I reanalyze Laurendeau and Pinard's data from the clinical interview, as well as data of my own from a slightly modified version of the Laurendeau and Pinard protocol. I show that although the phenomenon of childhood animism is both robust and nonartifactual, the data do not actually support Piaget's (and Laurendeau and Pinard's) characterization of the stages. Instead, it appears that the youngest children have not mapped the distinction between "alive" and "not alive" onto the biological distinction between living and nonliving entities at all. However, some children who provide animistic judgments are indeed interpreting the questions as the experimenter intends, and they bring all of their biological knowledge to bear on their judgments. In these cases, animistic responses are partly the result of inadequate biological knowledge.

By age 10, childhood animism has virtually disappeared, and inanimate objects are no longer judged alive. One goal of chapters 1 and 2 is to place this developmental phenomenon in the context of the acquisition and reorganization of biological knowledge. A second goal is to highlight the importance of analyzing such an ontologically important concept as *life* in terms of the theory in which it is a core concept.

Appearance vs. Reality
Young children are notoriously appearance bound. Indeed, it has often been claimed that preschool children are not able to distinguish appearance from reality (but see Flavell, Flavell, and Green 1983). If this claim were true, such young children would certainly be severely limited theory builders, since one goal of all theory construction is the discovery of the deeper reality underlying appearance. There would be no need for science if things were as they seem; scientific study has taught us that whales are not fish, that the sun does not circle the earth, etc.

Gelman and Markman (1984) have recently asked at what age knowing an animal's classification overrides knowing what it looks like in supporting inductive projection of new properties. For example, suppose I show you a picture of a lizard and tell you, "This lizard has moveable eyelids." I also show you a picture of a snake and tell you, "This snake has transparent unmovable eye coverings." I then show you a picture of a legless lizard that closely resembles the picture of the snake, but I tell you it is a lizard. I ask whether you think it has moveable eyelids or unmovable eyecoverings. Adults expect biological classification to predict such properties; Gelman and Markman tested whether 4-year-old children have such expectations. Their results are described in chapter 6. Also discussed there are data from an even more difficult appearance-reality problem involving biological classification (Keil (in press)).

Judgments of Category Errors
The last source of data brought to bear on these issues is also Keil's (1983a). Following recent philosophical practice (e.g., Sommers 1963), Keil distinguishes between category mistakes and mere falsehoods. *The idea is green* is a category mistake; an idea is not the kind of thing that can be green or any other color. On the other hand, *The Empire State Building is green* is merely false. It could be green; it has some color that just happens not to be green. *Green* can be predicated of *building, table, animal, grass,* etc., without creating category errors, but not of *idea, war, hour,* etc. Keil (1979) claims that certain concepts (the ontologically basic ones) have a special status in our conceptual system and that the set of ontologically basic concepts can be diagnosed from patterns of category mistakes. These claims are explicated and defended in chapter 6.

In one study Keil (1983a) looked intensively at two ontologically important distinctions, those between objects and events and between living and nonliving things. In chapter 6 I describe Keil's methods for obtaining judgments from children about whether given predicate-term combinations are category errors, and I summarize his data concerning biological predicates.

Conclusions

In this brief overview I have introduced the rich variety of phenomena that show that the child's knowledge of animals and living things is reorganized between the ages of 4 and 10. In the concluding chapter I return to two fundamental questions. I consider the nature of the restructuring that occurs during these years, arguing that it is at least of the weak sort and perhaps is an example of restructuring in the strong sense. I also argue that ontologically important concepts must be viewed in the context of the theories in which they are embedded, and that doing so has deep implications for the study of cognitive development.

Implications for Cognitive Development: A Preview
A new view of cognitive development is emerging, one that challenges Piaget's description of child development (see Gelman and Baillargeon 1983, Carey 1983, and Fischer 1980 for recent reviews). Many students of cognitive development now feel that there are no across-the-board changes in the *nature* of children's thinking. The new view denies that preoperational thinking or concrete operational thinking exists. Although this is not the place to enter into this debate, I do wish to emphasize one extremely undesirable consequence of the new view. Piaget's theory brought order to otherwise bewilderingly diverse developments. In giving up the stage theory, we seem to be left with tracing large numbers of piecemeal developments through the childhood years.

Piaget's theory offered the hope of reducing the task of explaining developmental changes to manageable proportions. For example: Piaget claimed that the child undergoes a general egocentric-nonegocentric shift between the ages of 5 and 7. That is, children under 7 (i.e., children in the preoperational period) are supposed to be generally unable to appreciate that other people have points of view different from their own. Being able to appreciate another's point of view is one of the putative achievements of the stage of concrete operations. The theory holds that this one change underlies diverse developmental changes in spatial reasoning, communication across barriers, moral reasoning, etc. Indeed, Piaget documented several developmental changes during the years from 5 through 7, in each of which the 5-year-old failed to take the other person's point of view while the 7-year-old succeeded in doing so. As Flavell (1985) points out, Piaget's theory is critically undermined by the fact that it is possible to find phenomena that exemplify a shift from ignoring to appreciating another's point of view that occur at 18 months, 30 months, 4 years, 10 years, etc. Piaget's work on egocentricity records a deep insight: for every task where point of view is an issue, one can find an age such that children younger than that age usually err by failing to see the other person's viewpoint. But this is quite different from the generalization of Piaget's stage theory, which states that before age 5 children are generally egocentric and that they first become able to take another's point of view in diverse domains around the age of 6 or 7.

When we give up Piaget's stage theory, we give up the ideas that held the promise of reducing the hundreds (thousands) of individual developmental changes that occur in early childhood to a manageable number. This is a high price to pay for the new view, and no doubt explains, in part, why many developmental psychologists have resisted abandoning Piaget's stage theory.

I believe there is an alternative analysis that allows us to see diverse developmental changes as reflections of the same single change and yet avoids the problems Piaget's stage theory came up against. This analysis holds that children represent only a few theory-like cognitive structures, in which their notions of causality are embedded and in terms of which their deep ontological commitments are explicated. Cognitive development consists, in part, in the emergence of new theories out of these older ones, with the concomitant restructuring of the ontologically important concepts and emergence of new explanatory notions. Such restructuring encompasses the entire domains of the theories. Since children have relatively few theory-like conceptual structures, and their domains include a wide variety of phenomena, some unification in the description of developmental change is achieved by interpreting individual changes in terms of the overall restructuring.

Chapter 1
What Is Alive?

Cut flowers with buds can be made to bloom faster if a piece of rotting fruit is put below them. So claimed a gardening expert on TV. This prompted a 7-year-old viewer to write in with a possible explanation:[1]

Is the reason that the flowers bloom because rotting is getting too ripe and blooming is also just getting ripe? Does the plant get the idea of getting ripe from seeing the apple rot?

The child's reasoning contains an element of the correct explanation. Rotting and blooming are alike, and both are like ripening in the relevant respect. However, the mechanism by which one case of ripening might affect another is totally unavailable to this 7-year-old. He knows nothing of the role of chemicals in biological processes. He produces, then, a classic case of animistic reasoning. The explanation he suggests imputes intentional states to a plant.

Piaget (1929) placed the phenomenon of childhood animism in the context of the child's causal reasoning. According to Piaget, young children derive ideas of causality from cases in which they themselves intentionally make things happen. In particular, children do not have a notion of mechanical causation distinct from intentional causality. In support of this thesis, Piaget showed that children under 10 interpret physical phenomena in terms of the intentional states of inanimate objects. For example, a 6-year-old might suggest that the sun is hot because it wants to keep people warm. Directly probing beliefs about intentional states, Piaget found that young children said that the sun, cars, the wind, bicycles, clocks, fires, etc., "know where they are" and "can feel a pin prick." When simply asked what is and what is not alive, they judged these same objects to be alive. According to Piaget, these three threads of childhood animism—(1) animistic causal reasoning, (2) overattribution of intentional states to inanimate objects, and (3) overattribution of "alive" to inanimate objects—are woven together. Because children feel the need to come up with explanations and causes of phenomena not involving people and animals, and because the only schema available is intentional, they attribute intentional states to the active objects involved in those phenomena. Thus, the story goes, since intentionality is attributed to active inanimate objects, so are consciousness and life. Piaget's account of why activity becomes the *criterion* for life is not entirely clear. Nonetheless, his data have been taken to show that activity and movement do become the basis for children's decisions about what is alive. (The status of this evidence will be examined below.)

Piaget's claim that the only causal schema available to young children is intentional, and that only late in the first decade of life does mechanical causality become distinguished from intentional causality, has been criticized from various points of view. Gelman and her collaborators (e.g., Bullock, Gelman, and Baillargeon 1982) and Shultz (1982) have established that the preschool child does *not* lack an appreciation of mechanical causation. Phenomena involving propagation of physical forces through space, whether involving contact or not, are interpreted mechanistically. If this is true, then childhood animism cannot be the result of the absence of a schema of mechanical causation, and we will have to look elsewhere for its interpretation.

Here I will be concerned with only one of the three threads of Piaget's phenomenon: the overattribution of life to inanimate objects. Through his interviews concerning which things are alive and which are not, Piaget sought to discover the meaning for the child of the word "alive" and to chart how this meaning changes with age. In this way he sought to diagnose the child's changing concept of life. He began by asking children to tell him what it means for something to be alive, and he asked them to judge whether certain animals, plants, and inanimate objects are alive or not, requesting explanations for each judgment. He followed up each justification with another object that would further probe the children's commitment to their current formulation of the meaning of "alive." A sample protocol reads,

VEL (8, stage 1) Is the sun alive? *Yes.* Why? *It gives light.* Is a candle alive? *No.* Why not? *(Yes) because it gives light. It is alive when it is giving light, but it isn't alive when it is not giving light.* Is a bicycle alive? *No, when it doesn't go it is not alive. When it goes it is alive.* Is a mountain alive? *No.* Why not? *Because it doesn't do anything.* Is a tree alive? *No; when it has fruit it's alive; when it hasn't any it is not*

Table 1.1
Stages in the meaning of "alive"

	Piaget	Laurendeau and Pinard
Stage 0	No concept Random judgments, or inconsistent or irrelevant justifications	No concept Random judgments, or inconsistent or irrelevant justifications
Stage 1	Activity Things that are active in any way (including movement) are alive	Activity or movement Things that are active, that move, or both are alive
Stage 2	Movement Only things that move are alive	Autonomous movement Things that move by themselves are alive
Stage 3	Autonomous movement Things that move by themselves are alive	Adult concept Only animals (or animals and plants) are alive
Stage 4	Adult concept Only animals (or animals and plants) are alive	

alive. . . . Is an oven alive? *Yes, it cooks the dinner and the tea and the supper.* Is a watch alive? *Yes.* Why? *Because it goes. . . .* Is a bench alive? *No, it's only for sitting on. . . .* (Piaget 1929:196)

Piaget found five distinct patterns of attribution and justification from which he derived five stages in the acquisition of the concept *alive* (table 1.1). Many young children appear to have no concept of life; they can give no definition and no consistent justifications. Some say everything is alive, some say nothing is, and others respond unsystematically, denying life to some animals as well as granting it to some inanimate objects. This initial period of uninterpretable responses is followed by four systematic stages. In the first stage, things seen to be active in any way are judged to be alive, as in VEL's protocol. In the second, the relevant kind of activity is movement. In the third, only things seen to move by themselves are judged alive, and in the fourth, being alive is restricted to animals and plants, or to animals alone. Inanimate objects are not judged alive in this last stage.

Piaget's results have been subject to many replications, the major one being that of Laurendeau and Pinard (1962). They tested 500 subjects between the ages of 4 and 12 on a standardized version of the clinical interview. Their data essentially agreed with Piaget's, except that they found no evidence for a distinction between Stages 1 and 2.

The modification of Piaget's stages proposed by Laurendeau and Pinard is also shown in table 1.1. Henceforth, when I refer to Stages 0 through 3, I mean the stages as described by Laurendeau and Pinard.

Piaget's goal was the diagnosis of the concept *alive*. Given that the meanings of words are concepts, Piaget's approach is on target, with one proviso. The child's meaning of the word "alive" bears on the child's concept *alive* only if the word has been mapped onto that concept. One cannot simply assume that the word "alive" is a direct pipeline to children's concepts of life. Even if children have a concept of life, "alive" may have some other meaning for them. That is, they may have a concept of life that plays some role in organizing inferences and in the acquisition of new knowledge, even though they have no word that expresses that concept. It is possible that attributions of life to inanimate objects reflect semantic rather than conceptual problems.

It is not clear from scrutiny of table 1.1 just which concept the word "alive" is supposed to be mapped onto. Clearly, it is not the biological concept of life. Both animals and plants are alive in this sense, but the last stage, the adult concept, is credited to children if they attribute life to animals alone, as well as if they attribute it to animals and plants. Further, the criteria summarized in the table do not transparently apply to plants. Plants are not active; nor do they move, autonomously or otherwise. Indeed, Laurendeau and Pinard state that Stage 1 and Stage 2 children deny that plants are alive. According to the picture in table 1.1, then, animistic attribution of "alive" to inanimate objects reflects children's struggle to distinguish animals from nonanimals more than their struggle to distinguish living things (including plants) from non-living things.

However, this hypothesis is problematic. There is now abundant evidence that the young child (age 2–6, Anglin 1977; age 3–5, Gelman, Spelke, and Meck 1983; Dolgin and Behrend 1984; see also chapter 3 below) represents a concept *animal* that does not include inanimate objects. Anglin found that for preschool children, the word "animal" has a *narrower* extension than for adults; when judging which objects are animals, children exclude people, some peripheral animals, and inanimate objects. Gelman, Spelke, and Meck found, as did Dolgin and Behrend, that a variety of psychological and biological properties, such as eating, having parents, having brains, thinking, and remembering, are not attributed to inanimate objects, even those judged alive in the Piagetian paradigm (see also chapter 3). Thus, although the criteria summarized in table 1.1 are more relevant to the distinction between animals and nonanimals than to the distinction between living and non-living things, it does not seem likely that the word "alive" is simply mapped onto the child's concept *animal*.

The word "alive" may not actually be mapped onto the child's concept that most closely approximates the adult's concept *living thing*. If not, then studying the development of the meaning of "alive" is not the best way to study the child's developing concept of life. Whether or not this concern is justified, the development of the meaning of the word "alive" is undoubtedly an interesting case study in semantic development. However, Piaget's claims for this case study come up against what seems to be an insurmountable obstacle. Beyond Stage 0, Piaget's stages, and Laurendeau and Pinard's, presuppose a view of the nature of word meanings that has come under severe criticism. Piaget saw the meaning of the word "alive" as passing through a succession of different necessary and sufficient conditions for something to be judged alive. At each stage the concept is identified with a definitional intension that provides a criterion for an object's being in its extension. This classical view of concepts is associated with an implicit model of how children actually generate their judgments. When asked whether something is alive, they apply their present criteria for life to that thing, say "yes" if the criteria are true of it and "no" if they are not. In his work on classification, Piaget explicitly endorsed this model of concepts as an achievement of the stage of concrete operations. Stage 0 children, being preoperational, putatively lack the conceptual machinery for holding any concept of this structure; Piaget held this to be one reason that preschool children are at Stage 0 with respect to the concept of life. However, if the widely held criticisms of the classical theory of meanings are correct, then the acquisition of the concept *alive* proposed in table 1.1 cannot be right.

The criticisms of the classical view may be briefly summarized. For most concepts it is simply not possible to provide definitions. That is, exemplars of most concepts bear a family resemblance to each other, rather than meeting a single set of necessary and sufficient conditions for category membership (Rosch 1978, Wittgenstein 1953). Also, the distinction between definitional components of a concept and merely empirical components (the analytic-synthetic distinction) has been shown to break down (Quine 1951, Putnam 1962). That is, even for scientific concepts like *living thing* or *energy,* no definition is immune from empirically driven revision. Finally, philosophers have recently argued that definitions of concepts cannot determine category membership (Schwartz 1979; see Carey 1982 and Smith and Medin 1981 for summaries of the criticisms of the classical view of concepts).

To appreciate the force of these arguments, consider how adults decide whether something is alive or not. For adults, as well as children, there will be unclear cases. What of bacteria, viruses, imagined discoveries on other planets? In these cases adults will defer to experts—biologists—but if forced to make a decision, they will consider complexity of structure, mechanisms of reproduction, metabolism, and myriad other factors. There is no single criterion for life; all of the adult's biological knowledge is brought to bear upon the decision.

In spite of these problems—the ambiguity of what concept "alive" is mapped onto and the presupposing of the classical theory of meaning—Piaget (1929) provided *evidence* that his description is right. Laurendeau and Pinard (1962) reported data from 500 children to back him up. The case rests on this evidence. Let us begin, then, by looking at it closely.

A Close Look at the Published Data: Single-Criterion Definitions

Does the child decide that something is or is not alive by evaluating it with respect to one of the criteria in table 1.1? This model of how children generate their judgments predicts two kinds of consistency in the data: (1) patterns of judgments across items should be consistent with the criterion the child is using in his or her definition of life, and (2) justifications should make consistent appeal to this criterion. The data given by Piaget in his books—fragments of protocols—provide this kind of evidence, but they are difficult to interpret since Piaget used his protocols to exemplify his points, and selected accordingly. In contrast, Laurendeau and Pinard tabulated all of their data, which may be examined with respect to these two kinds of consistency. Strikingly, their data show the child to be consistent in neither of the two ways.

Many Stage 1 and Stage 2 children attribute life to only one or to just a few inanimate objects, even though other objects in the set probed would clearly meet the criterion that characterizes each stage. That is, patterns of judgments are not consistent with single-criterion definitions. Furthermore, consistent appeals to a single criterion in justifications are extremely rare (only 25 of the 500 cases, 5%). Almost every single child produces many different kinds of justifications. This lack of consistency not only is apparent from Laurendeau and Pinard's tables, but also is tacitly acknowledged in their explicit instructions for classifying children into stages. To be at Stage 1, a child must attribute life to at least one inanimate object and justify at least one judgment with an appeal to activity or movement. For example, if the only inanimate object deemed alive is the sun, and the child just once mentions movement in a justification (for instance, claiming that an insect is alive "because it crawls around"), that child is classified as being at Stage 1. To be at Stage 2 the child must attribute life to at least one inanimate object and justify at least one judgment with an appeal to autonomous movement. In sum, in order to be classified into one of the Piagetian stages, children need not, and do not, provide patterns of data as if their answers were generated by appeals to the criteria in table 1.1.

One final fact belies the developmental story summarized in table 1.1. Laurendeau and Pinard report a class of justifications, "anthropomorphic traits," that is not reflected in the putative stages of the child's definition of "alive." Some examples are: tables are alive because they have legs, or tables are not alive because they do not have faces or because they do not breathe. Anthropomorphic traits are mentioned as commonly in justifications as movement or activity, more commonly than autonomous motion. Thus, not only do children fail to produce patterns of judgments and justifications that are consistent with single-criterion definitions, they commonly produce a type of justification that is ignored in the characterization of stages.

Piaget commented on this class of justifications, maintaining that such justifications do not reflect true criteria for life. Laurendeau and Pinard expanded Piaget's argument, suggesting that sometimes children have merely been told that animals (or animals and plants) are alive and have not yet formulated a criterion for life. They then sometimes judge a particular animal alive because it is considered an animal, and produce a justification (an anthropomorphic trait) relevant to its being an animal. Alternatively, they may judge an inanimate object not alive because of knowing it is not in the extension of the concept *animal,* and produce a justification (an anthropomorphic trait) relevant to its not being an animal. This is, of course, a quite different model of judgment generation than the one presupposed by the single-criterion characterizations in table 1.1. It is one that might be used by adults.

There are two very serious problems with Laurendeau and Pinard's attempt to rescue the single-criterion stage analysis in table 1.1 from the fact that children frequently cite anthropomorphic traits to justify calling something alive. First, their argument that anthropomorphic traits are epiphenomenal justifications could apply equally well to movement, activity, and autonomous motion. How are the latter justifications established as the "true" criteria for life? They may be merely salient anthropomorphic traits, produced in support of judgments based on category membership. That is, a child might judge an animal alive because of knowing the extension of the concept, and produce a justification relevant to its being an animal—that it is active, or moves, or moves by itself. The second problem is even more damaging. How do children know the extension of the concept *animal*? How do they decide that worms are in, and dolls, the sun, the wind, and so on, are out? In some cases they simply may have been told. But they classify previously unknown objects as animals (for evidence to this effect, see chapter 3 and Anglin 1977), and they also make many errors, as their judgments that inanimate objects are alive attests. Some productive process must underlie their judgments, even if they are based on decisions of category membership. The stage analysis depicted in table 1.1 is an attempt to sketch that productive process, as well as how it changes with age. If this sketch is wrong, we must replace it with a more accurate one.

I am not doubting the replicability of the Piagetian data. There is a long history of claims of nonreplication of Piagetian animism (e.g., Huang and Lee 1945, Klingensmith 1953, Klingberg 1957). But as two extensive reviews (Looft and Bartz 1969, Laurendeau and Pinard 1962) point out, as long as the scoring method described above is employed, the phenomenon is very replicable. My claim is quite different. Table 1.1 provides a highly theoretical summary of the results of a case study of semantic development: the development of the meaning of the word "alive." These results purport to show that with development the child adopts several different single-criterion meanings for the word. My argument is that the data, although replicable, do not support this description of development.

The first experiment to be reported here was a very modest replication of Laurendeau and Pinard's massive study. Most important to me was whether the child, like the adult, is attempting a biological classification—either into animals and nonanimals or into living things and nonliving things. I wanted some more direct information about what conceptual distinction the child spontaneously maps the contrast "alive–not alive" onto. To this end, Laurendeau and Pinard's protocol was slightly modified. The child was asked at the beginning of the procedure to give examples of some things that are not alive as well as of some things that are alive. Also relevant was a closer look at the justifications given. A particularly important category was that of anthropomorphic traits, since some such traits, like growing and reproducing, are highly relevant to the biological concept of living things, including plants, whereas others, like having eyebrows, talking, having legs, etc., are relevant only to the concepts of people and animals. Laurendeau and Pinard do not distinguish these two types of anthropomorphic traits.

Experiment 1: A Replication of Laurendeau and Pinard

Ten children at each of three ages (4, 7, and 10) participated in the study. They were drawn from an elementary school in an upper middle class suburb of Boston and from a nursery school for the MIT community.

As in the Piagetian procedure standardized by Laurendeau and Pinard, children were first asked if they knew what it means for something to be alive. After answering, they were asked to name some things that are alive, and then some things that are not alive. After this orientation to the task, the children were told that they would be shown several pictures, and they were to try to figure out, for each object pictured, whether it was alive or not. Laurendeau and Pinard's series was then presented, in the same order as in their study: mountain, sun, table, car, cat, cloud, lamp, watch, bird, bell, wind, airplane, fly, fire, flower, rain, tree, snake, bicycle, and pencil. After each judgment the children were asked for a justification by inquiring "How do you know?" Several times during the session, they were encouraged with the phrases "Uh huh, how did you know that?" or "Uh huh, why do you think that?" Such encouragement did not depend upon the correctness of the judgment. In addition to the tester, a scorer was present to note the judgments and justifications. The sessions were taped and the scorer's protocols checked against the tapes.

Results
Patterns of Judgments   Two judges independently scored the 30 protocols according to Laurendeau and Pinard's criteria. Agreement on placement was perfect. Stage 0 children (no concept) either said that all of the objects were alive, said that none were, or answered unsystematically, denying that some animals were alive and affirming that some, but not all, inanimate objects were. Stage 1 children attributed life to at least one inanimate object, appealed to activity or movement in their

justifications, and did not appeal to autonomous motion. Stage 2 children differed from those placed in Stage 1 in that they at least once made the distinction between autonomous movement or activity, on the one hand, and movement or activity caused by human agency, on the other. Stage 3 children made no animistic overextensions.

Table 1.2 shows the distribution of stages. Laurendeau and Pinard's data from these age groups are included for comparison. Despite the fact that we tested only 30 subjects, compared to their 199 (100 at age 4, 49 at age 7, 50 at age 10), agreement was substantial. Over half of both groups of 4-year-olds were at Stage 0 and roughly half of both groups of 10-year-olds were at Stage 3. Our 7-year-olds were slightly more advanced, being significantly more represented at Stages 2 and 3 than were Laurendeau and Pinard's ($p < .01$, Fisher exact test, 2-tailed). But although our 7-year-olds were more represented in the higher stages, the two groups did not differ in the overall level of animistic responses (table 1.3). Table 1.3 shows the percentage of all inanimate objects judged alive, excluding data from Stage 0 children. Again, the two studies largely agree.

Table 1.2
Percentage of children in each stage

Age	Stage 0		Stage 1		Stage 2		Stage 3	
	Exp. 1	L&P	Exp. 1	L&P	Exp. 1	L&P	Exp. 1	L&P
4	60	73	10	23	10	4	20	0
7	0	8	10	43	40	10	50	39
10	0	0	20	22	30	24	50	54
Overall Average	20	27	13	29	27	13	41	31

Table 1.3
Percentage of all judgments of inanimate objects
that were animistic.
(Stage 1, 2, and 3 children only.)

Age	Experiment 1	Laurendeau and Pinard
4	21 ($n = 4$)	49 ($n = 27$)
7	20 ($n = 10$)	20 ($n = 45$)
10	11 ($n = 10$)	16 ($n = 50$)

Laurendeau and Pinard's subjects spanned a greater range of social classes than did ours. Also, we used photographs of the objects probed, whereas they did not. Either of these factors could account for the slightly lower level of animistic responses by our subjects. Nonetheless, tables 1.2 and 1.3 show that the procedural and sample differences between the two studies had little effect on the outcome. The phenomenon of judging inanimate objects alive, tapped by Laurendeau and Pinard's procedure, is remarkably stable.

The Introductory Questions   Only 3 of our 30 subjects failed to provide examples of living things (all 3 were among our Stage 0 4-year-olds). The remaining 27 gave as examples "people" (16 times), "animals" (11 times), specific animals such as "turtles" or "my puppy Betsy" (11 times), "plants" (5 times), and specific plants such as "trees" (4 times). These numbers total more than 27, since many children gave multiple answers ("people, cats, animals"). Animals are clearly more salient examples of living things than plants, and of the animals, people are the most so.

In sharp contrast to the ease with which the children produced examples of living things was the difficulty they had in coming up with examples of things that are not alive. Only one of the 4-year-olds managed to provide any appropriate inanimate objects ("bricks, pipes, doors"). Even at age 10 three children failed to do so. Some children remained mute, while others provided examples of nonliving things that reflected a distinction other than the intended one between animate and inanimate objects. These were of three or four types:

the distinction between alive and dead: "dead animals," "George Washington"

the distinction between real and imaginary: "monsters," "fairies"

the distinction between real object and representation: "pictures," "people on TV"

the distinction between alive and extinct: "dinosaurs" (this may be the same as the distinction between alive and dead, or between real and imaginary, depending upon the child's beliefs about dinosaurs)

It is clear that many children do not immediately fathom just which abstract distinction the experimenter intends with the contrast "alive–not alive." Several are available, including alive-dead, real-imaginary, and real-representation. Which does the experimenter mean? Young children have plenty of linguistic evidence for each of these possible interpretations: "not alive" usually means "dead," and sometimes "extinct." The child is assured that the scary image in a movie, in a book, or on TV is "not alive" or "not real." Moreover, the candidate interpretations are closely intertwined conceptually, all related through the child's concept of death.

Aside: A 3-Year-Old's Struggle with the Concept of Death   Observations of my preschool daughter, Eliza, illustrate what every parent knows: the concept of death is conceptually difficult for young children. Over an 18-month period Eliza brought the matter up many times: it was one of the things that she thought about and wanted to talk about. Table 1.4 shows five vignettes, all but one initiated by her. Besides illustrating the importance of immobility to Eliza's concept of death (vignettes 2 and 3), these vignettes show that nonexistence is closely related to the concept of death, at least to her mind. The emotional impact of death follows from its being a transition from existence to nonexistence. This is especially clear from vignette 4, in which Eliza is denying this implication of death. Surely, life goes on as usual for the dead, just underground. (Not only Eliza is denying the finality of death. My "they just lie there" is a misleading description of the transition from body to dust.) In vignette 5 Eliza equates "not alive" with "dead," and "dead" with "nonexistent" ("you can't see him"). Both vignettes 5 and 3 show she has not grasped the distinction between living or dead, on the one hand, and living or inanimate, on the other. Statues, and her bear, are not alive, which to her means they are dead; but they are not dead either, at least not in the sense her grandpa is. Her resolution (vignette 3) that the bear is "middle-sized" between alive and dead is obviously unsatisfactory, and my attempted explanation (vignette 5) that some things are not alive and never were, whereas others are first alive and then die, sails right over her head.

The emotional and conceptual salience of the concept of death may make the young child assume that the distinction being probed in the Piagetian paradigm is that between alive and dead—hence, "George Washington" as an example of something not alive. But the concept of death itself is not clear, and it is closely tied to the concept of nonexistence—hence, "monsters" and "dinosaurs" as examples. Finally, Eliza's difficulty in straightening out the two distinctions suggests that she, at least, did not yet see death as solely a property of animals or living things. This may also be true of some of the young subjects in Experiment 1.

Table 1.4
One preschooler's struggle with the concept of death

Vignette 1 (2:6)
Eliza first became interested in the concept of death at about 2:6 when she was told that her grandfather, Eli, had died before she was born. Out of a long explanation she gathered that when somebody is dead you can't talk to them. For several months, she would bring up the fact that her grandpa was dead and that was sad because you couldn't talk to him.

Vignette 2 (3:6)
Watching a TV program where somebody was shot, she said excitedly, "He's dead—I can tell because he's not moving."

Vignette 3 (around 3:6)
S. What do you have in you?
E. Skin.
S. Inside?
E. Bones.
S. Anything else?
E. Blood.
S. Does your bear have bones and blood inside her?
E. No, because she's not a big, real person.
S. Are you?
E. Yes, well, not very big—she can never die, she'll always be alive!
S. Is she alive?
E. No—she's dead. HOW CAN THAT BE?
S. Is she alive or dead?
E. Dead.
S. Did she used to be alive?
E. No, she's middle-sized—in between alive and dead. She moves sometimes.

Vignette 4 (around 3:6)
E. How do dead people go to the bathroom?
S. What?
E. Maybe they have bathrooms under the ground.
S. Dead people don't have to go to the bathroom. They don't do anything; they just lie there. They don't eat or drink, so they don't have to go to the bathroom.
S. But they ate or drank before they died—they have to go to the bathroom from just before they died (triumphant at having found a flaw in my argument).

Vignette 5 (around 3:8)
E. Isn't it funny—statues aren't alive but you can still see them?
S. What's funny about that?
E. Grandpa's dead and you can't see him.
S. Oh, I see. Well, you know, people and animals can be alive and dead—first they are alive and then when they die, they're dead. But other things, like chairs—they aren't ever alive, so they can't die.
S. That's right. Tables and chairs are not alive and they're not dead and you can still see them. Isn't that funny, they're not alive, but you can still see them.

Von Hug-Hellmuth (1964) reports extensive diary records of a young German boy's spontaneous questions and comments about death. The diary was made by the boy's parents at the turn of the century, beginning in 1908 when the boy was 3½ years old. It is uncanny how similar the entries are to those in table 1.4. Ernie asks questions such as "And when we are dead, can we only speak softly?" He asks whether a dead person can "make a rumpus" in his coffin; when talking about a dead child, he suggests questioningly, "So the men can shovel the sand away and pull the flowers away from the grave and can sell the little boy to his mother again, so she can have her child again?" Von Hug-Hellmuth stresses that the idea that a person cannot feel and think after death is something completely incomprehensible to Ernie at this age. The question recurs again and again, "But what does a man say while he is dead?" I return to the child's conception of death in chapter 2; here I simply recommend Von Hug-Hellmuth's article for a rich portrait of the conceptual and emotional aspects of the preschooler's concern with death.

The Introductory Questions, Concluded   When asked to give an example of something that is not alive, all Stage 0 and Stage 1 children in Experiment 1 responded irrelevantly or not at all. In contrast, two-thirds of the Stage 2 and Stage 3 children gave examples of inanimate objects ($p < .001$, Fisher exact test). This suggests that for Stage 0 and Stage 1 children, part of the problem in childhood animism is semantic.

All of the nonintended distinctions (exists–does not exist, real-imaginary, alive-dead, alive-extinct) are related, directly or indirectly, to the contrast between life and death. In one of the first major replications of Piaget's animism studies, Russell and Dennis (1940) introduced their protocols by saying, "Do you know what it is for something to be alive? A cat is alive, but when a car runs over it, it is dead." They then proceeded to query, of a series of objects, whether each one was living or dead! Of course, buttons, tables, rocks, and the sun are neither living nor dead, but the children dutifully answered all of the questions and produced data exactly like those of Piaget and those of Laurendeau and Pinard. The same sorts of justifications appeared, with the addition of usefulness. Broken things were judged dead, because they were no longer any good to anyone, and this reasoning sometimes was extended to objects such as rocks. The results from the present experiment help make sense of these findings. Apparently many children in the Piagetian interviews spontaneously interpret the questions as Russell and

Dennis instructed their subjects to and are trying to decide how to apply the distinction between living and dead to the sun, cars, the wind, and so on. Since inanimate objects are neither living nor dead, it is not surprising that such subjects do not perfectly draw the animate-inanimate distinction.

Safier's (1964) data make the same point. She sought the relation between the young child's concepts of what things are alive and what things die. She asked about each of several objects (e.g., a dog, a ball, a bike, the moon) whether it is alive, whether it hurts when it is hit, whether it grows, and whether it dies. She found that her youngest subjects (4 to 5 years old) interpreted "living" and "dead" in opposition to each other, and judged that objects are in flux from one state to the other. Example protocols (Safier 1964: 290–291): "A ball is living when it goes up in the air and when the ball goes down, it dies dead," "The moon is dead today, but at night it lives," "The ball dies when the air is let out, but when you blow it up again, it lives."

These data reveal a mapping component in the phenomenon of childhood animism. Many young children do not interpret the question as intended by the experimenter. To say this is not to deny that conceptual differences between young children and adults are the main source of animistic attributions of life to inanimate objects. Most probably, conceptual differences are the reason that the words "alive–not alive" are not mapped onto the child's concepts that most closely approximate the adult's concepts *alive–not alive*. After all, the distinctions *alive-dead* and *alive-inanimate* are not conceptually independent, and conceptual problems children have with one have implications for conceptual problems they have with the other. Further, some attributions of life to inanimate objects occur in the absence of any semantic confusion. Two-thirds of the Stage 2 children produced relevant examples of nonliving objects when asked to list some things that are not alive (e.g., "rocks," "tables," "machines") but also made at least one animistic judgment. Even some children who are trying from the beginning to distinguish the class of living things, such as animals, from the class of nonliving things, such as tables, sometimes include the sun, the wind, etc., among the living.

Justifications   The children in Experiment 1 provided justifications that exemplify the purported stages in criteria for life: activity, movement, and autonomous movement. They frequently gave justifications in other categories as well. Examples are provided in table 1.5, along

Table 1.5
Justifications of responses in Experiment 1

Group	Percentage of responses	Justifications
I	18	Use: A table is alive because you can eat on it. Facts: A mountain is not alive because grass grows on it. Existence: Trees are alive because I've seen them.
II	33	Movement: A mountain is not alive because it just stays there. Activity: A clock is alive because it goes tick-tock.
III	25	Anthropomorphic trait: A watch isn't alive because it does not have eyes. Comparison to people: A bird is alive because I am.
IV	11	Built by people: A car is not alive because people made it. Autonomous motion: A bicycle isn't alive because you have to pedal it.
V	13	Growth, death, reproduction: A tree is alive because it grows. Composition: A cloud isn't alive because it's just made out of water.

with the percentage of all codable justifications of each type. A total of 4% of all justifications were not codable: "I just know," "I don't know," "My mommy told me," etc. The list in table 1.5 contains eleven categories of justifications that have been further divided into five groups. Two independent judges scored each justification into one of the eleven categories. Agreement was over 99%; the few disagreements were resolved by discussion. Although the basic categories should be self-explanatory, a few comments are in order concerning their further subdivision.

The most important subdivision comes between the first three (use, facts, and existence) and all the rest. Often, children simply mentioned true facts about the objects in their justifications, facts not biologically relevant in any way. These were dubbed "facts" and were produced by almost 40% of the sample. Appeals to use and existence are also irrelevant to the biological distinctions between living and nonliving things and between animals and nonanimals. Such appeals probably reflect the semantic problem discussed above, the child interpreting the questions as being about death. Death is associated with being broken and with no longer existing. Life, in contrast, is associated with being functional and simply with existing. Two Stage 0 children appealed to the objects' existence fairly consistently. Both said all of the items probed were alive, and mentioned having seen them, being able to point to examples, etc., in their justifications. One of these children gave "dead animals" and one gave "monsters" as examples of nonliving things.

All of the remaining types of justification are biologically relevant, to greater or lesser degrees. They all refer to properties of people or animals, and some refer to properties relevant to the adult characterization of all animals or all living things. Activity and movement (Group II) are properties of people and of all animals. These are the most frequent justifications. Anthropomorphic traits (Group III) are properties of people that some but not all other animals share (e.g., having faces, having legs). These justifications underscore the salience of people as exemplars of living things. Children often feel that "because people are" or "because I am" is sufficient justification for judging some other object alive; such reasons are classified as "comparison to people." The justifications in Group IV, autonomous motion and being built by people, are also relevant to the biological distinction between animals and nonanimals. Some children are aware of classes of objects that move or are active, but not autonomously so, because they are machines built by people or because they require a human agent to activate them. Finally, growth, reproduction, and death (Group V) are biological properties of all living things, including plants. What things are made of (composition) was mentioned only when justifying that inanimate objects are not alive (clouds are *just* water; rocks are *just* made out of stone, etc.). These rarely observed justifications were placed in Group V because they reflect a relatively sophisticated piece of biological knowledge—that living things are made of complex, variegated materials and parts.

No child used autonomous motion as *the* justification for attribution of life, nor did any use only movement, only activity, or only anthropomorphic traits. Rather all children, at all ages and stages, appealed to several types of justifications for their judgments. For example, a Stage 3 10-year-old mentioned activity, movement, composition, growth, and comparison to people; a Stage 0 4-year-old mentioned facts, movement, use, and activity. As with Laurendeau and Pinard's data, these results provide no evidence for single-criterion definitions of life.

It might be argued that no subclassification of the child's reasons is justified. Given the prevalence of simple facts as justifications, how are we to know that the child is not always merely stating a salient fact

Table 1.6
Percentage of all codable justifications in each category

Group	Type of justification	Stage 0	1	2	3
I	Biologically irrelevant	57	8	4	14
II	Movement; activity	28	67	42	22
III	Anthropomorphic trait; comparison to people	12	16	17	38
IV	Autonomous motion; built by people	0	0	20	13
V	Growth, reproduction, death; composition	2	10	17	13

(Groups III–V combined totals: Stage 0 = 14, Stage 1 = 25, Stage 2 = 54, Stage 3 = 64)

about the object? It may be accidental that the salient fact sometimes has something to do with the biological notions *animal* or *living thing*. Similarly, why aren't all of the justifications in Groups II through V merely anthropomorphic traits? Every property of all living things is a property of people; why are we licensed to draw distinctions among them? One reason is that the prevalence of justifications in the different categories changes systematically with stage (table 1.6). All Stage 0 children produced biologically irrelevant justifications; 57% of all codable responses were placed in Group I. Movement and activity were mentioned by children of all stages, but they dominated the justifications of the three Stage 1 children; 67% of all their justifications referred to motion and activity. All three of these children produced dead beings as examples of nonliving things, namely, "George Washington," "my grandmother," and "dead bears." Movement and activity are highly relevant to telling whether something is dead or alive. Instances of the remaining three groups of justifications increase with stage, the sharpest break generally occurring between Stages 1 and 2.

For no child does movement or activity (autonomous or otherwise) constitute the single criterion for life. Indeed, the analysis in table 1.6 suggests that we must interpret reference to movement and activity differently according to the stage of the child. For some Stage 0 children, movement and activity are no more than salient properites of some objects. These children produced mainly biologically irrelevant facts to justify their judgments. For other Stage 0 children, and for Stage 1 children, appeals to movement and activity, like appeals to existence, reflect the child's attempt to decide whether each object is living or dead. Finally, for Stage 2 and Stage 3 children, movement and

Table 1.7
Percentage of judgments that plants are alive

Stage	4- to 7-year-olds	10-year-olds	Overall
0	100	—	100
	$(n = 12)^a$		$(n = 12)$
1 and 2	93	100	96
	$(n = 16)$	$(n = 8)$	$(n = 24)$
3	17	100	58
	$(n = 12)$	$(n = 12)$	$(n = 24)$

[a]n = the number of judgments probed of plants. Each subject was asked about two plants, so the number of subjects in each group is half the number given.

activity are simply two of a large number of biologically important properties of living things.

The Classification of Plants (Flower and Tree)   According to the developmental progression summarized in table 1.1, virtually no Stage 1 and Stage 2 children should judge that plants are alive, and only some Stage 3 children should. Stage 1 and 2 children putatively define life by activity and movement, hardly salient properties of plants. Indeed, although they do not present their data on the matter, Laurendeau and Pinard state that Stage 1 and Stage 2 children do not attribute life to plants. Table 1.7 shows that these generalizations are not true of the data collected in Experiment 1. Instead of denying life to plants, Stage 1 and Stage 2 children called flowers and trees alive on 96% of all opportunities. Stage 3 children were less likely to attribute life to plants.

A closer look at the data makes clear what is going on. Young Stage 3 children (4- to 7-year-olds) differed from older children (10-year-olds) with regard to their classification of plants. Young Stage 3 children denied that plants are alive, while children of the same age in Stages 1 or 2 credited plants with life ($p < .01$, Fisher exact test, 2-tailed). In other words, young children who interpreted "alive" to refer to animals alone made no animistic overextensions. But those who attempted to encompass animals and plants in a single category also judged some inanimate objects alive. This suggests that 4- to 7-year-olds have a clear concept of animals, as distinct from inanimate objects, but that they do not have a concept of living things, as distinct from inanimate objects. By age 10, many children have achieved the biological concept *living thing* and have mapped it onto the word "alive."

Conclusions from Experiment 1

The phenomenon is not in doubt. In Piagetian clinical interviews children do attribute life to inanimate objects, and this demands an explanation. But there is not just one explanation; rather, there are two distinct sources of childhood animism. First, some young children are answering the wrong question, valiantly trying to decide whether a bicycle is alive or dead. It is easy to see, for these subjects, why objects obviously capable of activity are judged alive. The way you tell whether an animal—your pet gerbil or fish, a cowboy on TV—is dead is to see whether it is moving. Further, adults speak of "dead batteries," "dead cars," "dead parties," "dead telephones," etc., all characteristically active things no longer functioning. Second, other young children are indeed attempting to answer the right question, but still make animistic judgments. At least one source of their attribution of life to inanimate objects may be incomplete biological knowledge, for these judgments are more likely when the child is attempting to rationalize the inclusion of both animals and plants in the category of living things.

The above account, although consistent with the data presented so far, goes well beyond them. Support for it could come from the study of the young child's biological knowledge. What does the child know? How is that knowledge structured? How is it deployed in making judgments about life and in making other inferences? What knowledge is acquired between the ages of 7 and 10, and how is this new knowledge deployed in the 10-year-old's inferences? Can the 4- to 7-year-old's attribution of life to inanimate objects, and the lack of it in 10-year-olds, be understood in terms of these characterizations of biological knowledge? The rest of this monograph will focus in part on these questions.

Even if we can understand why 4- to 7-year-olds do not represent the biological concept *living thing* and hence why they have difficulty rationalizing the inclusion of animals and plants in a single category, we must also explain the particular animistic overattributions. Why especially the sun, the wind, cars? For this I believe we must appeal to the semantic source of the children's judgments. For the child for whom the distinction between living and nonliving things is not yet well motivated by biological knowledge, the ambiguity of "not alive" may pose a problem. The preschooler's difficulty in appreciating the two distinctions (alive-dead and alive-inanimate) may persist until the biological distinction is well established. Whenever the distinction between living and dead things intrudes, activity and movement become all the more salient.

My account differs from Piaget's in three essential respects. First, I argue that the patterns of attribution of "alive" partly reflect a semantic confusion. Second, and more important, I dispute the characterization of the development of the meaning of the word "alive" summarized in table 1.1. Children, no less than adults, have no simple definitions of life. The method by which children generate their judgments does not differ in kind from the method by which adults generate theirs; both appeal to a systematic body of knowledge rather than to single criteria. Finally, I would place the disappearance of animistic attributions in a slightly different context than Piaget did. He considered the essential development to be the growing distinction between intentional and mechanical causation. For this I would substitute the child's developing biological knowledge.

A Final Possible Source of Childhood Animism

In the Piagetian procedure children are made very conscious of the predicate "alive." They must define it, justify each judgment, and partition a set of objects with regard to whether each is alive or not. This procedure might trap the child into animistic judgments. For example, having just said that a bird is alive "because it flies," a child might feel compelled for the sake of consistency to judge an airplane alive. Perhaps the Piagetian procedure induces conscious theory building about life on the part of children, and does not simply diagnose their concept of life. That is, the procedure may reflect how the child comes to adopt a conscious criterion for life by trying various ones, testing them against intuitions, modifying them, and finally settling on one, then making all further intuitions consistent with that criterion. In the course of a clinical interview, the process of settling on a criterion may take some time. A crude test for this possibility is to see whether consistency in justifications is greater among the questions in the second half of the protocol than among those in the first half. The answer is no. Children produced an average of 3.8 different kinds of justifications in the first half of the protocol and an average of 4.2 different kinds in the second half. There was no hint of settling on one criterion as the interview progressed. Still, it is possible that the phenomenon *does* depend upon the self-conscious search for criteria. Being trapped into animistic judgments may reflect only local, short-lived attempts at consistency, which would explain why so many children judge only 1 or 2 inanimate objects alive.

Klayman (1979) has provided evidence against the possibility that animism is an artifact of conscious criterion search on the part of the child. He contrasted two groups of 4- to 7-year-olds. One group was required to provide a definition of "alive" and also to give justifications for judgments; the other group was required to provide neither. The two groups were identical in their degree of animistic overattribution of life to inanimate objects. However, Klayman's procedure is like the Piagetian clinical interview in that the child is still required to focus entirely on attribution of life. Even without definitions or justifications, this may induce conscious criterion building on the part of the child. Perhaps animistic judgments would disappear if the task were different, not requiring the partitioning of a set of objects solely with regard to being alive or not. In the second experiment to be reported here, children do not say what it means for something to be alive, nor do they give examples of living and nonliving things. They are questioned about several objects, and for each object many properties, not just life, are probed. All of the questions about a single object are asked before the next is presented. Finally, no justifications are required. Thus the procedure of Experiment 2 removes all those aspects of the Piagetian clinical interview that encourage the child to consciously reflect on principles that distinguish living from nonliving objects.

Experiment 2: Removing the Trap of Conscious Criterion Building

The primary purpose of Experiment 2 was to suggest a model of how children generate responses to questions such as "Does a dog breathe?" (see chapter 3). Here only the data relevant to the pattern of attribution of the word "alive" will be discussed.

There were two sets of materials. In one, all of the objects were highly familiar to the child; in the other, many were unfamiliar:

Familiar objects	Unfamiliar objects
person	person
dog	aardvark
fish	hammerhead (a hammerhead shark)
fly	stinkoo (a stinkbug)
worm	annelid (a worm)
tree	baobab (a tree)

Familiar objects	*Unfamiliar objects*
flower	orchid
car	harvester (a harvesting machine)
table	rolltop (a desk)
sun	sun
cloud	cloud
hammer	garlic press

Because some of the objects were unfamiliar to the child and had to be pictured (e.g., harvester, stinkoo), three drawings of each object were prepared. The properties probed included some true of all living things (is alive, grows), some true of all or many animals (eats, breathes, sleeps, has a heart, etc.), and some true of specific genera or species of animals (lives in the water, makes honey, etc.). Many were not properties of any living things (e.g., needs gasoline, is bigger than a house, is kept in the refrigerator). All the questions about one object were asked before the next object was introduced. The questions for each object were separately randomized once, and the order of presentation kept constant throughout all of the testing. The order of presentation of the objects was separately randomized for each child.

The experimental session was introduced by telling the children that they would be asked questions about a number of things. For the unfamiliar series they were warned that they might never have seen or heard of some of the things. All children were told that some questions would be easy, some silly, and some hard, and they were told to say what they thought was the right answer when they did not know for sure. Before being asked any questions about an object, children were shown three 4 × 6 index cards, each with a slightly different hand-drawn rendering of the object, and it was named for them.

Subjects were 50 children from the same population as those in Experiment 1. The familiar series was given to 10 children at each of the ages 4, 7, and 10. The unfamiliar series was given to 10 children at each of the ages 4 and 10. Three sessions of about 20 minutes each were required for 4-year-olds, two for 7-year-olds, and one for 10-year-olds. The 4- and 7-year-olds were tested individually; the 10-year-olds were tested in small groups of 3 or 4 children, working from prepared booklets.

Table 1.8
Percentage of children in each stage

Age	Experiment	Number of subjects	Stage 0	Stages 1 and 2	Stage 3
4	L&P	100	73	27	0
	Exp. 1	10	60	20	20
	Exp. 2	20	5	45	20
7	L&P	50	8	53	39
	Exp. 1	10	0	50	50
	Exp. 2	10	0	60	40
10	L&P	50	0	46	54
	Exp. 1	10	0	50	50
	Exp. 2	20	0	30	70
Overall, each	L&P		27	42	31
age weighted	Exp. 1		20	40	40
equally	Exp. 2		12	45	43

Results

Laurendeau and Pinard's Stages 1 and 2 are distinguished only by appeals to autonomous motion in justifications. Since children were not asked for justifications in Experiment 2, these two stages cannot be differentiated. Therefore, children were classified as Stage 0 (random responding, all objects judged alive, or no objects judged alive), Stage 1 or 2 (at least one inanimate object judged alive), or Stage 3 (no animistic overattributions of life). Responses on the familiar and unfamiliar objects did not differ, so the results from the two series were combined. Table 1.8 compares the data from Experiment 2 with those from Experiment 1 (Laurendeau and Pinard's data are also included). There were fewer Stage 0 4-year-olds in Experiment 2 than in Experiment 1, although the difference did not reach statistical significance. Among the 7- and 10-year-olds, the two sets of data did not differ. The procedural differences did not decrease the level of animistic responding. The phenomenon of attribution of life to inanimate objects does not depend for its manifestation on the Piagetian clinical interview.

Besides differing in how they encourage the child to reflect upon what makes something alive or not, the procedures in Experiments 1 and 2 differ in other ways that bear on the interpretation of the phenomenon of animistic judgments. In Experiment 2 more than half of the objects probed were animals and plants. Further, many biological properties, such as eating, growing, and breathing, were probed. Laurendeau and Pinard's series contain only a few animals and plants and probes only the property of being alive. The procedure of Experiment 2

Table 1.9
Percentage of animistic overgeneralizations by
non–Stage 0 children

	Age 4	Age 7	Age 10
L&P[a]	43	20	18
	(n = 27)	(n = 45)	(n = 50)
Exp. 1[a]	20	20	10
	(n = 4)	(n = 10)	(n = 10)
Exp. 2	35	16	7
	(n = 13)	(n = 10)	(n = 20)

[a]Based on sun, cloud, table, car, pencil for comparability to Experiment 2.

may orient the child toward the biological distinction between animals and inanimate objects, or between living and inanimate objects. This may be the reason for the slightly lesser degree of Stage 0 responding observed in Experiment 2. However, if even in the Piagetian procedure children beyond Stage 0 are basing their decisions on a variety of biological considerations, but their biological knowledge is inadequate, then highlighting the biological context should not affect the level of animistic responses. And this was indeed the case: non–Stage 0 subjects provided the same level of animistic responses here as in the standard Laurendeau and Pinard procedure (table 1.9). This finding—as much animism in Experiment 2 as in Experiment 1—supports two arguments. First, childhood animism is not an artifact of the testing method of the Piagetian clinical interview. Second, it would seem that young children, like adults, are applying their biological knowledge to the question of what is or is not alive, but that they simply do not know enough biology to draw the same distinction that adults draw.

Conclusions

In this chapter I have stressed my disagreements with the standard Piagetian treatment of the phenomenon of childhood animism. I have denied the developmental description illustrated in table 1.1. I have suggested that one source of animistic responses is inadequate biological knowledge and that one source of the decline of animism is the acquisition of biological knowledge in the years before age 10.

Let me conclude by underlining the points on which I instead agree with Piaget's treatment. First, the phenomenon of animistic attribution of life is real, nonartifactual, and important. The meaning of the word "alive" does change with age. And although one source of the young child's responses is a mapping problem—the child interprets the distinction in a way not intended by the experimenter—Piaget is also correct that the underlying concept of life itself develops during these years, attaining its recognizable adult form around age 10. These are major points of agreement. What follows in this monograph is an attempt to shed light on the developing concept of life in the years before age 10. In order to explore the suggestions that emerged from Experiment 1, I shall analyze the development of the concept of life in terms of the acquisition and reorganization of biological knowledge.

Piagetians will argue that my account misses the heart of Piaget's work on childhood animism. His primary concern was not the development of the meaning of the word "alive," nor even the development of the concept of life. Rather, he was concerned with the child's causal notions. At the same ages when children say that the sun, the wind, cars, etc., are alive, they also maintain that the sun knows where it is, that it shines in order to keep us warm, that it can feel a pinprick—in short, that it exhibits intentional states and purposeful activity. As I will spell out in the next chapter and in chapter 7, I agree that the development of the concept of living things and animals is entwined with developing notions of causal explanation. I agree that the separation of intentional causality from other types is central to what is changing over the years from 4 to 10, although mechanical causality is not at issue. But that part of the story must await presentation of the results from more studies.

Chapter 2
The Human Body

To evaluate the suggestion that young children judge inanimate objects alive partly because they do not know enough biology to rationalize the inclusion of plants and animals in a single category, we must examine what young children in fact do know about biology. In this chapter I review the extensive literature about one aspect of children's biological knowledge—their understanding of themselves as biological entities. Children have been questioned about their knowledge of their bodies, what is inside themselves, and the function of internal organs, and for their understanding of reproduction, growth, and death. In reviewing this literature, I develop three arguments. First, supporting the conjecture of chapter 1, published studies underscore the lack of biological knowledge among 4- to 7-year-olds. Young children's understanding of *these* aspects of biology, at least, would not support the inclusion of plants and animals in a single category. On the other hand, ages 9 and 10 witness a surge of biological understanding. Second, adding new pages to the story, I begin to describe the nonbiological framework into which children place their knowledge of bodily functions, death, growth, reproduction, gender, etc. In each case, 4-year-olds see these processes as aspects of human behavior, and their understanding of them is incorporated into intentional accounts of behavior—that is, accounts offered in terms of the desires and beliefs of the actor. It is because their explanations are intentional that I call this framework "psychological" in contrast to "biological." In contrast, by age 9 or 10, children have acquired an intuitive biological theory, and they understand these processes in terms of biological principles. Finally, I show how the documentation of this sort of conceptual change provides a framework for unifying the description of a wide variety of specific developmental changes.

The chapter is organized as follows. The data from the first concepts reviewed (internal organs, digestion, circulation, and respiration) demonstrate the increase of biological knowledge in the years right before age 10, and only obliquely exemplify the alternative framework the young child has for thinking about these processes. Data from the later concepts reviewed (the brain, gender, reproduction, death, and growth) make both points. Finally, I discuss the relationships among the developmental courses of all these concepts.

People's Insides

A half-dozen projects or so, the earliest from the 1930s, have probed children's knowledge of internal organs, including their knowledge of organ function. By far the most extensive is Gellert's study published in 1962. She asked 96 children, ages 4 to 16, to list what they have inside them; she probed where major organs (e.g., the heart, stomach, liver, lungs, bladder, nerves, bones) are found inside the body, what the role of each is, and what would happen if one were to be without it. Every aspect of Gellert's interview demonstrates the increase in biological knowledge over the school years. Though the years from 12 to 16 witness substantial elaboration of the child's understanding of bodily functions, by far the most striking changes occur between the ages of 4 and 9. Consider children's answers to the simple question of what is found inside a person. The sheer numbers reveal the pattern. Five-through 8-year-olds come up with about 3 things found inside people; 9- and 10-year-olds list over 8. Still more revealing are the developmental changes in the nature of the responses. The youngest children think of the contents of the body in terms of what they have seen being put into it or coming out of it. The dominant responses in Gellert's study are food and blood. The children also know about bones, which, of course, they can feel. The next group (7- and 8-year-olds) adds the heart to the list, but the heart also can be felt, in its beating. The third age group studied (9- and 10-year-olds) adds a wide variety of internal organs proper to bones and blood, common ones being the stomach, lungs, brain, glands, muscles, blood vessels, kidneys, and bladder.

Though Gellert emphasizes that young children have a more articulated picture of their insides than that painted by Fraiberg (1959), their spontaneous responses to the free listing task do not belie Fraiberg's description:

The child, until a surprisingly late age, even 8 or 9, imagines his body as a hollow organ, encased in skin. It is all "stomach" in his imagination, a big hollow tube which is filled with food at intervals and emptied of food at other intervals. It is interesting to ask a 6- or 7-year-old to draw what he thinks he looks like inside and to see the drawing of an undifferentiated cavern into which the child may, upon reflection, insert a "heart" in some out-of-the-way place. If you ask the question, "Where is the stomach?" the child will usually point to the interior of his drawing, indicating all of it. And since the child, at an early age, has discovered that if his skin is scratched or cut, blood will appear, he visualizes the interior of this body as a kind of reservoir in which blood, food and wastes are somehow contained. (Fraiberg 1959:129, quoted in Gellert 1962:387)

Only around age 10 is the inside of a person seen as composed of many different body parts, just as the outside of the body is.

At the very end of Gellert's interview, after children had been probed about the heart, blood vessels, lungs, brain, nerves, stomach, liver, bladder, and intestines, they were asked, "What do you think is the most important part of your body?" In spite of an hour's interview about the functions of all of the above-mentioned internal body parts, over five-sixths of the 4-, 5-, and 6-year-olds responded with *external* parts (legs, hair, nose, feet, eyes, etc.). To a few, the amount of care required served as the measure of the chosen part's importance. For example, a 5-year-old who chose feet explained, "You have to take good care of them." Why? "Because you have to scrub them between your toes, which is real hard." By age 10, children respond with internal body parts, justifying the chosen part's importance in terms of biological functions.

In sum, young children do not know much about what is inside their bodies, what they do know is not very salient to them, and they do not seem to grasp the function of internal body parts. The data from Gellert's free listing tasks underscore two points, then: the paucity of the young child's knowledge of internal bodily organs and the great strides, on this score, made by age 10.

Bodily Functions: The Digestive System

An understanding of digestion has several components. Many things are ingestible—liquids and foods, both wholesome and unwholesome—and eating has many consequences—growth, increased weight, health, strength, and energy. In addition to knowledge of input-output relations, an understanding of digestion includes a model of what mediates them. Recent work by Wellman and Johnson (1982) and Contento (1981) documents that preschool children have some knowledge of input-output relations, as well as many misconceptions, but that children have virtually no model of what mediates these relations until the end of the first decade of life.

Wellman and Johnson constructed two tasks to assess what children know about the variety of nutritional inputs and the consequences of different diets. In one task, pictures of two children who differed along one salient dimension (e.g., fat-skinny, tall-short, strong-weak) were presented, and the child was asked what might account for the difference. In the other task, pictures of identical twins were presented, and the child was asked to predict what would happen if the diet of one twin were changed (e.g., if she were to eat only green beans, or drink twice as much water, or eat twice as much dessert). Even preschool children know that some diets are wholesome (ensure growth and health) and some are not (lead to weight gain and laziness). Preschool children differed from third and sixth graders in thinking that increases in consumption of anything (water, green beans, desserts) would lead to weight gain and in thinking that differences in height are as direct a function of differences in consumption as are differences in girth. Given Gellert's findings about preschool children's ignorance about the insides of the human body, it is not surprising that they have no model of what mediates those input-output relations they have learned.

"Stomach" is an ambiguous term, referring to the abdomen as well as to the internal organ. Young children know it in the former sense and rarely list "stomach" as one of the things found *inside* a person. But whether or not they knew of the stomach as an internal organ, even the youngest children in Gellert's study (70% of the 5- to 7-year-olds) knew its function was related to food, although a substantial group (30%) of the youngest children thought it was related to breathing, presumably because of the movement of the abdomen in respiration. That food undergoes a process of transformation in the stomach was not generally known until age 11. Younger children held either that food goes to various parts of the body or that food is discharged. Those who held the latter believed the discharged food is the *same* food that is earlier circulated through the body. The digestive process was understood by analogy to chewing—making the food smaller and smaller. The phrase "Food turns into . . . (blood, part of you, things the body can use, fat, bones, etc.)'' was used by only one child under 8, and this process became widely understood only by age 12.

A more detailed study of children's understanding of digestion (Contento 1981) confirms and extends Gellert's findings. Contento showed that young children have no understanding of nutrients. About vitamins, young children know that they are pills that come in lion, bear, and monkey shapes, and that the purpose of the pills is to make people strong and healthy. Only 2 of 34 5- to 11-year-olds in Contento's study realized that vitamins are assimilated into the body, and only 3 of the entire sample (all were 9- to 11-year-olds) realized that ordinary food contains nutrients such as vitamins. Contento's questions about the relation between nutrients and food primarily tapped the child's developing conceptions of material kind (see Smith, Carey, and Wiser (in press)). In addition, her interview more directly accessed the child's notions of physiological processes, as she probed her subjects' views of the functions of eating and of what happens to food once it is eaten.

Five-year-olds know that fruits, vegetables, and milk are good for them, but they do not know why. One subject was asked what eating spinach does for Popeye. "Makes him strong," was the reply. When asked how spinach makes him strong, the child answered, "Because he likes it." This interchange, typical of the data, exemplifies the psychological explanatory framework available to children. Upon further probing, most said that food makes people grow and makes them strong and healthy, but they had no idea how this is accomplished. When asked what happens to the food, most 5-year-olds knew that it goes to the stomach, but thought that it stays there unchanged. A few knew that it is transported to other parts of the body, but imagined that it is transported unchanged. By age 6 almost all children knew that food makes its way to all parts of the body, but as mentioned above, only 3 of 34 subjects, all ages 9 to 11, knew that food is changed in the stomach and brings about its desired effects by being broken down into altered substances that are carried to tissues throughout the body.

How should we characterize young children's knowledge of eating? They do know that there is a relation between food and various processes and states of affairs—growing, being strong, being healthy, not dying. But such knowledge should not be viewed as being incorporated in an autonomous biological domain, for two reasons. First, young children are totally ignorant of the physiological mechanisms involved. They know *that* there is a relation between eating and these other processes but know nothing about what mediates these relations. Second, the explanatory notions they *do* have are psychological. That is, they are articulated in terms of wants and beliefs. Food ensures desirable states of affairs (growing, being healthy, not dying); that is why we eat it.

Gellert (1962) probed children's views about defecation as well as about digestion. Her young subjects viewed bowel movements as a social requirement rather than as a mechanical or biological necessity. The function of bowel movements is to allow us to go to the toilet, so we won't go in our pants. Almost half of the youngest children knew that defecation is related to food, but no biological function was articulated until the age of 9 or 10. At that age, the common explanation was that we need bowel movements so we won't get too full, so we won't burst. It was not until ages 13 to 14 that children get the idea that some of the materials in food are useless or even noxious to the body and must therefore be eliminated.

Bodily Functions: The Circulatory System

As we have seen, the heart is generally the first internal organ that children know about. When asked to draw the heart in the human body, even the youngest in Gellert's study were accurate in the location they assigned to it (children of all ages gave it a Valentine shape). However, the two youngest groups, those age 9 and under, knew little or nothing of its physiological function. These children assigned it a psychological or social significance ("It's so you can love," "It makes you do the things you should"), or they mentioned its behavior ("It ticks," "It pounds when you run fast," "You can hear it beat"). Such responses were given by over half of the children below age 9. The next most common response at these ages was the simple assertion that the heart is essential for life, with no further elaboration. Although one-fifth of the 4- through 6-year-olds mentioned blood in their explanations, only 1 (of 19) had any idea about circulation. Rather, they offered such statements as "It makes blood" or "Blood comes from the heart." Seven- through 9-year-olds had more idea of physiological function— approximately one-fourth knew about circulation and some of these even knew something of the blood's relation to breathing. By the third age group (10- and 11-year-olds), the psychological components of the children's explanations, though still present, were subordinated to the physiological functions. Well over half of the children at this age knew about the circulation of air through the body and realized that the heart is a pump. Although "circulation" referred to blood flow, there was no evidence that even the older children (16-year-olds) realized that the blood *returns* to the heart. Clearly, the expertise gained by age 10 is relative. Biology has become a separate domain, but there is still a great deal to learn.

Bodily Functions: The Respiratory System

Many of the youngest children in Gellert's study had never heard of the lungs, and more than half of those under 7 either had no idea of lung function or were wildly inaccurate (e.g., "They are for your hair. Without them you couldn't have hair"). More generally, although young children know that air is necessary for life, they know nothing of the relationship of air, or of the lungs, to vital bodily processes. Both Nagy (1953) and Gellert (1962) noted that children under 9 do not know what happens to air after it is inhaled. Nagy claimed that children of this age think of air as remaining in the head.

By the age of 9 or 10, well over half of Gellert's subjects associated the lungs' activities with breathing. After age 9 most could articulate the role of the lungs in purifying blood, some form of the interaction between pulmonary and cardiac function, the exchange of gases in the lungs, and/or the fact that air gets to the rest of the body.

Conclusions: Digestion, Circulation, Respiration

The above review has something of the flavor of a list: young children do A, B, C, and D; older children do W, X, Y, and Z. Crider (1981) has tried to bring theoretical order into these lists by describing the key differentiations the child makes between ages 4 and 11. The youngest child does not consistently distinguish the inside of the body from the body itself, either in terms of parts or in terms of function. The child knows no internal organs, proper, and thinks about the processes probed in terms of the whole person (you eat, you breathe). Nagy (1953) found that children say that internal organs (e.g., the heart, stomach, and brain) are made of bones, skin, blood, flesh, and food— the same answers they give when asked what the body itself is made of. Thus, one important differentiation to be made is between properties of the whole body and properties of its internal parts. When the young child comes to know some internal organs, each is assigned a static function: the heart is for love, the lungs are for breathing, the stomach is for eating, and the brain is for thinking. Next, the organs are more widely differentiated as an explanation for each function is given in terms of the properties of its organ: the heart is a pump that causes the blood to circulate, the stomach is a container for food, and so on.

Next, the child builds a coherent system: the functioning of all of the organs is conceptualized in terms of the movement of tangible substances such as food, air, and blood. The organs are all containers, with channels of various sorts (e.g., blood vessels) connecting them. This stage of understanding is reached by age 8 or 9. The final stages involve adding still another microlevel of description, the metabolic and cellular; the child comes to understand that bodily substances are transformed into different kinds of things (e.g., food is used for energy, after having been broken down into other substances and transported through the body via the circulatory system).

Crider's account is consistent with the characterization of the shift between ages 4 and 11 as a shift from psychological explanation to biological explanation. First, the child understands eating, breathing, thinking, etc., as human behaviors, and explains them in terms of the same kinds of considerations that account for other human behaviors. Second, until the child builds either the container theory or the physiological theory, there is no system of ideas in which these processes are related to each other. As children begin to build such a theory, they begin to establish biology as a separate domain. There is a considerable difference between the kinds of relations among internal organs and biological processes articulated in the container model and the kinds articulated in the substance transformation models, as Crider insists. The latter, not achieved until the end of the first decade of life, would better support seeing animals and plants as fundamentally alike.

A recent study of children's understanding of the brain confirms Crider's account. Young children see the brain as the locus of mental activity, in just the one-organ, one-function manner in terms of which they conceptualize the functions of all internal organs they know about. Coming to see neural processes as part of a system of biological functions is a late achievement.

Bodily Functions: The Nervous System

Johnson and Wellman (1982) questioned 3- to 14-year-old children about the location and nature of the brain, about its function, and most crucially, about what activities require a brain. Three-year-olds were mostly ignorant about the brain: they could not reliably judge that the brain is found inside the head, and they could not reliably judge that although dolls have noses they do not have brains. By age 5, and to a large extent also by age 4, the children knew that the brain is an internal body part of people, but not of dolls. Also by age 4 children had a very clear idea of the function of the brain: it is for mentation, broadly conceived.

Four-year-olds judged the brain necessary for thinking, dreaming, remembering, and knowing the ABCs, but denied it was needed for telling a story, shaking one's head, making a face, wiggling one's toes, walking, or picking up a glass. By age 4 children had a category of mental processes distinct from overt behavior, and they judged the former to be the province of the brain. In two additional studies, Johnson and Wellman traced through to adulthood the developing views of the functions of the brain. The brain was deemed necessary for mental acts by subjects from age 5 on, as it was for school tasks such as spelling, counting, reading, telling a story, and drawing. Feelings related to cognition, such as feeling curious or feeling sure, were judged to require the brain, even by 5-year-olds. The significant finding was that 5-year-olds, like the preschoolers, do not think the brain necessary for motor acts such as walking, grabbing something, or kicking a ball, or for involuntary acts such as coughing, blinking, or sleeping. Nor do they yet realize that the brain has a role in the senses—they do not judge that a brain is needed to see, hear, taste, or smell.

At ages 4 and 5, then, the brain is a *mental* organ. The domain of the mental is somewhat narrower than for the adult (it does not yet include emotions and sensations), but it encompasses a wide variety of cognitive activities. With increasing age the brain is seen as required for more and more of the activities probed, until by adulthood *all* are deemed to require a brain. The increase has two distinct sources. First, the domain of the cognitive expands. Children see that thought is needed for all sorts of activities; for example, you need a brain to walk "because it helps you know where your feet are going." Second, the brain in particular, and the nervous system in general, becomes conceptualized in its biological role, integrated in the functioning of the whole body. One aspect of the Johnson and Wellman interview most directly reflected the latter change. Children were asked whether the brain helped each of a series of body parts (e.g., nose and legs) and whether each body part helped the brain. Over half of the 5-year-olds considered the brain autonomous from all of those parts, whereas by age 10 about 80% of the children saw the brain as helping the body parts. Almost half also realized that the body also helps the brain. The biological understanding of the brain is by no means complete by age 10. It was not until age 14 (and adulthood) that the brain was seen as essential for all behaviors, including noncognitive involuntary responses.

Johnson and Wellman set out to explore the child's conception of mental phenomena (questions about the mind as well as the brain were included in the studies). Their goal was not to characterize the child's understanding of the brain as a biological organ. However, Nagy (1953), who did have this goal, also found that young children believe that the brain performs mainly intellectual activities, especially thinking. Gellert (1962) showed the same to be the case for the nervous system more generally. Not surprisingly, given what we have seen of children's understanding of the brain, children below age 9 have little knowledge of the nature and function of nerves. About one-fourth claimed they themselves did not have any nerves, at least not all the time, although other people might. Under age 9 no child attributed to nerves the functions of conducting messages, controlling activity, stabilizing the body. After age 9 more than half assigned nerves one or more of these roles. The young children were able to think of no role at all for nerves, or came up with the uninformative "necessary for life." Specific functions mentioned were always psychological: anger, mental illness, and thinking.

For the young child the nervous system supports psychological functioning. There is no mystery here: there is plenty of linguistic support for children's usage: "Use your brains," "Don't be nervous," "He has a lot of nerve," "He had a nervous breakdown." What *is* surprising, at least on some reading of young children's cognitive powers, is the systematic and elaborate theory they have constructed. An unseen body part (the mind, or the brain—the two are both seen as internal organs by 5-year-olds) is responsible for diverse cognitive functions. This theory is elaborated in the years from 5 to 10, as other psychological functions are attributed to the brain and as "mind" becomes differentiated from "brain," but the brain remains primarily a mental organ throughout that period.

The school in which Johnson and Wellman carried out one of their studies had a unit on the brain in the 5th grade science curriculum. This unit taught about the nervous system and about the brain's role in controlling all voluntary and involuntary behavior. Johnson and Wellman's study took place before their subjects had studied the brain in school, so they tested an additional 14 subjects after the unit had been taught. The curricular unit had absolutely no effect on the results. The subjects who had completed the unit were just as likely to deny that the brain is needed for coughing, sleeping, and blinking as were those tested before the unit was taught. Such a failure of training is reminiscent of the dramatic failure of college physics courses to influence students' intuitive mechanics. By age 10 children have worked out an elaborate picture of mental functioning, and understand the brain to be the organ responsible for it. This picture cannot be easily rearranged.

Summary: Bodily Functions

The studies reviewed above show that by age 10, and decidedly not by age 7 or 8, the child understands that the body contains numerous organs that function together in maintaining life. For instance, the 10-year-old knows something of the mechanisms by which eating and breathing support the body's functioning. This knowledge is by no means perfect, and early adolescence brings further changes in the child's conceptualization of these mechanisms. Ten-year-olds do not understand that food is broken down into nutrients and wastes in the course of digestion (Contento 1981); it is not until age 14 that children conceptualize defecation in terms of elimination of waste (Gellert 1962). And the nervous system still fulfills primarily psychological functions for 10-year-olds (Johnson and Wellman 1982). Nonetheless, by age 10 or so children have achieved a view of the body as a biological machine. They know how the circulatory, respiratory, and digestive systems are related, and they are beginning to conceptualize the relations between the brain and the body. They are beginning to command a domain of knowledge about humans that is clearly separate from knowledge of why individuals behave as they do.

Gender and Gender Constancy

Within an intuitive biological theory, a fundamental distinction is that between male and female. Gender organizes one mechanism of reproduction that is found throughout both the animal and plant kingdoms. Of course, the concept of gender is central to the child's intuitive social theories as well. Gender organizes social roles as well as biological roles. It is because of the social importance of the child's concept of gender that it has been widely studied (see Damon 1977 and Maccoby

1980 for extensive reviews). These data provide information about the child's knowledge of the biology of gender as well.

Thompson (1975) studied the very beginnings of the child's knowledge that he or she is a boy or a girl. At 2:0 children know some of the words *boy, girl, mommy, daddy, brother, sister* and are beginning to know some sex-appropriate objects (e.g., that neckties go with Daddy and that lipsticks go with Mommy). However, they do not know their own sex. By age 3 they do know their own sex and can label photographs of adults and of other children with sex-appropriate words, but as Maccoby (1980) puts it, at this age *boy* and *girl* are labels, like the child's own name, with little implication of class membership.

Thompson and Bentler (1971) sought to discover how older children (ages 4 to 6) conceive boyness or girlness. They showed children naked dolls on which genitals, upper torso (breasts vs. muscular masculine body), and hair varied. For each doll the child had to choose a name, decide which clothing was appropriate, and predict whether the doll would grow up to be a mommy or a daddy. The overwhelmingly salient cue was hair length. Most of the children never chose on the basis of either genitals or upper body, when the latter cues conflicted with hair style.

Consistent with their view that hairstyle and clothing determine gender, children under age 7 maintain that if a person changes his or her hairstyle, clothes, and behavior, he or she can thereby change gender (Kohlberg 1966, Emmerich 1982, Marcus and Overton 1978). In the most massive study, Emmerich (1982) showed almost 1000 4- to 7-year-olds a stylized picture of a girl, named Janie, and asked a graded set of questions, beginning with "If Janie really wants to be a boy, can she be?" and "If Janie played with trucks and did boy things, what would she be? Would she be a girl, or would she be a boy?" and ending with "If Janie has her hair cut short like this and wears boy clothes like this, what would she be? Would she be a girl, or would she be a boy?" (A comparable set of questions was posed about a boy, named Johnny.) Note that the use of a gender-stereotyped name and the appropriate pronoun supported judgments of *gender constancy* (that is, the belief that a person's gender is maintained despite such transformations). Nonetheless, on three-fourths of their judgments Emmerich's subjects maintained that Janie can freely change into a boy. Emmerich described three phrases in attaining gender constancy. In the first phase, children have no problem accepting that a person could change gender, although they see such an act as morally wrong, calling for the application of negative sanction. "That a person could change gender practically at will was hardly in doubt as a physical reality matter to our Phase 1 children. Rather, during this phase, children may hold a purely social identity rule that states that such a willful act is socially unacceptable" (Emmerich 1982:262). In this early phase, if children judge that gender is maintained in spite of Janie's or Johnny's desires, behavior, hairstyle, or clothing, they justify their choice with social considerations, such as "My daddy would yell and tell him to get off all those girl clothes," or "He's supposed to stay a boy. He's a good boy," or simply "I want her to be a girl."

In the second phase, the child usually denies gender constancy, but the purely social justifications typical of phase 1 children have disappeared. Phase 2 children define gender in terms of clothing, hairstyle, and so on, and if they judge that gender is maintained under one of Emmerich's transformations, they appeal to one such cue to gender that has not changed—for example, "She's still got girl shoes." Finally, in the third phase, children consistently judge that gender cannot change under these transformations, justifying their judgments with statements such as "She was born a girl." Emmerich's subjects were disadvantaged children, ages 4 to 7; very few reached phase 3 by this age. Other investigators, looking at more advantaged children, have replicated lack of gender constancy in children under age 6, but have found gender constancy fairly secure by age 7 or 8 (e.g., Marcus and Overton 1978).

Kohlberg (1966) has suggested that an understanding of gender constancy precedes and triggers identification with adults of the same gender. Kohlberg's idea is that children's knowledge that they will remain the same gender influences them to pay attention to and emulate sex-specific roles. An alternative hypothesis is supported by Marcus and Overton's (1978) finding of no relation between gender constancy attainment and same-sex preference. As Emmerich (1982) spells out the alternative, before children understand that gender is an unalterable biological given, they are more anxious about learning sex roles, and anxious to be sure to behave in the way that will maintain their gender. A study by Damon (1977) illustrates the changes that occur over the ages of 4 to 10 in children's views of the importance of conforming to sex stereotypes. Damon told his subjects a story about a little boy, George, who liked to play with dolls, and asked whether it was OK for George to do so, whether it would be fair for him to be punished, whether it would be OK for him to wear a dress, and so forth. Four-year-olds thought it was fine for George to do whatever he wanted. In contrast, six-year-olds viewed it as a punishable wrong for George to behave in that manner. But by age 9 or 10 the children understood that George probably wouldn't want to be teased by other kids, but that if he wanted to play with dolls and wear dresses, it would not be wrong to do so. Just prior to the time when gender constancy is attained, children see sex-appropriate behavior and wearing sex-appropriate clothing as a matter of right and wrong; after attaining gender constancy, they can relax a bit about what they must do to maintain their sexual identity.

Clearly, there is a lot more going on in children's conceptions of gender than their coming to see maleness and femaleness as basic biological categories. But it is perfectly clear from the studies reviewed above that for children below age 7, gender is not a basic biological fact about people. Rather, its meaning to children is social: what they wear, how they cut their hair, what they like to play with, and how other people react to these choices. Coming to see gender as a biological given is part of the emergence of biology as a separate domain of intuitive theorizing that occurs during the first decade of life. One source of this change is very likely learning about reproduction, for gender differences play a crucial role in explaining the origin of babies. Indeed, the child's understanding of reproduction also undergoes reorganization between the ages of 4 and 10, as we shall see next.

Reproduction

Parents and schools are concerned with how to broach the subjects of sex and birth. Understanding reproduction involves knowing the mechanics and purpose of sexual intercourse. Furthermore, understanding how human beings reproduce involves solving a major conceptual problem, grasping that there is a transition from nonexistence to existence, and proposing some mechanism by which this transition might be achieved.

Two extensive studies of developing concepts of reproduction are Bernstein and Cowan 1975 and Goldman and Goldman 1982. Both teams queried children ranging widely in age (3 to 12 in the former case; 5 to 16 in the latter). Although the actual wording of the two interviews differed slightly, both probed the origin of babies and the role of the mother and the father in producing babies. Both found substantially the same developmental progression.

The Origin of Babies

The responses of the youngest children (3- and 4-year-olds, some 5-year-olds) presuppose that babies have always existed. Before birth, the baby lives somewhere else—at a store, in its mother's tummy, in some other person's tummy. The child interprets the question "How do people get babies?" as "Where do babies come from?"—that is, as being literally about the "where" of the matter. As Bernstein and Cowan put it, "The problem is to discover where the baby was before it was present in the family, no need to explain how." Asked how people get babies, the child may answer "You go to a baby store and buy one" (age 3:8) or simply "From tummies" (age 3:2). Table 2.1 presents an example of level 1 responses to the question "How does the baby happen to be inside the mother's tummy?"

The second level of responses to "How are babies made?" is also profoundly nonbiological; the child focuses on the word "made" and describes a process of manufacture. How does the baby get in the tummy? "Just make it first." How? "Well, you just make it. You put some eyes on it . . . put the head on, and hair, some hair all curls." With? "You make it with head stuff." How? "You find a store that makes it . . . Well, they get it and then they put it in the tummy and then it goes quickly out" (age 3:7). Also characteristic of this stage is the "digestive fallacy," whereby the baby gets into the tummy by being ingested as food and exits as in elimination. Table 2.1 provides further examples.

Bernstein and Cowan studied the children of highly educated middle class families in Berkeley, California; 90% of the 3- to 4-year-old sample responded at level 1 or 2 to questions about the origin of babies. Goldman and Goldman's subjects were from North America, Australia, England, and Sweden and spanned a wider range of social classes. Level 1 or 2 responses were provided by 84%, 90%, 82%, and 54% of the 5-year-olds, respectively. When it comes to reproduction, the preschool child's information is exceedingly scanty and is placed in the context of purposeful human activity.

The next level is transitional. The child is aware of three aspects of the explanation of "where babies come from": the social relationship (some affective and/or marital bond between man and woman), the mechanics of sexual intercourse, and some components of the creation of new life (the egg, sperm, fluid). However, the child's explanations are tinged with animistic attributions to the components—the sperm "makes a little hole and then it swims into the vagina." How? "It has a

Table 2.1
How the baby happens to be inside the mother's body

Level 1

(How did the baby happen to be in your mommy's tummy?) It just grows inside. (How did it get there?) It was there all the time. Mommy doesn't have to do anything. She waits until she feels it.

Level 2

(If the seed is in the daddy, how does it get on the egg?) I don't know. 'Cause he can't really open up all his tummies. (Then how?) It rolls out. (How does it get to the egg?) Well, I think that the daddy gets it. (How?) Puts his hand in the tummy. (Whose?) His tummy. (Then?) He puts it on the bottom of the mommy and the mommy gets the, gets the egg out of her tummy, and puts the egg on top of the seed. And then they close their tummies . . . and the baby is born . . .

Level 3

People have children if they get married. (How?) They sleep together and cuddle. (How does the baby get inside the mother's tummy?) The baby just grows from the food the mother eats. The father warms her tummy in bed and it grows.

Level 4

(Knows that the seed from the father is united with the egg from the mother inside the mother.) Or else the baby, the egg won't really get hatched very well. (How does the baby come from the egg and the seed?) The seed makes the egg grow. It's just like plants; if you plant a seed a flower will grow. (There's no egg with plants.) No, it's just a special kind of seed, that makes an egg hatch. (Why must the seed touch the egg for the baby to grow?) The egg won't hatch. (What about its coming together makes a baby?) I don't know. Well, I don't think . . . I don't know.

Level 5

(Knows that the sperm fertilizes the egg.) (What does "fertilize" mean?) Kind of give it food and things like that . . . (How is it that the baby starts growing when the sperm goes into the egg?) I guess when it gets in there it just does something to the egg, and it makes it start growing . . . (Can the egg grow if no sperm goes into it?) I don't think so. (Can the sperm grow with no egg?) No, that doesn't have the baby. It's the egg that would have the baby in it.

Level 6

(Knows that the sperm fertilizes the egg.) Well, it just, it starts it off, I guess. You know. Mixes the genes, or, well, puts particles or something into the egg, to make it, you know, fertilized. And so it will, you know, have genes and different kinds of blood and stuff like that, I guess. Because if it didn't, it would be more like the mother, I guess. (What do the genes have to do with it?) Well, genes are the things from the father and the mother, you know, and they put a little bit of each into the baby so the baby turns out to be a little bit like the mother or father or something. Not all ways, but a little bit.

Table 2.2
Attainment of levels 4, 5, or 6 on origin-of-babies scale (percentage)

Age	N. America[a]	N. America[b]	England[b]	Australia[b]	Sweden[b]
7	30[a]	0	2	7	56
9		17	52	40	83
11	100[a]	80	63	87	97

[a]Bernstein and Cowan (1975) study. 7-year-olds actually 7 and 8; 11-year-olds actually 11 and 12.
[b]Goldman and Goldman (1982) study.

little mouth and it bites a hole" (age 4:6). Also classified as level 3 responses are elaborate literal interpretations of the agricultural metaphor—the seed is planted in the mommy's tummy (often by her swallowing it or by manual insertion), the fluid from the daddy's penis waters it, the stomach is lined with soil in which the baby grows, etc.

The fourth level of responses is free of animism and artificialism. The child understands the mechanics of sexual intercourse and knows that babies result from the fusion of sperm and eggs. That is, the child is aware of the facts of life. Still missing is any understanding of how this process causes the new life to begin. Level 4 responses are distinguished from level 5 and level 6 responses in that the latter two involve explanations for what it is about the sperm and the egg coming together that produces a baby. Level 5 children create a preformation theory—either the baby exists in the sperm, but requires the egg for food and protection, or the baby exists in the egg and requires the sperm as a trigger to growth. Level 6 children have some understanding of genetic mixture.

Table 2.2 shows the proportion of children classified at level 4 or higher in the five samples of subjects. There is a sharp increase in the proportion of such responses between ages 7 and 8, on the one hand, and age 11, on the other. Ninety percent of Bernstein and Cowan's 11- and 12-year-olds responded at levels 5 and 6, as did between 15% (Australian sample) and 47% (Swedish sample) of Goldman and Goldman's 11-year-olds. The Swedish subjects were several years ahead of the other groups.

The Role of the Mother and Father in Procreation
Goldman and Goldman directly asked, "Does the mother do anything to start a baby?" and "Does the father do anything to start a baby?" Most of the 5- and 7-year-olds, at levels 1 and 2 on the origin-of-babies

scale (again excepting the Swedish subjects, who were approximately 4 years ahead of their peers from other countries), either could specify no role for parents in getting babies started or outlined activities parents engage in after conception: the mother rests, diets, exercises, eats special food, visits the doctor; the father drives the mother to the hospital, helps with housework, etc. When activities leading to the actual starting of the baby were mentioned, by older children, responses were consistent with the origin-of-babies responses. For example, level 2 children who have the digestive model say that the mother must eat the food that turns into the baby, and level 3 children who have the agricultural model discuss the father's role in planting the seeds. Only at age 11 (age 9 in Sweden) do children have an understanding of sexual intercourse in which both parents are seen to play a symmetrical role in the starting of babies, namely, doing what is necessary to get the sperm and egg together.

Conclusions: Reproduction
These data point toward familiar conclusions. Preschool children see the origin of babies only in terms of the intentional behavior of the parents, who go out to a store to buy them or who make them and place them in the mother's tummy. Young children know nothing about how a person's body produces a baby. Primary grade children have been told the facts of life and might well mention sperms and eggs, but their understanding of the process of birth is based on analogies to activities for which physiological mechanisms are not yet known. So the egg is assimilated to a chicken's egg; the sperm protects it like a shell. For a child who uses the agricultural metaphor, the semen waters the seed implanted in the soil lining the mother's tummy. These beliefs are truly transitional. Like 10-year-olds, these children are now imagining internal bodily processes; but like younger children, they understand them in terms of human behavior. Since they do not yet understand the roles of eating and watering in promoting growth, their talk of planting and watering seeds is continuous with talk of buying parts and manufacturing a baby. By age 10 they make a clear distinction between the role of the body and the role of the parents: to have intercourse is intentional; from then on the body takes over. A distinct level of bodily processes results in a new baby. Again, understanding in terms of human activities has been supplemented by an additional level of understanding in terms of processes in which wants and beliefs play no explanatory role.

The child's role as theory builder is very clear. The preformation model was articulated by more than 30% of the children age 11 and older in all five groups studied. It is unlikely that preformation is taught. Rather, preformation is a sophisticated way of understanding, in the absence of an understanding of genetic mixing, exactly how the body produces new life. Younger children's responses are also constructions. Obviously, they are not taught that parents go to special stores to buy babies or the materials out of which babies are constructed; these are theories fabricated from their own experience and understanding. For example, Bernstein and Cowan describe the child who gravely explained that to create a baby, parents first buy a duck, which then turns into a rabbit, which then turns into a baby. When asked how he learned this, he replied, "From a book," the book being one that tries to defuse the issue of the mechanics of sex by starting with the birds and the bees (in this case, the ducks and the rabbits).

The data on children's understanding of the role of mothers and fathers in creating babies complements the literature on their understanding of sex roles. As we have seen, gender is a social matter to young children—partly because they do not yet grasp its biological nature.

The fact that Goldman and Goldman's Swedish subjects were several years ahead of their peers from other countries in their understanding of reproduction no doubt reflects cultural differences in attitudes toward sex and the quality of information available to young children in the various countries. Should Swedish children also show early command of the other indicators of the establishment of a separate domain of intuitive biology in the years before age 10? This is an interesting question, for it bears on the issue of what drives the conceptual reorganization documented in this monograph. I would venture to say no, that Swedish children would not be advanced in their understanding of death, growth, internal organs and their functions, etc. My guess is that the reorganization occurs when enough *different* aspects of biological knowledge have been mastered that some critical mass has been reached. (This is a deliberately vague statement; I will return to the mechanism of change in chapter 7.) What about gender constancy, then? Would Swedish children attain gender constancy earlier, since they understand the role of sex in reproduction earlier? Here the answer may be yes, if coming to see gender as part of the biological essence of each person is indeed one factor that drives the attainment of gender constancy.

Death

Adults faced with the difficult task of explaining the death of a loved one to a child have sought advice from psychologists. Also, children's conceptions of death are of some theoretical import in psychoanalytic theory. For these reasons there is a robust clinical literature on the child's understanding of death. The methods used in the research have ranged from diary studies to projective techniques (drawings, story completions, etc.) to clinical interviews structured around basic questions such as what makes people die, whether death is irreversible, whether death is inevitable, and so on. I have reviewed only the literature in English, which covers studies done over the past 80 years in Hungary, Germany, England, and the United States. A remarkably consistent picture emerges from this research. All authors agree on three periods in the child's emerging understanding of death.

In the first period, characteristic of children age 5 and under, the notion of death is assimilated to the notions of sleep and departure. The emotional import of death comes from the child's view of it as a sorrowful separation and/or as the ultimate act of aggression (Anthony 1940). In this period death is seen neither as final nor as inevitable. Just as one wakes from sleep or returns from a trip, so one can return from death. Although children associate death with closed eyes and immobility, as in sleep, they do not grasp the totality of the cessation of function. Nor do they understand the causes of death. Even though they might mention illness or accidents, it is clear that they envision no mechanisms by which illness or accidents cause death. As Anthony summarizes it,

The realization that human beings die overshadows the greater generality of death as a biological fact. . . . Death is thought of in terms of human experience. To think of it as biological process . . . is a distinctly later stage. (p. 93)

As Nagy (1948) characterizes the conception of death in terms of human experience,

. . . in general these children do not accept death. To die means the same as living on, under changed circumstances. Death is thus departure. If someone dies no change takes place in him. Our lives change, inasmuch as we see him no longer, he lives with us no longer. This, however, does not mean that the child has no disagreeable sentiments about death, because for them the most painful thing about death is just the separation itself. (p. 11)

When these authors say that death is not yet understood biologically, they have two things in mind. Children do not yet see death as the last stage in every animal's life cycle. Also, they do not understand death in terms of the cessation of biological functions required to support life. This is utterly predictable from the data on the child's understanding of bodily functions; the young child knows next to nothing about the biological functions death is the cessation of. In the absence of a bio-logical framework for understanding death, the concept is placed in the context of the child's understanding of human activities and emotions. The evidence for this characterization of the child's first understanding of death is culled mainly from diaries and clinical interviews. Table 2.3 reproduces protocols in support of it (see also table 1.4, protocols from my 3-year-old daughter). The first group exemplifies children's assimi-lation of sleep and death and their denial of the finality and totality of death. The second and third exemplify the emotional impact of death as separation and punishment. And the fourth demonstrates the arbitrari-ness of children's notions of the causes of death. That is, children have been told some things that cause death, but they know no mechanisms by which death results from going with a stranger or eating a dirty bug. In all four of the protocols reproduced in Koocher 1974, children in this first stage mentioned poison as the cause of death.

Just as preschool children fail to see the real conceptual problem of birth—the transition from nonexistence to existence—so too they fail to grasp that death is a transition from existence to nonexistence. The second stage (early elementary years) in the child's understanding of death is transitional and is characterized differently in the different studies. All authors agree that children now understand the finality of death, and that they understand the sense in which a dead person no longer exists. However, children still see death as caused by an exter-nal agent. In Nagy 1948 death was personified in this stage as "Father Death" who caught people. Safier (1964) and Koocher (1974) report little personification, but agree that their subjects see the causes of death as external to the dying person. In Koocher's study, in which subjects were asked directly what makes things die, children in this stage listed myriad specific causes (p. 407):

Knives, arrows, guns, lots of stuff. Do you want me to tell you all of them? . . . Hatchets and animals, and fire and explosions too.

Cancer, heart attacks, old age, poison, guns, a bullet, or if someone drops a boulder on you. (Anything else?) That's all.

Table 2.3
The child's first conception of death

Death is reversible, assimilated to sleep and departure

T. P. (age 4:10; from Nagy 1948:10)

T. P. A dead person is just as if he were asleep. Sleeps in the ground, too.

G. Sleeps the same as you do at night, or otherwise?

T. P. Well—closes his eyes. Sleeps like people at night. Sleeps like that, just like that.

G. How do you know whether someone is asleep or dead?

T. P. I know if they go to bed at night and don't open their eyes. If somebody goes to bed and doesn't get up, he's dead or ill.

G. Will he ever wake up?

T. P. Never. A dead person only knows if somebody goes out to the grave or something. He feels that somebody is there, or is talking.

G. Are you certain? You're not mistaken?

T. P. I don't think so. At funerals you're not allowed to sing, just talk, because otherwise the dead person couldn't sleep peacefully. A dead person feels it if you put something on his grave.

G. What is it he feels then?

T. P. He feels that flowers are put on his grave. The water touches the sand. Slowly, slowly, he hears everything. Auntie, does the dead person feel it if it goes deep into the ground? (i.e., the water).

G. What do you think, wouldn't he like to come away from there?

T. P. He would like to come out, but the coffin is nailed down.

G. If he weren't in the coffin, could he come back?

T. P. He couldn't root up all that sand.

J. M. (age 3:11; from Nagy 1948:10–11)

G. What does he do, since he is in the coffin?

J. M. Sleeps. Covered with sand. It's dark there.

G. Does he sleep as we do at night, or differently?

J. M. He puts sand there, lies on it. If you die the bed will be sandy, then the sheet will be black.

E. S. (age 3:11; from Von Hug-Hellmuth 1965:502)

He asks his parents, with voice nearly failing, not to eat any more of the fishes they were having for dinner so they could be put back in the water and come alive and swim again.

The emotional impact of death: separation

E. S. (age 4:2; from Von Hug-Hellmuth 1965:504)

Upon being told that a dead child would never wake up, he sighs, then brightens up. "So the men can shovel the sand away and pull the flowers away from the grave and can sell the little boy to his mother again—so she can have her child again."

F. R. (age 9:10; from Nagy 1948:11)

F. R. I was six years old. A friend of my father's died. They didn't tell me, but I heard. Then I didn't understand. I felt as when Mother goes travelling somewhere—I don't see her anymore.

Table 2.3 (continued)

The emotional impact of death: punishment
E. S. (age 4:4; from Von Hug-Hellmuth 1965:505)
On seeing a funeral procession the boy became upset about the gravedigger
who was going to shovel earth over the coffin. He apparently blamed this
man for the death, *and only with the matter of burying-in-the-earth did he
connect the idea of being dead,* for now he can already imagine that deep
under the earth a person can no longer breathe and live. Very agitatedly he
called out: "The old gravers (gravediggers) shouldn't always dig such a
grave and put people in it. But I'll get rid of the sand and the flowers and *let
the people out again. And I'll take the old graver and throw him into the
water.* And then I'll crawl up to the sky on a ladder and shovel a lot of ice
into my bucket—there's a lot of ice up there, you know; the other time lots
of ice came from the sky (memory of a recent hailstorm)—and then I'll pour
the ice on the bad man's head, and then he'll get a cold, and his nose will
be bloody, all bloody, and *then the graver will be completely dead,* and I'll
pour out more and more ice, *and he'll be deader and deader."*

The avoidable, magical causes of death
N. (age 6:5; from Koocher 1974:407)
Asked what makes people die, replies, "When they eat bad things, like if
you went with a stranger and they gave you a candy bar with poison on it."
(Anything else?) "Yes, you can die if you swallow a dirty bug."

Certainly all of the things these children have listed are possible causes
of death, as is the poison listed by children at an earlier stage. But all
are things that *happen to* people (or that people catch, like a disease),
usually through the agency of another person. The child does not yet
conceptualize death in terms of what happens within the body as a
result of these external events. The psychoanalytic literature points out
that by externalizing death, children try to have it both ways. If
pushed, they admit that death is inevitable; but their answers seem to
imply that if Father Death does not come for you, or if you can avoid
cancer, bullets, and boulders, you need not die.

One way that children's concept of death is still embedded in their
knowledge of human behavior, even in this second transitional period,
is that they often take death as punishment for evildoing. When asked
why people die, children in Nagy's study credited Father Death or God
with coming after people who have been bad. An American study
(White, Elsom, and Prawat 1978) showed that contemporary upper
middle class American children have the same views. White, Elsom
and Prawat told children stories about a woman who died. For half of
the subjects the character was a mean, selfish, unpleasant person; for
the other half she was a sweet, generous, warm person. After the story,

subjects were asked, "Do you have any idea why Mrs. Wilson died?" About one-fourth of the 85 children (ages 5 to 9) who heard about the unpleasant Mrs. Wilson attributed her death to some unkind act she had committed. Although this finding no doubt reflects demand characteristics of the task and misplaced faith that there is justice in this world, presumably older children would not make this inference. They understand much more clearly just where in the process of dying intentional behavior could play a role. Character does not intervene in the causal chain leading to the cessation of bodily functions, unless one person drives another to murder.

In the final stage death is seen as an inevitable biological process. Such a view of death first becomes evident around age 9 or 10 (Koocher 1974, Nagy 1948, Safier 1964, Anthony 1940, Mitchell 1967). To Koocher's question about the causes of death, one sage 12-year-old answered, "When the heart stops, blood stops circulating, you stop breathing, and that's it. . . . Well, there's lots of ways it can get started, but that's what really happens." Another example from a 10-year-old in Koocher's study: "When someone gets too old. You could also die of a sickness or if you couldn't have enough to eat. . . . Well, when you get old you can just wear out eventually." Or from a 10-year-old Hungarian in Nagy's study: "It means the passing of the body. Death is a great squaring of accounts in our lives. It is a thing from which our bodies cannot be resurrected. It is like the withering of flowers." Only in this last stage is death restricted to biological organisms (Safier 1964).

Cultural differences can be seen in the details of the children's beliefs. Only the Hungarian children personified death in the second stage: these children also blended the biological and the religious in the third stage. That is, many knew that the body suffers biological death, but considered that the soul lives on. Surprisingly, this religious notion is little evident in the American protocols. Underneath the cultural variation, however, the same developmental sequence over the years 4 to 10 emerged in each study: from seeing death in terms of human activities and emotions to seeing it as the cessation of bodily processes.

Conceptualizing death as a fundamental biological process does not *replace* seeing it in the context of human activity and emotions. The emotional impact of death remains attributable to its being an irreversible loss; human beings can contribute to the deaths of others and there are things humans can do to minimize the likelihood of dying at any given time. What the literature on the child's concept of death shows is that by about age 10 the child has constructed *another* framework for conceptualizing death—an intuitive biology.

Growth and Personal Identity

As people grow, they change. The landmarks of the human life cycle are as inevitable as they are bewildering: infancy, childhood, adolescence, adulthood, old age. Through all this change, each person maintains his or her essential identity. The literature on the child's understanding of growth and the maintenance of personal identity through growth is scanty, especially compared to the literature on the child's understanding of death. But what there is suggests that (1) growth for preschool children is merely getting bigger, (2) the explanation for why people grow is given in terms of human activities; preschool children have no account of growth in terms of the functioning of the bodily machine, and (3) the maintenance of personal identity through the life cycle is beyond the young child's understanding.

Interchanges initiated by my daughter between ages 3 and 4 illustrate these points (table 2.4). The earliest one, about what would happen to the little girl Eliza when she grew up, shows dramatically that she considered being a little girl essential to Eliza's identity; though she had heard that she would grow up, she thought that meant there would no longer be an Eliza. (Notice also the spontaneous level 1 view of the origin of babies.) At this point, growing up entailed becoming someone else—a grown-up, a teacher, Satu. In the next three or four months she repeatedly brought up this issue, grappling with what would happen to her friends when they grew up, what it meant that her father and I had once been little children. She came to be able to mouth the "right" answers—that she would always be named Eliza, that her friend Daniel would always be named Daniel, that her father and I had been children in somebody else's family but we had always been Ned and Susan. Her constant return to this question, like her constant return to the question of death (table 1.4), shows the conceptual salience and emotional charge of the issue of what would happen to the *real* her when she grew up.

I know of two studies of children's understanding of the maintenance of personal identity through growth. G. Voyat (reported in Piaget 1968) had children draw themselves as a baby, at their current age, as a grown-up, and as an old person. They then made analogous drawings of the experimenter at each of these stages. Finally, they witnessed the

Table 2.4
Personal identity and growth

Personal identity

E. (age 3:9) When I grow up, there won't be a little girl named Eliza around here anymore.

S. That's right.

E. Will you go out and buy another one?

S. Oh no, we love the Eliza we have, and we won't need to; what do you think will happen to you when you grow up?

E. I'll be a teacher.

S. But what will your name be?

E. Satu (the name of her favorite teacher at day care).

Growth

E. (age 4:0) Sings song with words "nor you nor I nor anyone knows, how oats, peas, beans, and barley grow."

S. I don't even know how Eliza grows.

E. I do; I have birthdays.

E. (age 4:0) Watching *The Wizard of Oz* on TV. Very much interested in the Munchkins, played by dwarves, understanding that they are adults but are smaller than Dorothy, a child. Asks, "Why are they so small? Why didn't they grow? Oh, I bet I know; I bet their mothers didn't let them eat birthday cake."

S. Asks Eliza (about 4:5) to name some things that can roll, that can be eaten, etc. Then asks for a list of things that can grow.

E. People, and animals.

S. Anything else?

E. Flowers.

S. Anything else?

E. I can't think of anything.

S. What about baths? (Eliza is taking a bath at the time.)

E. Oh yes, and sand castles.

S. What does a sand castle need to grow?

E. More sand.

S. What about a bath?

E. Water.

S. What about a flower?

E. Water, and sun.

S. What about people and animals.

E. Food, and birthday parties, birthday cake.

S then asks Eliza to say of a list including people, flowers, sand castles, balloons, and birds, which are most alike in the ways they grow.

E. People and birds go together. Flowers, balloons, and sand castles go together.

---

rapid growth of "seaweed" resulting from a grain of potassium ferro-cyanide seeded in a solution of copper sulphate, and made a series of drawings representing the plant at successive points in its development. They were then questioned whether the pictures depicted one and the same plant. The youngest children (under 7 or 8) claimed that pictures depicting the plant close in size showed the same plant, but that those differing in size did not. "It grew, but it isn't the same any more; here it's a little plant and there it's a big plant, it's not the same plant" (Piaget 1968:28). This fragment of protocol is somewhat bizarre—what is the "it" that is a little plant over here and a big plant over here, if not one and the same plant? Nonetheless, children did explicitly deny that it remained the same plant. In contrast, the children tested by Voyat had no problems understanding the maintenance of their own ("It's still me") or the experimenter's identity; Piaget does not report the ages of Voyat's youngest subjects.

Guardo and Bohan (1971) asked 6- to 9-year-old children how long they had been the boy (or girl) they now were. The proportion of "always" responses rose from 19% at age 6 to 71% at age 9. Children who denied they were the same child all their lives claimed they were different when they were babies or before they went to school. These responses must partly be due to the specific wording of the question; after all, when I was a baby I wasn't the "same girl" I was when I was 7. But there is a dramatic increase from ages 6 to 9 in ignoring the implications of the wording, due to the older child's firmer grasp of the maintenance of personal identity throughout growth. Guardo and Bo-han also asked their subjects whether each would be the same person in the higher grades and as a grown-up. There was little developmental change in the proportion of "yes" responses (about 85% for the near future questions and only 65% for the far future questions). Younger children (ages 6 and 7) appealed to the fact that their names would not change in support of their assertion that they would still be the same person. Eight- and 9-year-olds were more likely to try to refer to their singular and personal identity. One 8-year-old, for example, said "I'll still be the same person." E.: "What stays the same?" "My per-son-al-i-ty" (Guardo and Bohan 1971:1920).

The importance of the children's names in maintaining their sense of identity over time was assessed by asking them if they would remain the same person if their names were to be taken away or changed. Over 25% of the 6- and 7-year-olds said they would not remain the same person if their names were changed, whereas only 5% of the 8- and 9-year-olds answered this way.

The stark confusion about the maintenance of personal identity as one grows, seen in Eliza at age 3, persists through the early elementary years, as shown by the studies of Voyat (Piaget 1968) and Guardo and Bohan (1971). By age 5 or 6, children *know* that as they grow they keep the same name, but they have a very fragile idea of any other senses in which they stay the same person. They do not yet have a concept of an individual person's life cycle (let alone of a plant's) around which to organize their sense of personal identity. As Guardo and Bohan stress, not only the biological concept of the life cycle is being developed before age 10. The concept of a person, in psychological terms, is also enriched during the early elementary years (for a review, see Maccoby 1980).

A bit after Eliza was concerned with what would happen to *her* when she was replaced by an adult, the topic of growth came up several times. When she was around 4:0, it became clear that she believed that people grew on their birthdays and that birthday cake was crucial to the process (see table 2.4; there were several other interchanges similar to those reproduced in the table). These anecdotes illustrate several points. Eliza's view of growth was related to her knowledge of social activities—birthday celebrations and the eating of birthday cake. More-over, growth was not biological in any sense that encompassed all living things, even though she knew that both animals and plants grow. It meant simply "getting bigger." Finally, just as the causes of death are somewhat magical for children of this age (e.g., "You eat a dirty bug"), so the causes of growth were too, at least for her.

The conceptual problems with the idea of growth come not only from lack of biological knowledge. The child of this age also has difficulty conceptualizing time (Piaget 1946). This contributes to the preschool child's identification of getting older with getting bigger (Looft 1971). These confusions came together when Eliza wondered whether I would suddenly be taller than her father after eating my birthday cake, for there is a short period each year when I am counted as one year older than he is (i.e., I am actually three months older).

I know of no investigation of when children see biological growth (as it applies to both animals and plants) as a single process, different from other cases of getting bigger, but from the research presented so far we would expect them to achieve this understanding around age 9 or 10, for this is both the age when children understand digestion in terms in which a mechanism for growth can be stated and the age at which bodily functions have become firmly differentiated from the intentional activities of the person as a whole.

Conclusions

The literature on the young child's intuitive theory of human behavior is much too vast to review here. An entire branch of cognitive development—developmental social cognition—is devoted to the topic, and the literature on the child's concept of self, moral development, sex role development, metacognition, and even aspects of language acquisition are all relevant. What I have reviewed in this chapter affords a partial sketch of the young child's concept of a person. For a much fuller account, see reviews by Maccoby (1980) and Flavell (1985).

The core of preschool children's conceptions of people is their attempt to understand human behavior. They catalogue and classify it (just what behaviors there are, and just what kinds) and make generalizations about its consequences (both specific consequences such as gaining weight from eating too much candy and general consequences such as approval and punishment) and its causes (in terms of wants and beliefs). Although preschool children are deeply concerned with understanding human behavior, they are not behaviorists (see Wellman 1985 for a review). Thus, I have spoken of the framework young children have for understanding human behavior as an *intuitive psychology,* because it is based on intentional causality. Death, growth, eating, sleeping, breathing, the heart's beating, playing boys' or girls' games, and having babies are all assimilated into this framework. It is enough to explain the function of the heart by mentioning its behavior ("it ticks"), although some young children see the heart as the organ of emotion and morality just as the brain is the organ of mentation. There is no biological inevitability to death and growth; the causes of each are seen in terms of human behavior, as are the consequences. There is nothing wrong with the assimilation of all of these behaviors in an intuitive psychology; they all have a valid role there. However, by age 10 children have another framework for understanding all of these behaviors: in terms of the integrated functioning of internal body parts. Intentional causation plays no role in the explanation of the workings of the bodily machine: the stomach does not want to digest the food; the heart does not believe that circulating the blood will distribute food throughout the body. That's just the way the body works.

In this chapter I have described children's knowledge of the circulatory, respiratory, and digestive systems and of the role of the body in death, growth, and reproduction. In each case, vast differences have been documented between the 4-year-old's understanding and the 10-year-old's. Indeed, the 10-year-old largely resembles the naive adult with regard to this domain of knowledge. The developmental advances between ages 4 and 10 are conceptually interrelated. Understanding the functions of internal organs in maintaining life supports understanding death as the cessation of vital bodily function. Understanding digestion as the transformation of food supports understanding growth in biological as well as social terms. Understanding the body as a functioning machine in these domains supports understanding reproduction in this way. Finally, knowing the biology of reproduction supports seeing gender in biological as well as social terms. Thus, all of these developments are deeply interconnected—none is logically required for the other, and all support each other. Such is the nature of theory emergence (Kuhn 1962).

The argument for an interconnection among these developments is conceptual. Empirical evidence that the developments are causally related is indirect—namely, that they occur together between ages 4 and 10. The studies reviewed in this chapter were carried out independently of each other, by different investigators, on different subjects, sometimes even in different cultures. Massive training studies would be required to sort out just how these developments can influence each other. As yet, no such study has been attempted.

A good half of the studies reviewed in this chapter were placed by their authors in the context of Piaget's general stages of development. For example, Koocher (1974) discussed children's preoperational, concrete operational, and formal operational views of death, Contento (1981) described the same three stages in children's views of digestion, Crider (1981) the same three stages in their understanding of bodily processes, and Bernstein and Cowan (1975) the same three stages in their conceptualization of reproduction. The earliest stages in each case are seen as preoperational because the child indulges in magical reasoning or fantasy. The middle stages are seen as concrete operational because the child is now thinking in terms of mechanisms, but not in terms of mechanisms stated at two levels of analysis. The final stage includes mechanisms stated at two levels of analysis and is therefore deemed formal operational. The proper description of the successive conceptualizations in each case does indeed encompass these differences, but what is added by labeling them preoperational, concrete operational, and formal operational? Piaget intended these stages to refer to characteristics of the logic available to children. But preschool children's views of death, digestion, and reproduction are not illogical (in any sense of illogical) because they think that vitamins are pink and purple bear-shaped pills and that eating vitamins staves off death whereas eating dirty bugs invites it, and because they think that babies are bought at stores. Nor are the 10-year-old's views more logical (in any sense), although they certainly conform to the adult's more closely than do the preschooler's. Labeling the stages in the child's understanding of reproduction as preoperational, concrete operational, and formal operational commits one to the claim that there is something about the nature of the child's thought that limits understanding digestion or the origin of babies—something about the child's thought that would also limit understanding in any other domain of knowledge. There is an alternative view: the changes in conceptualization of the human body reviewed in this chapter are indeed interrelated, as suggested above, but are not constrained by limitations on the child's thinking. The restructuring we have witnessed is within the domain of understanding human activity. The increasing complexity of this understanding typifies all examples of novice-expert shifts, all examples of theory emergence, regardless of the age of the people involved.

I began this excursion into the published literature on children's knowledge of the human body in order to learn something about their biological knowledge. I wanted to examine whether children below age 9 or 10 do not know enough biology to rationalize the inclusion of animals and plants in a single category. Though we have seen a dramatic increase in biological knowledge between the ages of 4 and 9 or 10, we do not yet really have an answer to this question. We do not yet know what "enough biology" would be to support the biological concept *living thing*. Indeed, we do not even know at what age children understand that all animals are like people with regard to certain aspects of biological functioning, and that each animal is a unique solution to common biological problems. These questions are logically independent of how one conceptualizes the human body. However, we might expect that changes in the child's understanding of humankind's membership in the animal kingdom accompany the developmental changes described in this chapter. The next four chapters document several ways this expectation is realized.

Chapter 3
The Biological Concept *Animal*

The studies in chapter 2 probed children's understanding of people as biological organisms—their knowledge about human internal organs and their functions, where human babies come from, what makes people grow, what happens when people die. Four-year-olds know little about what is inside their bodies, and they see a person's gender, growth, death, eating, breathing, etc., in terms of what the person wants and thinks. By age 10 a new framework for understanding people has emerged, an intuitive biology. Ten-year olds see death, reproduction, gender, digestion, circulation, and respiration in terms of internal bodily processes. They have achieved a new kind of explanation: explanation in terms of the integrated functioning of body parts. The studies reviewed in chapter 2 raise the question of how young children conceive of nonhuman animals. What do they think is to be found inside a dog's body, a fish's body, a worm's body? What do they know about animals as a class? If human babies are bought at stores or constructed by their parents, what about dog babies, fish babies, worm babies? Do children even know that all animals have babies, or that all animals eat and breathe? To the extent that young children's knowledge of such processes is embedded in their understanding of human behavior, and to the extent that they do not understand the role of such processes in maintaining life and activity, one would not expect them to credit these processes to nonhuman animals. On the other hand, these animals also behave. To the extent that children apply their understanding of human behavior to nonhuman animals, they might understand that other animals also eat, breathe, grow, etc.

This chapter is the first of three exploring the reorganization of the child's concept of *animal* over the years from 4 to 10. I explore the relation between the new framework for understanding people that has emerged by age 10 and the sense in which the child considers people to be just one kind of animal among many. No less than the concept of life, the concept *animal* plays a major organizing role in biological theory. Animals are one main branch of the biological kingdom, and children are more likely to know that the biologically important anthropomorphic traits—eating, breathing, being active—are properties of animals than that they are properties of plants. In this chapter I begin to examine at what age the child represents a concept with the same extension as the adult's concept *animal,* and when this concept begins to constrain the child's inferences about these biologically important traits.

One might trace the development of the child's concept *animal* by tracing the meaning of the word "animal," just as Piaget tried to trace the concept of life by studying the acquisition of the meaning of "alive." Anglin (1977) has shown that the word "animal" functions differently in the young child's lexicon than in the adult's. When asked what things are animals, children under 7 exclude people and tend to exclude nonprototypical animals such as insects. Inanimate objects are not called animals. Anglin's results, taken together with those reviewed in chapter 1, also show that for the preschool child the word "animal" is not synonymous with the word "alive." The pattern for judging things to be animals contrasts markedly with that for judging things to be alive. There is no "stage 0" for the term "animal." Even 2-year-olds use the word to pick out a systematic subset of what adults call "animals." Further, "animal" does not include all animals, and it excludes inanimate objects. In contrast, "alive" includes some inanimate objects in its extension, as well as all animals.

The difference between the child's meaning for "animal" and the adult's may have a conceptual basis, in that the child may not represent any concept with the same extension as the adult concept *animal.* It is also possible that the child *has* the adult concept, but does not use "animal" to express it. The English word "animal" is ambiguous among three dominant uses. Sometimes it contrasts with plants and with inanimate objects, as in "the animal kingdom." This is the sense I intend with the phrase "the biological concept *animal.*" Sometimes it contrasts with people, as in "Don't eat like an animal." And sometimes it means roughly "mammal," as in "birds, bugs, snakes, and animals." Anglin's data show that the young child's meaning for the word is some amalgam of the latter two of its adult senses. It is an open question whether the young child's conceptual system represents the concept *animal* in the sense in which it contrasts with *plant* and *inanimate object*. Because the word has not been mapped onto the inclusive concept, we must look to some other method for finding the answer.

Data from chapter 1 suggests the technique adopted here to probe the child's conceptual system for the concept *animal*. Animal properties like breathing, having legs, and eating were often mentioned in children's justifications for the attribution of life. For example, one child said that snakes are alive because they breathe, and another said that airplanes are not, because "even though they fly, they do not breathe." In order for an animal property to be used in such a justification, the child must know that that object does, or does not, have it. Some anthropomorphic traits are salient surface properties, such as having legs or a face. Others, like eating and breathing, pose an interesting question. How did the children mentioned above know that snakes breathe and that airplanes do not? Although it is possible that they actually picked up these specific pieces of information somewhere, it is more likely that both beliefs were inferences. If so, it is possible that the concept *animal* plays some role in the generation of such inferences.

Studies by Gelman, Spelke, and Meck (1983) and by Dolgin and Behrend (1984) confirm that animal properties of various types—internal and external parts, physiological functions, psychological functions, characteristic activities—are not attributed to inanimate objects, even by children as young as age 3. Both studies conclude that even very young children are not animistic, in the sense that they distinguish very clearly the kinds of objects that have animal properties from those that do not. This conclusion is consistent with that reached in chapter 1, where we found that children who restricted attribution of "alive" to animals alone did not make animistic errors; only those who tried to encompass animals and plants in a single category judged any inanimate objects alive. However, neither Gelman, Spelke, and Meck nor Dolgin and Behrend found children to be as good as adults in their attribution. Gelman, Spelke, and Meck did not study a wide range of animals (people and cats were the animals probed), and young children were not clear on whether to attribute to cats the one internal organ studied (the stomach). In contrast, Dolgin and Behrend did study a wide range of animals (people, mammals, birds, fish, and insects) and found that young children did not universally judge that animals grow, have brains, sleep, etc. The purpose of these two studies was to examine the pattern of attribution of animal properties to inanimate objects.

Neither examined the patterns of attribution across all animals. Thus, although they both confirm that the child represents some concepts that include people and some other animals and exclude inanimate objects, they do not settle the question of whether the child represents the biological concept *animal* (including people and all other animals, excluding plants and inanimate objects; henceforth, unless otherwise noted, I intend this inclusive sense whenever I speak of the concept *animal*).

In the research to be reported here, I asked subjects of various ages whether each of a series of objects eats, breathes, sleeps, has babies, has a heart, has bones, can get hurt, and thinks. I sought to constrain a model of how children answer questions such as "Do snakes breathe?" Once we have a satisfactory model for the generation of such judgments, we may ascertain the role, if any, that the concept *animal* plays in the process. If the concept *is* needed in the model, we can also use the data to begin to characterize it. To answer a question such as "Do snakes breathe?" children must combine information they have represented about snakes with information they have represented about breathing. At the outset, one may distinguish three classes of models:

Model Type I (Deductive inference or direct representation). In this class of models the only knowledge of breathing that the child uses is his current knowledge of which things breathe. If the child has not directly represented the fact that snakes breathe, he checks whether snakes are included in any class of things he knows to breathe, such as animals. If so, he answers "yes"; otherwise, "no." This class of models is characterized by deductively valid inference.

Model Type II (Application of definition). In this class of models the child retrieves a definition of the property in question. For breathing it might be "sucks air in and blows air out of its nose." The object is then examined with respect to applicability of the definition. Snakes might be deemed not to breathe because they have no noses, or they may be deemed to breathe because the child either knows they have nose holes or assumes they have noses because they have faces.

Model Type III (Similarity to exemplar). In this class of models the relevant knowledge of breathing is an exemplar of things that breathe. For example, the child might retrieve that people breathe, or that dogs do, or that fish do. He then compares the animal in question (in this case the snake) with the retrieved exemplar, and makes a judgment on the basis of the similarity between the two.

These three types of models differ in terms of the kinds of inferential processes that are deployed, and in terms of what knowledge of the objects and properties children appeal to in generating responses. A claim about which model actually underlies children's judgments does not entail that the knowledge used exhausts what they have represented about the properties or objects. For example, children may well generate an answer on the basis of deductive inference, or even comparison to a retrieved exemplar, even though they know a definition of the property in question.

A fourth model will also be considered—a guessing model. On this model, children simply guess, unless they definitely know the answer. For example, children may be certain that dodos breathe because they know that birds do, and they may be certain that tables do not breathe because they know that man-made artifacts do not, but they may have no idea whether worms breathe. In the case of worms, they guess. This guessing model is not listed separately because it could be combined with any of the three types we have distinguished on principled grounds: whenever some threshold of certainty (however generated) is not crossed, the child guesses.

The concept *animal* plays an explicit, direct role only in deductive inferences in which the property is listed as a property of animals and the object in question is evaluated for animalhood. Other models of Type I need not use the concept *animal*. In Model Types II and III the role of the concept *animal*, if any, is more indirect. In Type II (application of definition) the concept may be reflected in the definition itself or in the decision of applicability. The definition may mention parts of animals, animal functions, etc. If so, knowledge that the object in question is (or is not) an animal may contribute to the decision about whether the definition applies. In Type III (comparison to exemplar) the concept *animal* could have two different roles. The similarity metric used in the comparison between the object and the retrieved exemplar could reflect children's concepts of animals. Also, children may distinguish between animal properties of the exemplar, such as breathing, and nonanimal properties, such as laughing or going to school, in this way deploying their concepts of animals.

The data from the experiments in this chapter are analyzed in two steps. They are first examined as they bear on the child's biological knowledge. Of special interest here is whether the child knows that all animals must eat, breathe, and have babies, and whether the child knows that people are the same as other mammals with respect to these properties. The data are then examined as they bear on deciding among the three model types and on the role the concept *animal* plays in generating judgments. To anticipate the conclusions of this and the next two chapters: the model that characterizes how 4- to 6-year-olds generate their judgments differs from the model that characterizes the judgments of 10-year-olds and adults. Further, there are several respects in which the concept *animal* plays different roles in constraining the inferences of 4- to 6-year-olds and those of 10-year-olds and adults. Thus, deciding among the three models of inference is important to making precise how the child's knowledge is reorganized over the years from 4 to 10.

Experiment 2 of chapter 1, analyzed there only for the patterns of judgment about which things are alive, is also Experiment 2 of this chapter. Experiment 1 here preceded it, both temporally and logically, and so will be presented first.

Experiment 1: Attribution of Animal Properties

Because we wished to ensure inferences in the generation of responses, most of the objects included were objects unfamiliar to children. The animals were people, aardvarks, dodos, hammerheads (sharks), and stinkoos (stinkbugs). The plants were orchids and baobabs. The inanimate objects were harvesters, garlic presses, volcanoes, and clouds.[1] The animal properties probed were eating, breathing, being able to get hurt, sleeping, and having a heart. For older children and adults, an even more peripheral animal than the stinkbug, the annelid (worm), was added to the objects, and thinking was added to the properties, while the properties of eating (except for stinkoos and annelids) and being able to get hurt were omitted.[2] The animal properties were fewer than one-third of all the properties probed, others being properties of living as opposed to nonliving things (grows, is alive, dies), or of particular animals (e.g., makes honey), or of inanimate objects (e.g., needs gasoline, is bigger than a house, has wheels, is made in a factory). For each object roughly half of the questions received "no" responses from adults and roughly half received "yes" responses.

Subjects were shown pictures of each object. The order of objects was separately randomized for each subject, and all of the questions for one object were asked before beginning on the next object. The child's spontaneous comments were noted, and each child was asked for justifications for one or two judgments per object.

There were 9 subjects at each of ages 4, 5, 7, and adult, all from middle class populations. Children were tested individually; adults were tested in groups and wrote their responses in booklets.

Results

The data from the animal properties are the only results presented in detail. Error rates on properties of inanimate objects and individual animals (e.g., lives in water, needs gasoline) were uniformly low at all ages, less than 2% overall. These properties are treated as fillers with respect to those of interest here.

As can be seen from table 3.1, at no age were animal properties attributed to inanimate objects. In this respect, these data are confirmed by those of Gelman, Spelke, and Meck (1983) and Dolgin and Behrend (1984). It is notable that they differ from the patterns of attribution of "is alive," "knows where it is," and other properties probed by Piaget. Also, all subjects of all ages attributed all of the animal properties to people. In this respect, the pattern differs from that of "is an animal" in Anglin's (1977) data. At first glance, then, these data show promise as possibly reflecting the inclusive concept *animal*.

The most striking result is the young child's underattribution of animal properties to animals other than people. Adults judge all of the tested properties to be true of all mammals. As can be seen from table 3.1, 4- and 5-year-olds do not universally credit the aardvark with these properties. At these ages, even eating and breathing are underattributed. That is, 4- and 5-year-olds do not know that all animals eat and breathe. In this regard, too, these data are corroborated by unpublished findings of Dolgin and Behrend (personal communication, 1984). They also found that 4-year-olds' attribution of properties such as sleeping, having a brain, and even growing falls off regularly from about 100% attribution to people to about 50% attribution to fish and insects.

The insights these data provide into children's understanding of basic biological processes and internal morphology complement those of chapter 2. Not only are preschool children ignorant of any mechanisms articulated in terms of internal bodily processes, they also do not view human beings as just one mammal among many with respect to these processes. Further, their lack of understanding of the biological functions of eating and breathing most probably accounts for their failure to attribute these properties to all animals. Experiment 2 of the present chapter investigates whether the reorganization of the child's understanding of the human body that has occurred by age 10 is accompanied by the emergence of the adult pattern of attribution of these properties to all animals. For now, we can only say that the concept *animal* does not organize the 4-year-old's attributions of these properties in the same way it organizes the adult's.

Two salient features of the data begin to constrain a model of the child's generation of responses. The first is the regular decline in attribution of properties to the animals when ordered: people, aardvark, dodo, stinkoo, hammerhead, and annelid. The second is the lack of differentiation among the patterns of attribution of the different properties. To a first approximation, the attribution of eating and breathing falls off from people to worm to the same extent as the attribution of thinking and having a heart. Neither of these is a feature of the adult's data.

The Ordering of the Animals   The ordering of the animals is evident in the summary rows of table 3.1. For example, the 5-year-olds attributed all of the properties to people but judged annelids to have them, on the average, only 33% of the time. Table 3.1 presents group data. Such group patterns could reflect several different combinations of individual patterns, each of which would have different implications for the processes by which the judgments are generated. The appendix presents several statistical analyses that establish that for children animals were ordered in such a way that the attribution of animal properties to them fell off monotonically. Each subject reflected that ordering in the number of properties he or she attributed to the animals, and each property reflected that ordering in the number of subjects who attributed it to the animals. Finally, each child reflected the same ordering in his or her attribution of *each* property (see the appendix).

The Lack of Differences among Properties   It is a matter of biological fact that some of the properties probed are properties of all animals, whereas others are not. Adults did not consider that all of the animals have hearts or that they all think, but they did judge that virtually all of the animals eat, breathe, sleep, and can get hurt. An analysis of variance on the adults' data checked for effects of the property probed (eats, breathes, sleeps, can get hurt, has a heart, thinks), the animal probed (people, aardvark, dodo, stinkoo, hammerhead, annelid), and the interaction between the two. All three effects were significant. That is, there was a main effect for property ($F = 5.18$, $p < .001$; the first four were more widely attributed than was having a heart, which in

Table 3.1
Percentage of attribution of animal properties to all objects probed

		Object											Garlic
Age	Property	People	Aardvark	Dodo	Stinkoo	Hammer-head	Annelid	Orchid	Baobab	Cloud	Volcano	Harvester	press
4	Breathes	100	78	67	33	89		0	0	0	0	0	0
	Sleeps	100	100	78	67	44		0	0	0	0	0	
	Gets hurt	100	67	67	56	56		22	22	11	0	11	
	Has a heart	100	89	56	56	44		0	11	0	0		0
	Eats	100	78	89	78	67		0	11	0	0	0	0
	Mean	100	82	71	58	60		4	9	2	0	3	0
5	Breathes	100	89	89	78	78	44	0	0	0	0	0	0
	Sleeps	89	100	89	89	67	33	11	11	11	11	0	
	Has a heart	100	67	56	78	78	33	0	0	0	0		0
	Thinks	100	56	67	56	44	22			0		0	
	Eats				(100)[a]		(89)[a]						
	Mean	97	78	75	75	67	33	4	4	3	4	0	0
7	Breathes	100	89	100	100	89	78	22	22	0	0	0	0
	Sleeps	100	100	100	100	78	78	78	11	0	0	0	
	Has a heart	100	89	89	89	78	56	0	0	0	0		0
	Thinks	100	89	78	56	56	44			0	0		
	Eats				(100)[a]		(89)[a]						
	Mean	100	94	92	86	75	64	33	11	0	0	0	0

	Adult											
Breathes	100	100	100	100	89	89	100	100		56		0
Sleeps	100	100	100	100	89	100	56	11	11		0	
Gets hurt	100	100	89	100	89	89	44	44		0		
Has a heart	100	100	89	89	100	56	0		0		0	
Thinks	100	89	89	67	67	44	0		0		0	
Eats	100	100	89	100	100	100	56	56	0		0	0
Mean	100	98	93	93	89	80	43	53	6	23	0	0

ᵃData from "eats" for 5- and 7-year-olds not included in means, since "eats" was probed on only two objects for these groups.

turn was more widely attributed than thinking, according to Neuman-Keuls analysis). There was also a main effect for animal probed ($F =$ 2.9, $p < .03$; the two mammals were credited with more properties than were the dodo, shark, and stinkoo, which in turn were credited with more properties than was the annelid). Finally, the interaction ($F =$ 2.37, $p < .001$) reflected the fact that some animals were credited with all of the properties whereas others were not.

Children's patterns of attribution could be less articulated than those of adults in two ways. First, children may not attribute any one property any more widely than any other; that is, there may be no main effect for property. Second, although some properties are more widely attributed than others, the slope of attribution across the animals might be the same for all properties; that is, there may be no interaction between properties and animal taught on. Both results were observed for 4-year-olds. In this group of subjects, the main effect for animals was significant ($F = 9.17$, $p < .0001$), but there was neither a main effect for property nor an interaction between property and animal probed. Five-year-olds and 7-year-olds both revealed main effects for animals and main effects for properties, but no interaction between animals and property (see appendix, table A4).

The number of subjects in this experiment was very small (9 per age group). It is possible that a main effect for property and an interaction between property and animal probed might have emerged if more subjects had been included. Further, subjects of different ages were probed on different animals and for different properties. It was therefore impossible to carry out an overall ANOVA including the four age groups. The relevant three-way interaction—age by animal by property—will be assessed in Experiment 2 in this chapter and in chapter 4.

The Acquisition of Biological Knowledge
Four-year-olds differ from adults in many ways with regard to biological knowledge. Adults honor the vertebrate-invertebrate distinction in two ways not reflected in the children's responses. First, children credit bugs with more animal properties than fish; adults do the reverse. Second, for adults there is a sharp break between vertebrates and invertebrates with respect to having hearts and thinking; no so for children. Since 4- to 7-year-olds do not understand the biological functions of internal organs and of processes like eating and breathing, they would hardly be expected to know about systematic differences in the ways animals have solved the same biological problems (e.g., exoskeletons

vs. endoskeletons). Nor can such children be expected to realize that certain biological problems must be solved by *all* animals. So it is not surprising that they exaggerate the distinction between people and other mammals with regard to these properties, and even underattribute eating and breathing to peripheral animals. As children become older, they conceive of eating and breathing more abstractly, and they attribute these activities to all animals. This development must be related to coming to understand the biological functions of digestion, respiration, and circulation.

Constraining a Model
Model Type I: Direct Knowledge or Deductive Inference   In addition to giving us some hints about the acquisition of biological knowledge, these data begin to constrain a model of how the child answers such questions as "Do stinkoos have hearts?" Two variants of Model Type I can be rejected outright. First, attributing a property does not require that the child have directly stored the fact that the object in question has that property. Since young children have never heard of aardvarks, dodos, stinkoos, and hammerheads, they could have no information about these animals directly represented. However, they freely judged that such animals eat, breathe, have hearts, etc. Second, attributing a property does not require that the property be generaly represented as a property of animals, and that the objects be evaluated with respect to membership in the category of animals. This model would predict that all of the animals would be credited with the property 100% of the time. Instead, the salient feature of these data is the denial of the animal properties to many animals. Only for adults, in the case of eating, does this pattern obtain.

One might argue that this model *does* underlie young children's judgments; the young child simply thinks of the peripheral animals that they are not animals. Some children might have a narrower concept of *animal* than do adults (see Anglin 1977). If the ordering of animals characteristic of the data for 4- to 7-year-olds reflects Model Type I reasoning from a narrow concept of *animal,* then some children should attribute no animal properties to the aardvark, more should attribute none to the bird, and so on. This is not what we found (appendix, table A3). Of the 4-year-olds, all children attributed at least one animal property to every animal, including the shark and the stinkoo. Of the 5-year-olds, three children failed to credit the annelid with any of the animal properties, but all three said that worms can die or that worms can both die and grow. Further, these three children do not account for the extremely low rate of attribution of animal properties to worms (33%). All other animals were credited with at least one animal property by each 5-year-old.

One final analysis rules out the hypothesis that the young child's judgments were generated by deductive inferences through a narrow concept of *animal*. After Experiment 1 was completed, each 4- and 5-year-old was presented with an array of one picture each of the objects from the study, plus several others: dog, bee, canary, goldfish, and bus. The children were instructed to give the experimenter the pictures of all of the animals. After they were finished, they were asked, "Is that all?" If they then added more, they were again asked, "Is that all?" until they asserted that there were no more animals. As reported by Anglin (1977), all 4- and 5-year-olds omit people. However, only one 4-year-old omitted the stinkoo, and all of the 4-year-olds included all other animals and excluded all inanimate objects. The sorting of the 5-year-olds was similar. Without question, then, all of the youngest children knew that all of the nonhuman animals were animals. Thus, we may reject the version of Model Type I in which these properties are listed as properties of animals and the child's concept of *animal* is narrower than the adult's.

We may conclude, then, that some productive process underlies children's responses, since they attribute animal properties to animals they can have no direct knowledge of. This process does not, in general, involve a deductive inference from the knowledge that all animals have the property in question.

There is a third version of a Type I model (deductive inference) that is *not* ruled out by these data. Breathing, eating, having a heart, and so on, could be retrieved as properties of classes less abstract than the class of animals. Suppose one child has learned that people, mammals, and birds breathe, and a second has also learned that insects do. When asked if stinkoos breathe, the second child notes from the picture that a stinkoo is a kind of insect and so says "yes," whereas the first says "no." Within each child, as well as across children, these properties could be known to be true of different classes of animals. As long as they are represented with decreasing frequency on people, mammals, birds, bugs, fish, and worms, the observed results would obtain.

When shown the pictures of each object, the children were asked if they knew what it was. For unfamiliar objects such as the dodo, typical responses were "I don't know, something like a duck" or "Some kind of bird." The child categorized each unfamiliar animal as some particular kind, and it is certainly possible that the child's knowledge of animal properties is articulated at this intermediate level of the hierarchy. Indeed, their justifications indicate that sometimes this is so. A small proportion (3% of the 4-year-olds' justifications, 0% of the 5-year-olds', and 17% of the 7-year-olds') appealed to inclusion in a subclass of animals. For example, one child said dodos breathe "because birds breathe."

Although the Type I model described above is certainly consistent with the data, two considerations militate against deductive inferences playing a major role in the generation of young children's responses. First, it seems implausible that 4- and 5-year-olds would have explicitly learned that bugs, birds, or fish sleep, breathe, or have any other of the properties probed. At least some of these properties are sufficiently unfamiliar (e.g., having a heart) that it seems unlikely that young children would ever have encountered the question of whether nonhuman animals of any type have them. Second, for 4-year-olds attribution is identical from property to property. It seems unlikely that 4-year-olds, as a group, would have happened to have learned to just the same extent that the same classes of animals have hearts, sleep, eat, and breathe. These arguments are not conclusive, of course. Experiment 2 of this chapter and the study in chapter 4 will further assess whether such a model (Type I, deductive inferences based on intermediate levels of the hierarchy) underlies the young child's judgments. Nonetheless, the results from Experiment 1 do establish that if the correct model is of Type I, the concept *animal* is not the repository of such a list of properties.

Model Type II: Application of Definition   The key to models of Type II is the characterization of children's definitions and of the process by which they apply them to the objects in question. Under some assumptions, definition-based reasoning could generate at least some of the data from Experiment 1. The child's definitions could be couched in terms of the human activities these properties represent. Sleeping could be seen as lying down, closing one's eyes, and losing consciousness for a period of time. Eating could be seen as putting food in one's mouth and swallowing it. Breathing could be seen as sucking air into one's nose and mouth and blowing it out. The decision whether some other object has one of these properties would include checking for the parts of people mentioned in the definition. The stable ordering of animals might then reflect the decreasing likelihood that the more peripheral animals have the human parts mentioned in the definition.

Justifications provide some support for this type of model. (The children were asked to justify one or two judgments per object; thus, each child provided around 20 justifications.) Children were quite likely (age 4, 35% of the justifications; age 5, 44%; age 7, 54%) to justify their judgments by appealing to what might be an aspect of a definition—aardvarks breathe, for example, "because they have a nose." However, it is also possible that these justifications are post hoc appeals to some aspects of known definitions of the property in question, and do not reflect the actual basis of the judgments. This is clear in the case of the 5-year-old who said that annelids breathe "because they have a nose and a mouth . . . except they don't have a nose . . . or a mouth" (looking closely at the picture). Even though annelids do not satisfy this child's explicitly stated definition, she did not change her mind about whether they breathe.

Two considerations make it doubtful that the bulk of the young child's judgments reflect the application of definitions. It is easy to imagine definitions of breathing, eating, and sleeping that mention parts of people, but what plausible definition might there be of hearts or of getting hurt that would predict that the latter properties would be attributed less to nonhuman animals to exactly the same degree as the former? A second, related consideration is the same one leveled against Type I models. If a definition of each property were the basis for decisions, one might expect substantial variation among the patterns for the different properties, since the properties are of various types and the children would be expected to be more familiar with some properties than others. Quite the opposite; it is a salient feature of the young child's data that there are no differences among the attribution patterns for the different properties.

Model Type III: Comparison to Exemplar   A model of type III can most naturally generate the observed data. Since all subjects said that people had all of the animal properties, *human* is a good candidate for the most accessible exemplar for each property. The model predicts decreasing attribution as the animals become more dissimilar to people. If nothing is entering into a judgment of whether some object has some property besides an estimate of the similarity between that object and people, then we would also expect that the properties would not be differentiated from each other in their patterns of attribution. Both of these expectations are fulfilled. Further, some justifications reflected comparison to people (age 4, 8% of all justifications; age 5, 14%; age 7, 2%). For example, when the children were asked to justify a judgment that a nonhuman animal had a heart, three of them replied, "Every people has a heart," "People do," and "I have a heart."

In conclusion, versions of all three types of models could generate the data from Experiment 1. However, the lack of differentiation among the attribution patterns for the different properties is predicted by Model Type III (comparison to people) and is an embarrassment for Model Types I and II.

The above discussion presupposes that at a given age only one kind of model underlies the generation of all judgments about these properties. Obviously, this is a gross oversimplification. It is certainly possible that any one subject uses all three types of reasoning, depending upon the particular knowledge he or she has represented about each property and each animal, and depending upon the accessibility of that knowledge. For example, an anomalous point in the data is that 89% of the 4-year-olds said "yes" when asked if hammerheads breathe (table 3.1). It happened that the nursery school class of these 4-year-olds had visited the New England Aquarium the Monday of the week they were tested, and much had been made of the bubbles produced by breathing fish. Armed with this knowledge, the children made perfectly good deductive use of it. Also, children as young as 4 produce justifications that show they appreciate the force of all three types of arguments. Although all three types of reasoning contribute to the child's responses, it is still possible that one of the models is primarily responsible for them. This question will be addressed in chapter 4.

Experiment 2: Further Constraints on a Model

The goal of Experiment 2 was to replicate the main results of Experiment 1 and to further constrain a model of the processes by which children attribute animal properties to objects. Several additions were made to the basic procedure of Experiment 1.

To distinguish between Model Type I (deductive inference) and Model Type III (comparison to exemplar), having bones was added to the list of animal properties probed. No child could have learned that bones are a property of any superordinate category of bugs and worms, since bugs and worms do not have bones. Thus, if deductive inferences based on membership in categories less abstract than *animal* underlie the judgments, young children should deny that bugs and worms have bones. In contrast, if responses are generated by comparison to people, then having bones should yield the same attribution pattern as do the other properties, even where bugs and worms are concerned.

In Experiment 1 of this chapter, subjects did not attribute animal properties to inanimate objects. This contrasts with the attribution patterns for "alive" reported in chapter 1. However, the objects probed in Experiment 1 did not include the sun, the object that occasions by far the most animistic responses. Therefore, in order to establish whether life actually is attributed to inanimate objects more than properties such as eating, having a heart, etc., the sun was added to the battery of objects in Experiment 2.

Experiment 1 revealed many differences between 4- to 7-year-olds, on the one hand, and adults, on the other. In Experiment 2, 10-year-olds were included as a probe for the beginnings of the adult pattern of results.

The final modifications were made on the assumption that the child's judgments are based on a comparison to people. If this is so, we would like to know what role, if any, the concept *animal* plays in the comparison; and this in turn requires knowing what features the comparison is based on. To this end we added a mechanical monkey to the battery of objects. This battery-operated toy loudly bangs cymbals together, while screeching and baring its teeth. In terms of salient surface properties, it is intuitively more similar to people than is, for example, a worm. It has a face, a mouth, teeth, arms, and legs; it is wearing clothes; etc. However, it is *not* an animal. Subjects' failure to attribute animal properties to the mechanical monkey would provide evidence that the biological concept *animal* influences the comparison process. Gelman, Spelke, and Meck (1983) included dolls and puppets in some of their experiments and found that animal properties were denied such objects. Analogously, we expected no attribution of a heart, bones, eating, sleeping, etc., to the mechanical monkey, even by the 4-year-olds.

The youngest two groups of children in Experiment 1 judged the mammal (aardvark) to have many fewer of the animal properties than do people. This may be due to its unfamiliarity. The child might represent many more properties of familiar mammals such as dogs that would contribute to a positive outcome of the comparison to people. To test for this possibility, Experiment 2 contrasted a series of familiar objects with a series of unfamiliar objects. (These are listed in chapter 1.) The mechanical monkey was always presented last, to avoid a possible source of difference that might affect the comparison with Laurendeau and Pinard's procedure (chapter 1) or with Experiment 1 of this chapter.

The familiar series was presented to 10 subjects at each of ages 4, 7, and 10. The unfamiliar series was presented to 10 subjects at each of ages 4, 10, and adult. The procedure, described in chapter 1, was the same as in Experiment 1 of this chapter. The animal properties probed were eating, sleeping, having bones, having a heart, having babies, and thinking. Properties of living things (is alive, dies) were also included, as well as various kinds of filler properties, as previously described.

Results

Children attributed animal properties to inanimate objects, including the sun, much less than they attributed being alive (table 3.2). Also, as in Experiment 1, all children attributed virtually all animal properties to people (tables 3.3 and 3.4). Thus, the attribution of animal properties reflects the concept *animal* more than does attribution of "is an animal" (which excludes people) and more than does attribution of "is alive" (which includes inanimate objects).

Underattribution of Animal Properties   Two properties of all animals were probed: eating and having babies. As in Experiment 1, 4-year-olds did not think that these were universally properties of animals. Over the two series, they denied that nonhuman animals eat 20% of the time. "Have babies" was worded "have baby dogs," "have baby hammerheads," etc., to minimize the possibility that "baby" might be taken in its human sense, contrasted with such terms as "puppies," "kittens," and "chicks." Still, 4-year-olds denied that nonhuman animals have

Table 3.2
Percentage of attribution of "is alive" and of the animal properties to inanimate objects. (Familiar and unfamiliar series collapsed.)

		All inanimate objects		Sun only	
Age	Number of subjects	Is alive	Animal properties	Is alive	Animal properties
4	20	36	8**	70	16**
7	10	16	4**	40	7**
10	20	7	1*	30	5*

**p < .01 Wilcoxin, 2-tailed
*p < .05 Wilcoxin, 1-tailed

Table 3.3
Percentage of attribution of animal properties. (Experiment 2, unfamiliar series.)

Age	Property	Animals				
		People	Aardvark	Hammer-head	Stinkoo	Annelid
4	Eats	100	90	90	90	70
	Sleeps	100	70	80	70	90
	Has bones	100	70	80	70	50
	Has a heart	90	70	70	50	60
	Has babies	90	80	60	70	40
	Thinks	100	70	40	60	50
	Mean	97	75	70	68	60
10	Eats	90	100	100	90	80
	Sleeps	100	100	60	80	40
	Has bones	100	100	100	40	50
	Has a heart	100	80	90	70	50
	Has babies	100	100	100	100	60
	Thinks	100	80	80	70	40
	Mean	98	93	88	75	53
Adult	Eats	100	100	100	100	100
	Sleeps	100	100	80	90	90
	Has bones	100	100	90	20	10
	Has a heart	100	100	100	30	50
	Has babies	100	100	100	100	90
	Thinks	100	70	60	40	40
	Mean	100	95	88	63	63

Plants		Inanimate objects					
Orchid	Baobab	Sun	Cloud	Harvester	Garlic press	Rolltop	Mechanical monkey
50						10	40
	10	30		10	0		30
10			0			0	30
	0	0			0		10
30	20	20	20	10	10	10	20
	0		10	0			20
30	8	17	10	7	3	7	25
60						0	0
	10	10		0	0		0
0			0			0	0
	0	0			10		10
10	0	0	0	0	0		0
	0		0	0			0
23	3	3	0	0	3	0	2
10						0	10
	10	0		0	10		10
0			0			0	0
	0				0		0
20	0	10	10	0	0	0	0
	0		0	0			0
10	3	5	3	0	3	0	2

Table 3.4
Percentage of attribution of animal properties. (Experiment 2, familiar series.)

		Animals				
Age	Property	People	Dog	Fish	Fly	Worm
4	Eats	100	90	90	40	80
	Sleeps	100	90	70	50	90
	Has bones	80	80	60	30	40
	Has a heart	90	60	60	30	40
	Has babies	100	60	50	60	60
	Thinks	90	60	20	10	60
	Mean	93	73	58	37	62
7	Eats	100	100	100	100	100
	Sleeps	100	100	90	90	90
	Has bones	100	100	90	60	40
	Has a heart	100	80	90	80	70
	Has babies	100	100	90	90	80
	Thinks	100	70	70	50	80
	Mean	100	92	88	78	77
10	Eats	100	100	100	100	80
	Sleeps	100	100	80	70	70
	Has bones	100	100	90	20	20
	Has a heart	100	100	90	90	90
	Has babies	100	100	90	90	80
	Thinks	100	90	90	50	70
	Mean	100	98	90	70	68

Plants		Inanimate objects					
Flower	Tree	Sun	Cloud	Car	Hammer	Table	Mechanical monkey
20						0	50
	20	20		0	10		70
10			0			10	40
	20	20			0		50
20	30	10	30	10	10	20	50
	20		10	0			50
17	23	17	13	3	7	10	52
50						0	50
	0	10		10	10		0
0			0			0	10
	0	10			10		0
10	10	0	0	0	10	0	10
	0		0	0			0
20	3	7	0	3	10	0	12
60					0	0	0
	0	0		0			0
0			0		0	0	0
	0	0		0			10
10	20	10	0	0	0	0	0
	10		0				0
23	8	3	0	0	0	0	2

Table 3.5
Percentage difference in attribution of animal properties to people and another mammal

Experiment	Series	Mammal	Age				
			4	5	7	10	Adult
1	Unfamiliar	Aardvark	16**	23**	$8^{n.s.}$		$6^{n.s.}$
2	Unfamiliar	Aardvark	22**			$5^{n.s.}$	0
2	Familiar	Dog	20**		$8^{n.s.}$	$2^{n.s.}$	
Overall			19**	23**	8*	$4^{n.s.}$	$3^{n.s.}$

Significance levels: Wilcoxin signed ranks, 2-tailed
$^{n.s.}$not significant
**$p < .01$
*$p < .05$

babies 40% of the time. By age 7, and among 10-year-olds and adults, all animals were virtually always credited with eating and having babies.

Also confirming Experiment 1, 4-year-olds do not realize that all of the animal properties probed are as much properties of other mammals as of people (table 3.5). This is as true for the dog as for the aardvark. At age 7 the drop in attribution from people to other mammals is still present, although it is significant only when the data from both studies are pooled. By age 10, as for adults, people are simply one mammal among many with respect to these properties.

The Ordering of the Animals All of the analyses performed on the data from Experiment 1 were repeated on those from Experiment 2 and are presented in the appendix. Here I will comment on points of similarity and contrast between the two studies. Analyses of concordance both by subject and by property showed that each group of 4- to 7-year-old children agreed on stable ordering of the animals. In Experiment 2, unlike Experiment 1, adult subjects also agreed among themselves in their ordering of the animals. So too did the new groups of 10-year-olds.

The Differentiation of Attribution Patterns Separate ANOVAs were performed on the data from each age group within each series (see appendix). As in Experiment 1, there were main effects for animals within each group. That is, every group of subjects credited some animals with more properties than others. Unlike Experiment 1, there were also main effects for properties within each group. Even 4-year-olds attributed some animal properties more widely than others. This is probably because a greater variety of properties was being probed. As in Experiment 1, there was no animal-by-property interaction in the data for either group of 4-year-olds. That is, attribution of all properties fell off from people to worm at the same rate. This interaction appeared in the data for the 7-year-olds, however, and was highly significant in the data for 10-year-olds and adults.

The picture that emerged from Experiment 1 must be qualified somewhat. In Experiment 2, 4-year-olds attributed eating and sleeping more widely than the other four properties, and 7-year-olds attributed the different properties differently among the five animals probed. Nonetheless, these data confirm and extend the findings of the first study in an important way—the age-by-animal-by-property interaction was significant in both series. In other words, although properties are not completely undifferentiated from each other at the youngest ages, development consists of increasing differentiation.

Figure 3.1 depicts the three-way interaction. For 4-year-olds, attribution of eating, sleeping, and having babies falls off from vertebrates to invertebrates to the same extent as attribution of thinking, having a heart, and having bones. As subjects become older, the two curves increasingly diverge.

An analysis of patterns for each individual's attribution of each property was also carried out. When the child credited only some animals with a given property, the resulting pattern was judged either consistent with the overall ordering for that group, or inconsistent. As in Experiment 1, the consistent orderings were observed significantly more often than would be expected by chance.

Taken together, the results from Experiments 1 and 2 show that the animals are very strongly ordered with respect to the attribution of these properties. Each subject agrees with every other on an ordering (averaged over properties); each property agrees with every other on an ordering (averaged over subjects); and each subject, in attributing each property, respects that ordering more than would be expected by chance.

For adults, three properties are essentially attributed to all animals (eating, sleeping, and having babies), while there is a sharp division between vertebrates and invertebrates on the other three (has a heart, has bones, and thinks). This effect can be quantified as follows: take the average attribution of a heart, bones, and thinking to nonhuman vertebrates (87%) and subtract the average attribution to invertebrates

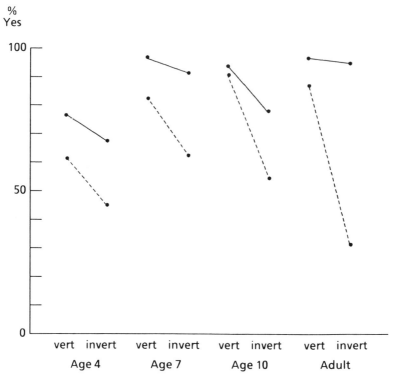

Figure 3.1
Attribution of animal properties to vertebrates (aardvark, dodo) and to invertebrates (stinkoo, worm). ●——● eats, sleeps, has babies; ●---● has a heart, has bones, thinks.

(32%; difference 55%). Then do the same for average attribution of eating, sleeping, and having babies: nonhuman vertebrates, 97%, invertebrates, 95%; difference 2%. The difference-of-difference score for adults, then, is 53%. For 4-year-olds, in contrast, the resulting figure is only 6%. At age 7 it still does not reach statistical significance (15%). Ten-year-olds, like adults, significantly distinguish vertebrates and invertebrates more on properties like having bones than on properties like eating. Figure 3.2 shows the regular increase in this difference-of-difference score with age; this represents the age-by-property-by-animal interaction that is seen in these data.

The Acquisition of Biological Knowledge
Two results from Experiment 1 were replicated in Experiment 2. First, 4- and 5-year-olds do not consider other mammals on a par with

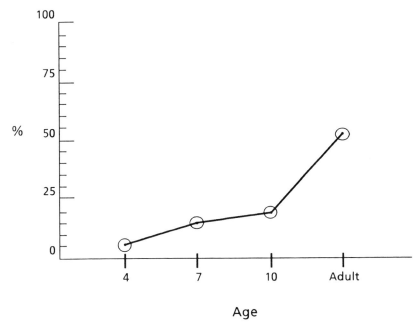

Figure 3.2
Difference of difference score: (Vertebrates[heart, thinks, bones] −
Invertebrates[heart, thinks, bones]) − (Vertebrates[eats, sleeps, babies] −
Invertebrates[eats, sleeps, babies])

humans as far as the tested properties are concerned. Second, 4- and
5-year-olds do not appreciate that all animals eat, sleep, and reproduce.
Of the 38 4- and 5-year-old subjects in the two studies, 29 (82%) denied
one of these properties to at least one nonhuman animal. Both reflections of incomplete biological knowledge are still present, in an attenu-
ated form, in the responses of the 7-year-olds, who exhibited a small,
but significant, drop in attribution between people and other mammals
(table 3.5). And of the 19 second graders in the two studies, 26% denied
that some nonhuman animal eats, sleeps, or has babies. By age 10, and
among adults, both of these reflections of incomplete biological knowledge have virtually disappeared.

Apparently the preschool child does not yet grasp that all animals
share a common set of problems to which eating and sleeping are
universal solutions. Nor does the preschooler understand that all complex animals, including people and other mammals, have common

internal organs with common functions. The 10-year-old has grasped both of these principles.

The interaction depicted in figure 3.1 shows that insofar as young children respect the vertebrate-invertebrate distinction in their judgments, they do so equally for the general biological properties (eats, sleeps, and has babies) and for the more restricted biological properties (has bones, has a heart, thinks). By age 10 the two classes of properties have become differentiated, but the 10-year-olds distinguish them far less than do adults (figs. 3.1 and 3.2). Ten-year-olds, unlike 4- to 7-year-olds, see eating, sleeping, and having babies as properties of all animals. Unlike adults, they seem to think that other properties of complex animals, such as having a heart and bones, are also part of the universal solutions to the problems of maintaining life.

In sum, 10-year-olds understand that all animals share certain biological processes, and they are just beginning to be aware that animals differ in their solutions to certain biological problems. The preschool child, in contrast, does not see these properties as common to all mammals, let alone to all animals.

Constraining a Model

Children's (and adults') justifications are dominated by appeals to definitions. For example, aardvarks breathe "because they have noses," harvesters do not eat "because they do not have mouths," and baobabs do not have hearts "because they don't have blood." Although partial definitions are the most common justifications, it is not safe to conclude that Model Type II (application of definition) processes actually underlie the child's judgments. In justifying a response, the subject often gives supporting evidence, rather than the actual basis of the judgment. In many cases the partial definition provided by the child is itself an inference. How does the child know harvesters do not have mouths and baobabs do not have blood? Furthermore, other types of justifications are observed. Children (but not adults) also offer comparisons to people as justifications—for example, dogs breathe "because I do." And subjects of all ages also mention membership in superordinate categories as justifications—for example, hammerheads breathe "because they're fish"—although this is rare among young children.

The best basis we have for constraining a model of children's inferential process is their actual patterns of judgments. Most relevant are the gradients of application across the different animals and the degree of differentiation among properties with regard to these gradients. By age 10, and certainly among adults, the attribution patterns for the various properties differ markedly from each other. As shown in tables 3.3 and 3.4, for some properties attribution patterns are flat across all animals (e.g., eating); for others they fall off regularly from people to worm (e.g., thinking); and for still others there is a sharp break between vertebrates and invertebrates (e.g., having bones). Categorical information and biologically rich definitions probably underlie most of the judgments at these ages. Comparison-to-exemplar reasoning could underlie those judgments that are distributed in the same way as similarity to people. Other data are needed to ascertain what that similarity function might be (see chapter 4).

The data from the younger children paint quite a different picture. Attribution of *every* property falls off gradually across the animals from people to worm. Typically, within each group of 4- to 7-year-olds the slope across the different properties was always the same (no animal-by-property interactions). This would be expected if most judgments were being generated by comparisons to people and if the same similarity metric underlay each comparison. Of course, as pointed out above, models of both Type I and Type II could also generate such data. The property of having bones was included in the battery of Experiment 2 to help decide between Model Type III (comparison to people) and Model Types I (deductive inference) and II (application of definition).

Three of the animals probed were invertebrates (the fly, the stinkoo, and the worm (annelid)). Children could not have explicitly learned that any of these three animals has bones. Nor could they have learned that any of these belongs to any superordinate category of animals that have bones. Thus, any attribution of bones to invertebrates could not result from Model Type I (deductive inference) reasoning. As can be seen from tables 3.3 and 3.4, children often attributed bones to invertebrates (4-year-olds, 48% of all opportunities; 7-year-olds, 50% of all opportunities; 10-year-olds, 38% of all opportunities). Adults do so much less often (15% of all opportunities). Not only do the youngest children attribute bones to invertebrates to a substantial degree, they do so every bit as much as they do having hearts and babies. Indeed, the 4-year-olds' attribution patterns for these three properties are virtually identical (tables 3.3 and 3.4).

Model Type I (deductive inference) reasoning cannot underlie the young child's judgments about what things in the world have bones.

Model Type II reasoning (application of definition) can also be ruled out. If the child were applying a definition of bones to the objects, what might that definition be? If it were something like "hard stick-like things inside arms, legs, fingers . . . ," we would expect high attribution to people and less to things that do not have the parts mentioned in the definition. If the parts were extremities, as in this example, then people, mammals, and bugs should be attributed bones, whereas fish and worms should not. Such a pattern was never observed—bugs were closer to worms than to fish at every age. If the definition were something like "hard stick-like things inside bodies," then the child's problem becomes one of deciding what counts as a body. As tables 3.3 and 3.4 show, plants and inanimate objects are virtually never attributed bones, so only animals must have bodies. But if a body is simply the main part of an animal, this definition would apply to all animals and should yield 100% "yes" responses. If what counts as a body depends upon similarity to people's bodies, this application of a definition (Model Type II) reduces to a comparison with people (Model Type III).

In sum, children attribute bones to invertebrates as much as they do several other properties. The inferential processes underlying these judgments cannot be deductions from the "fact" that flies, stinkoos, and worms (annelids) belong to superordinate categories known to have bones. That Model Type I reasoning does not underlie attribution of bones suggests that it does not underlie attribution of other properties either, especially those with patterns very similar to those of the child's judgments about bones. This implies that models of Type II or Type III must play a very large role in the 4- to 7-year-old's responses, and a significant role even in the case of 10-year-olds. Of these two, Model Type III (comparison to exemplar) is favored, given the difficulty of formulating a definition whose application would yield the observed patterns of attribution.

Even among the 4- to 7-year-olds, the judgment profiles for each property are not identical to each other. In Experiment 2 there were main effects for property at every age, and an animal-by-property interaction at age 7. This shows that children as young as 4 sometimes use specific information about classes of objects having particular properties and/or informative definitions to supplement the dominant process of comparison to people. The increasing differentiation with age of the attribution patterns for these properties reflects increasing reliance on Type I and Type II reasoning.

The Problem of Chance Responding: A Final Alternative Model
Since children were asked yes/no questions, guessing would yield 50%
attribution. With 20 subjects, "yes" response levels between 25% and
75% do not differ from chance; with 10 subjects, chance is anywhere
between 10% and 90%. Most of the response levels for each property
fall within these limits (tables 3.1, 3.3, and 3.4). However, even the
youngest children are not simply guessing, as can be seen by the systematic ordering of animals even within this region of chance responding, and by the sharp break between attribution to animals, on the one
hand, and plants and inanimate objects, on the other. Nonetheless,
considerations of guessing suggest another model for how young children might be generating their responses. A major component to young
children's undifferentiated patterns reflects their underattribution of
eating, sleeping, and having babies to bugs and worms, and their overattribution of having bones to these same two animals. But all of these
properties are attributed to these animals close to 50% of the time,
especially by 4- and 5-year-olds. Perhaps judgments are generated as
follows: if the object is known to have the property (from Model Type I
or II reasoning), say "yes"; if it is known not to have the property, say
"no"; otherwise, guess. On this view, the regular ordering of the animals results from each child's having some specific knowledge that
leads to certainty for some nonhuman animals, with decreasing frequency from mammals to worms. In the case of worms and bugs the
young child is guessing virtually all of the time.
    The model just proposed differs greatly from Model Type III. In the
latter case, children's judgments are determined by their assessment of
each object's similarity to people. On this view, that bugs and worms
are attributed the animal properties around 50% of the time is a consequence of their exact degree of dissimilarity to people. If we knew the
child's assessment of similarity between each object and people, and if
the resulting function matched the patterns in tables 3.1, 3.3, and 3.4,
then Model Type III would be supported over the guessing model just
proposed. The relevant data, with such a result, are provided in chapter
4. Data concerning within-child consistency would also be relevant. If a
model of Type III underlies the child's judgments, we would not expect
consistency in attribution of *particular* properties from occasion to occasion. This is because attribution of any given property to any given
animal is determined probabilistically on the basis of degree of similarity between the animal and humans. For example, if the probability
that dodos will be attributed any of these properties is .7, then having a

heart will be attributed to dodos by a child an average of 7 out of 10 times, and denied to dodos by that same child an average of 3 out of 10 times. However, if particular knowledge of classes of objects or of the individual properties determines the responses, then the child who attributes eating to all animals on one occasion should do so on another. A little study of 12 of the 20 4-year-olds from Experiment 2 examined this issue.

Experiment 3: From Properties to Animals

Experiment 3 was the work of Carol Smith. One of its purposes was to see whether the most accessible animal that has each of the tested properties is, indeed, people. Its second goal was a preliminary attempt at probing within-child consistency.

Experiment 3 was carried out two weeks after the completion of Experiment 2. The subjects were asked to say all the things they knew that can bounce, that can eat, that melt in the sun, that have a heart, etc. A total of 18 different properties were probed, including five of the animal properties from Experiment 2 (eats, sleeps, thinks, has a heart, has bones), one property of living things (grows), properties of subclasses of animals (says quack-quack, flies), and properties of inanimate objects (has a motor, can be seen through, etc.).

Results
Only the results for the five animal properties will be analyzed here. The dominant response was "people" (counting "people," "human," "person," or particular people such as the children's mothers or themselves). Such an item was found among those listed for each property 93% of the time. People were mentioned first 78% of the time. On 17 of 18 occasions where only one animal was provided, that animal was people.

For some properties a child might mention only one example (e.g., for having bones, "people"); for others, more (e.g., for eating, "cats, dogs, people, lambs, sheep, tigers, lions, ducks, fish, zebras, monkeys, caterpillars, and robins"). Table 3.6 shows the total number of times that a child mentioned at least one example of people, mammals, birds, fish, reptiles, or bugs. In this tabulation, the above child's 13 responses for eating would contribute one tally for people, one for mammals, one for birds, one for fish, and one for bugs. As table 3.6 shows, the dominant response is people, with mammals accounting for only a bit over

Table 3.6
Frequency with which children mention at least one instance
of each category

Property	People	Mammal	Bird	Fish	Reptile	Bug	Word "animal"	Total
Eats	12	8	3	2	0	2	5	32
Sleeps	12	7	3	2	2	1	5	32
Has bones	10	7	2	1	0	1	2	23
Has a heart	12	6	3	0	3	1	2	27
Thinks	11	6	1	2	2	0	3	25
Mean	11.4	6.8	2.4	1.4	1.4	1.0	3.4	

half as many. The ordering of animals seen in Experiments 1 and 2 is again observed, although here the slope is steeper.

It is unlikely that having been in Experiment 2 two weeks earlier had much effect on the children's responses. Most of the animals and plants listed were not those used in the earlier study. Also, responding became more systematic at the end of the free listing task. The proportion of "people first" listing was higher when the property came at the end of the list (89%) than when it came at the beginning (57%). The high accessibility of people as creatures who have these properties is probably not due to the child's having previously judged in Experiment 2 whether people have them.

That the children had been in Experiment 2 allowed their performance on the two tasks to be compared. Smith made this comparison in two ways: she looked for within-child consistency with regard to overall tendency to attribute animal properties widely, and she looked for within-child consistency within individual properties. The first type of consistency was present and the second was not.

The 12 subjects in the free listing task were divided into two groups: those who tended to list people only and those who tended to list many animals. Every child in the former group (narrow attributers) listed only people at least twice; no child in the latter group (wide attributers) did. The two groups were then compared for their attribution of these properties to nonhuman animals in Experiment 2. The narrow attributers denied nonhuman animals these properties an average of 10 times each; the wide attributers, 4.5 times each ($p < .05$, t-test, 1-tailed). Thus, children were either narrow attributers on both tasks or wide attributers on both tasks.

Looking for consistency within individual properties, Smith asked whether having credited all animals with a given property in Experiment 2 was predictive of the child's crediting at least some animal other than people with that property on the free listing task. The answer was no. A child who had attributed "has a heart" only to people on the free listing task, for example, was just as likely to say that all animals have hearts as one who attributed "has a heart" to people, turtles, and dogs.

Smith's study demonstrates that for 4-year-olds, at least, people are prototypical objects with these properties. It also shows that children whose similarity metric was restrictive on the picture question task also tended to list only people as having the animal properties in the free listing procedure. In contrast, there was no consistency within individual properties.

At the same time that they affirm that people and some other animals breathe, have babies, have hearts, sleep, think, and so on, young children deny that plants and inanimate objects do. Such a pattern of judgments suggests that young children have a concept with the same extension as the adult concept *animal* and that they know that breathing, having babies, having hearts, and so on, are properties only of animals. In other words, these data suggest that the concept *animal* plays a role in the attribution of these properties. But there is another possibility. Imagine that a single set of features, weighted for relative salience, underlies the young child's representations of all objects. (One could think of this feature space as Quine's (1969) innate quality space, imagining the features as perceptually salient aspects of the objects.) Suppose also that animals are more similar to people in this space than are inanimate objects or plants. After all, animals and people have similar shapes and move in the same ways. The inanimate objects probed in Experiments 1 and 2 differ greatly from people in these perceptually salient surface properties. If children attribute eating, sleeping, having babies, and so forth, on the basis of comparison to people along perceptually salient features, then we would expect them not to credit these properties to plants and inanimate objects. That is, the results presented so far may not indicate that young children know that the tested properties are properties only of animals.

The mechanical monkey is highly similar to people in appearance and in movement patterns. Nonetheless, it is not an animal. Do 4-year-olds judge that the mechanical monkey eats, sleeps, has a heart, has bones, thinks, and has babies? Before turning to the data on this question, we must check the intuition that subjects do in fact see the mechanical monkey as being similar to people in surface properties. Experiment 4 assessed judged similarity between the mechanical monkey and people, and compared this to judged similarity between other objects and people. It was expected that if subjects were not told the basis on which similarity was to be judged, both adults and children would rank the mechanical monkey as being highly similar to people.

Experiment 4: Similarity Judgments

In this study the subject was simply asked to rate the overall similarity between people, on the one hand, and a series of different objects, on the other. The ratings obtained were neutral in that subjects were given no instructions regarding what aspects of similarity they were to focus on. The purpose of the study was to see whether a different similarity ranking emerges when subjects are simply asked to rank similarity, as opposed to when they are judging which objects breathe, eat, sleep, etc. If it does, we can be confident that some concept of *animal* conditions the attribution of such properties to objects, even if the process underlying attribution involves the computation of similarity to people.

Subjects were presented with successive pairs of pictured stimuli, each consisting of a person and one other object from the pictured stimuli of Experiment 2. As in Experiment 2, the pair including the mechanical monkey was always presented last. Care was taken to mimic the order of presentation of objects in Experiment 2 so that context effects on similarity judgments would be constant.

Twenty adults and 20 6-year-olds from the same populations as those in Experiment 2 participated in the study. The instructions to the adults and to the children differed slightly. The adults were simply asked to rank the similarity between each object and a human being on a scale from 0 (very different) to 10 (extremely similar). Children were given a physical scale with a movable pointer, and were given practice in its use. Pairs of objects (an apple and a carrot, a pencil and a cigarette, a cake and an aspirin, and a sofa and a stool) were used for the practice session, and the children were encouraged to dwell on the functional similarity between apples and carrots, sofas and stools. This was to influence them not to base their judgments solely on how similar the items looked.

Results
People and the mechanical monkey share properties that are salient to both adults and children. When asked to judge similarity in no particular context, subjects judge these two objects as being very much alike.

Table 3.7
Judged similarity to people. (Scale: 0 to 10.)

Object	Age 6	Adult
Mechanical monkey	7.4	8.0
Mammal	2.2	6.6
Fish	2.4	5.6
Bug	3.0	6.0
Worm	2.3	4.0
Flower	2.4	4.3
Tree	2.7	4.8
Sun	1.8	3.2
Cloud	2.1	2.2
Vehicle	1.8	2.8
Furniture	1.8	2.0
Tool	1.5	1.4

In fact, of all the objects both adults and children ranked the mechanical monkey most similar to people (table 3.7). The rankings for the remaining objects do not resemble the patterns for attribution of animal properties. There is no sharp cutoff between animals, on the one hand, and plants and inanimate objects, on the other. Indeed, the 6-year-olds made no further distinctions among the objects; the only significant difference was between the mechanical monkey and all other objects. A more suitable method for getting 6-year-olds to generate similarity judgments could no doubt be found. But this method served our purpose of checking that all the subjects would see the mechanical monkey as highly similar to people.

Attribution of Animal Properties to the Mechanical Monkey
From age 7 on, the subjects in Experiment 2 virtually never judged the mechanical monkey to eat, sleep, think, have babies, or have bones or a heart (12% attribution of these six properties at age 7, 2% at age 10, and 2% among adults; see tables 3.3 and 3.4 for the data broken down by property). Each of these groups of subjects attributed the animal properties to the mechanical monkey significantly less than to the worm, the animal judged least to have them ($p < .01$ or better, Wilcoxin signed ranks test, 2-tailed). The attribution of these animal properties is clearly influenced by a concept *animal* with the same extension as the adult's biological concept, at least from age 7 on.

The 4-year-olds present a different picture. They judged the mechanical monkey to have an animal property on 38% of all opportunities. This is not significantly different from the level for bugs (53%) and worms (61%), the animals least attributed these properties. As can be seen from tables 3.3 and 3.4, the two groups of 4-year-olds differed in this regard. Those in the unfamiliar series were like older children in showing a lower level of attribution to the mechanical monkey (25%) than to their most peripheral animal, the annelid (60%, $p < .05$, Wilcoxin signed ranks test, 2-tailed). In contrast, the children in the familiar series treated the mechanical monkey (52%) as they did the fly (37%), the fish (58%), and the worm (62%). The latter group attributed animal properties to the mechanical monkey as much as they did to animals, significantly less only than their level of attribution to people.

Several factors may contribute to judgments that the mechanical monkey has a given property. Some of the 4-year-olds seemed confused about whether they were being probed about real monkeys or the toy itself; after all, in every other case they were being asked about what the pictures represented, not about the pictures themselves. Also, some of the judgments clearly reflected guesses about the construction of the toy. If so much care had gone into making it realistic in all of its details, why shouldn't it have bones? Many children felt the wires in the arms and legs and pronounced them bones. One child said it had a heart taken from a real monkey. Thus, even the child who distinguishes the mechanical monkey from real animals may attribute some animal properties to it. However, the 4-year-olds in the familiar series treated the toy exactly as they did nonhuman animals. The similarity metric underlying at least some 4-year-olds' comparisons to people does not seem influenced by whether or not the object actually *is* an animal. Perceptually salient surface features could underlie these comparisons, with the concept *animal* playing no role whatsoever.

The results from the 4-year-olds in the familiar series conflict with the data of Gelman, Spelke, and Meck 1983 and Dolgin and Behrend 1984. These studies found that a wide variety of animal properties were not attributed to inanimate objects, including objects such as dolls, stuffed animals, and puppets that perceptually resemble people. I do not have an explanation for this discrepancy, except to note that my method probably placed somewhat greater demands upon the child. This is because I probed many properties that are not relevant to the animal-nonanimal distinction as well as many that are. Since the distinction between animals and nonanimals was relevant to only some of the judgments in my study, children had the problem of deciding, for each judgment, whether or not it was. In the other studies the distinction was relevant to every judgment. Thus, my procedure required that children have a better grasp of the distinction itself and of the fact that it is relevant to attributing eating, having bones, sleeping, thinking, having babies, and having a heart.

My data show that some 4-year-olds know too little of the particular properties probed to automatically see the relevance of the animal-nonanimal distinction in this task. The data of Gelman, Spelke, and Meck, and of Dolgin and Behrend, show that in other circumstances all 4-year-olds and even 3-year-olds do invoke this distinction in attributing such properties. Even in my study, one group of 4-year-olds did so. Taking all of the data together, we should probably conclude that preschool children do condition their projection of these properties from people to other objects by considering whether the object is an animal or not. The present data indicate that such adjustment of perceptually salient similarity is problematic for some preschool children.

Blurring the Distinctions among the Three Types of Models
My characterization of Model Type III has so far glossed over the importance of the child's knowledge about the different properties. As I have stated, in the comparison-to-people model the only two kinds of information that are relevant to a decision are whether people have the property and how similar the object being probed is to people. If this were the only factor involved, all properties of people should be projected to other objects in the same way as those studied in this chapter. But we know this is not the case. In particular, "is alive" is not projected in this way, being much more widely attributed. It seems likely that wearing clothes, going to school, and a host of other properties would be restricted to people alone. Indeed, in Experiment 1 two properties were included in the battery, talking and laughing, which were little attributed to animals other than people (table 3.8). Like the properties in table 3.1, these were universally attributed to people. Children at each age judged other animals to talk and laugh significantly less than their next least widely attributed property (all comparisons, $p < .05$, Wilcoxin signed ranks test, 2-tailed).

In spite of the young child's relative lack of differentiation among the attribution patterns for eating, breathing, sleeping, thinking, having a heart, having bones, and having babies, some information about each of these properties, other than their merely being properties of people,

Table 3.8
Percentage of attribution to nonhuman animals

| Age | Property | Animal | | | | | |
		Aardvark	Dodo	Stinkoo	Hammer-head	Worm	Average
4	Talks	10	30	0	0		10
	Laughs	0	0				0
5	Talks	20	40	0	20	0	16
7	Talks	0	30	20	20	20	18

plays an important role in their attribution to other objects. The child distinguishes animal properties of people (such as thinking) from non-animal properties of people (such as laughing).

Conclusions

The experiments in this chapter have suggested that preschool children decide whether an object has certain animal properties by comparing the object to people. This model will be tested further, especially against the guessing model, in chapter 4. Establishing the correct model is important for two reasons. If we know how children are generating their judgments, we can better constrain our models of what knowledge they have and how that knowledge is organized. Second, should it turn out that 4- to 7-year-olds rely heavily on a type of reasoning that 10-year-olds and adults do not rely on, this would in itself be evidence for the reorganization of children's knowledge about animals during these years.

The aspects of biological knowledge probed here and in chapter 2 are complementary. The main concern in chapter 2 was what children know about the human body and about various bodily processes. Here it has been their knowledge of whether animals have those same internal organs and bodily functions. If children understand the human body in terms of the integrated functioning of internal organs maintaining life, it is difficult to imagine that they would not also conceptualize animal bodies in this way, given that they know animals are alive. The converse is easy to imagine: it is certainly possible that young children might know that all animals are alike with respect to the properties probed in this chapter, even though they have not achieved the view of the body as a machine documented in chapter 2. In fact, the two developments occur in parallel. Four-year-olds do not understand that people are just like mammals with respect to all of these properties, nor that all animals eat, breathe, and reproduce. By age 10, the age at which a view of the human bodily machine has been articulated, both generalizations have been achieved.

In chapter 1 I suggested that one source of animistic attributions of life to inanimate objects is lack of biological knowledge. Children's justifications for their judgments suggest that stage 1 and stage 2 children recruit all of their biological knowledge in their decisions about what objects are alive or not, but that for many 4- to 7-year-olds that knowledge is not adequate to drawing the distinction between living and nonliving things. The data from this chapter lend indirect support to this suggestion. Several biological functions universal among complex animals are not yet conceived sufficiently abstractly for the child to conclude that all animals must have them. How, then, is the child to understand how plants and animals are alike? If children do not even know that all animals eat, breathe, and reproduce, they are not likely to have a basis for justifying the inclusion of animals and plants in a single category.

Chapter 4 provides further evidence concerning the inferential processes by which these properties are attributed to nonhuman animals. Further, in the next three chapters I present several new reflections of the difference between the way the concept *animal* articulates the young child's knowledge and the way it articulates the 10-year-old's and adult's knowledge. These will allow a more precise characterization of how knowledge of animals is restructured between the ages of 4 and 10.

Chapter 4
The Projection of Spleen (Omentum)

In chapter 3 I suggested that preschool children decide what things in the world eat, breathe, have babies, think, have a heart, etc., on the basis of similarity to people. The first goal of this chapter is to provide a further test of Model Type III (comparison to exemplar) against the other models of the processes underlying the young child's judgments. Such a test requires an estimate of the similarity function relating people and other animals at each age. Therefore, since perceived similarity between any two objects depends upon the purpose of the comparison—the relevant similarity in this case being similarity with respect to internal organs and biological processes—I assessed patterns of inductive projection of a previously unknown internal organ from people to other objects.

Suppose I tell you that an *omentum* is a flat, thin, yellowish object, and that one thing that has an omentum is a person. I indicate a place, inside the abdominal cavity, where a person's omentum is located. By telling you that omenta are found inside people, I have suggested that they are some kind of internal organ, or part of one. (In fact, the omentum is the thin membrane that holds the intestinal organs in place.) I then ask you what else in the world has an omentum. Presumably, you proceed to attribute omenta to other objects by comparing those objects to people. Now suppose I teach a group of 4-year-olds about spleens in the same way. If the argument in chapter 3 is correct, these children, so instructed, will know about the spleen pretty much what they know about the heart and bones. That is, they will know that it is found inside a person, and they will know nothing about its function. If just such knowledge is the basis on which children attribute a heart, bones, having babies, sleeping, etc., to other objects, then their patterns of attributing spleens to new objects should be exactly the same as the patterns of attributing animal properties reported in chapter 3.

Subjects cannot attribute spleens on the basis of a definition, for they are given no informative definition. Nor can they attribute spleens on the basis of deductive inferences from categories of animals known to have them, for there are no such categories of animals, other than the category of people itself. Finally, if the guessing model suggested in chapter 3 is correct, subjects should attribute spleens to people 100% of the time and to all other animals 50% of the time. There should be no gradient of attribution between people and worm. In sum, if subjects attribute spleens as the subjects in the previous studies attributed all of the other properties, Model Type III will be supported over the other types of processes that could underlie young subjects' judgments.

In chapter 2 I suggested that preschool children's understanding of processes such as eating, breathing, and sleeping, as well as their understanding of the nature and function of internal organs, is embedded in their framework for understanding human behavior, whereas by age 10 this knowledge has become part of an independent domain of intuitive biology. The second goal of this chapter is to probe for further evidence for this reorganization of knowledge. To this end I will compare patterns of projection when subjects are told the new properties are properties of people and when they are told they are properties of dogs and bees. When Carol Smith asked preschool children to list those things in the world that think, breathe, eat, sleep, have hearts, etc., they frequently listed people first, and often listed only people (chapter 3, Experiment 3). It is possible, therefore, that children use people as their standard of comparison in generating answers to such questions as "Do dodos breathe?" simply because people are the most accessible animal that breathes, sleeps, eats, etc. On this view, if for some reason the child retrieved "dog" as the object known to breathe, then the process would involve a comparison between dodos and dogs. However, there may be other reasons why the child's judgments involve comparisons to people. Preschool children do not know the relations between eating, breathing, having a heart, and so on, in supporting life; nor do they realize that all animals must eat, breathe, and have babies. They conceive of these processes in terms of intentional human behavior, and explain them in terms of what the person (or animal) wants and thinks. By age 10, in contrast, children have constructed a first theory of the human body and understand that bodily processes underlie the functioning of all animals.

On this description of how the 4-year-old's understanding of these processes differs from the 10-year-old's, it is not surprising that people are the most accessible eaters, breathers, baby bearers, and thinkers, for to the 4-year-old these are fundamentally activities of people rather than of all animals. If so, it might be necessary for the child to retrieve that people breathe in order to decide that dodos do. Suppose a child's only example of a breathing animal is the dog (the child having seen a dog pant and having been told it was breathing, but not having focused on the fact that people breathe). The child knows many idiosyncratic properties about many animals—bees make honey, elephants have trunks, pigs go oink—and usually does not assume that other animals share these properties. Such a child might not expect other animals to breathe, just as such a child would not expect other animals to have trunks. Once children understand, as 10-year-olds do, the integrated functioning of internal organs in maintaining life, then they might assume that all animals have any internal organ known to be found in any particular animal.

In the present study, subjects of all ages are expected to project spleens (omenta) from people to other animals, on the basis of similarity between the animal and a person. For 4-year-olds this result is expected because they understand animal behavior and animal bodies by analogy to human behavior and the human body. For 10-year-olds this result is expected because they understand that internal organs have physiological functions and that people are identical to other animals with respect to these functions. Of interest is whether there are marked developmental differences in projection patterns from non-human animals, especially dogs.

Experiment: Patterns of Projection

Rips's (1975) paradigm was adapted for this study. Rips taught a new fact about some bird (or mammal) and analyzed the pattern of projection of that fact to other birds (or mammals). The main determinant of responses was the similarity of the two birds (or mammals), although there was a small effect of prototypicality as well. For example, robins are considered by adults to be prototypical birds; eagles are not. Projection from robin to eagle was greater than from eagle to robin. In the present adaptation of Rips's paradigm, children and adults were taught a new property of animals. Four- and 6-year-olds were taught about spleens; 10-year-olds and adults about omenta. At each age some subjects were taught that people have the property in question, others that dogs do, and still others that bees do. For adults, Rips's results should be replicated. Omenta should be attributed to other objects primarily on the basis of similarity, perhaps with a small prototypicality effect as well. That is, we might find greater generalization from people and dog to bee than vice versa. If people play the role of standard in the young child's comparison-to-exemplar reasoning merely because people are the most accessible owners of animal properties, then analogous results should be observed no matter which animal is used in teaching. When the child has been taught on dogs, dogs will be the most accessible spleen owner; similarly for bees. In contrast, markedly more generalization from people than from dogs or bees would suggest a central role for knowledge of humans and human activities in organizing the child's knowledge of animal properties.

Procedure

The most important aspect of the procedure is the teaching event. It is likely that the pattern of results crucially depends upon the wording used in this event. We wish to avoid the impression that we are primarily teaching something new about people (or dogs, or bees). Compare:

1. Dogs have omenta. Omenta are very thin, yellowish things found inside a dog's body.
2. Have you ever heard of an omentum? Omenta are very thin, yellowish things. Here is a picture of something (a dog) that has an omentum inside it.

To my ear, the first locution, more than the second, implies that dogs are the only animals with omenta. I did not want to study the effect of wording, and I wished to encourage projection, so I adopted the second locution throughout the studies of chapters 4 and 5. The exact wording for the two youngest groups was as follows:

I'm going to teach you a new word. Has anyone ever heard of a "spleen"? A spleen is round and green. Here's a picture of something that has a spleen. What is this a picture of? Good. I'm going to draw the spleen where it is found in the person's (or dog's or bee's) body.

Subjects were then each given a picture on which they drew a spleen. In addition, each child repeated the word "spleen" and the group produced as many rhyming words as they could. The older children and adults were told that the study they were to participate in was designed for very young children. It was stressed that what we were teaching them was true, and that we would give them an encyclopedia article about it after they completed the study. The crucial part of the instructions was the same as for the younger children:

Omenta are yellowish in color, and are flat and thin. Here is a picture of something that has an omentum. I am going to draw one approximately where it is found in a person's (or dog's or bee's) body.

Fifty-one subjects at each of four ages (4, 6, 10, and adult) participated. Within each age group, 17 were given people as the exemplar, 17 dogs, and 17 bees. Subjects who subsequently failed to attribute the property to the animal on which it had been taught were removed from the sample and replaced. Three children had to be replaced (2 4-year-olds and 1 10-year-old).

After the teaching event, the children were tested for projection of spleens to other objects. The procedure of chapter 3 was adapted, using "has a spleen" (or "has an omentum") as one of the properties probed. The other animal properties probed were breathing and having bones. Each object was also probed for growing and dying. In addition, as in chapter 2, filler items sampled categorization at different levels of the hierarchy. The objects included people, dogs, aardvarks, dodos, stinkoos, bees, and worms as animals, and flowers, the sun, clouds, harvesters, and garlic presses as nonanimals. The randomization of the order of questions for each object was as in chapter 3.

The objects for which projection of spleens was probed were arranged in 17 different random orders for the groups of subjects taught on people. The 17 orders for those taught on dogs was then constructed by switching the dog and the person in each of the orders. Similarly for bees. Thus, the subjects in each group received the animal on which they had been taught in the same positions during the testing series.

For 4- and 6-year-olds the teaching sessions preceded the generalization sessions by one or two days. The 4-year-olds were tested individually in two sessions and the 6-year-olds in a single session. Booklets were prepared for the 10-year-olds and adults, who were tested in groups immediately after the teaching session.

I will discuss the results in three steps. Because 51 subjects were tested at each age, and each subject was asked whether each animal has bones and breathes, these data provide an opportunity to replicate the findings of chapter 3 with respect to attribution patterns for such properties. I present these results first. Next I compare how subjects project spleens (omenta) from people to the way they attribute eating, sleeping, having bones, etc. The analysis provides a further test of the hypothesis that preschool children attribute animal properties on the basis of similarity to people, and that 10-year-olds and adults do not. Finally, I compare projection from people to projection from dogs and bees, in order to further elucidate the senses in which people are the prototypical owners of internal organs.

Results

Having Bones and Breathing
Breathing is a universal animal property; having bones is a restricted animal property. As in the two main studies of chapter 3, 4-year-olds failed, almost completely, to differentiate the patterns of attribution of breathing and having bones (table 4.1). Attribution fell off fairly regularly from people to worm, as if a single similarity metric underlay both patterns. As a consequence, breathing was underattributed to peripheral animals and having bones was overattributed to peripheral animals.

Adults presented a completely different picture. All animals were credited with breathing and only vertebrates were credited with having bones. And as can be seen from table 4.1, the results from ages 6 and 10 fall neatly in between the undifferentiated patterns of the 4-year-olds and the fully articulated patterns of the adults.

The data on breathing and having bones were analyzed with an ANOVA. Three findings are of importance. First, the animal taught on (people, dog, or bee) had no effect on the attribution patterns for these properties. (In the language of analyses of variance, there was no main effect of the animal taught on, nor any interaction of this factor with any other variable.) This is important since it shows that any differences in attribution of spleens or omenta based on the animal taught on are not due to differences in biological knowledge among the groups, at least as diagnosed by attribution patterns for breathing and having bones. Second, the three-way interaction among animal probed, age, and property was significant ($p < .001$). Figure 4.1 summarizes this interaction. For 4-year-olds, both breathing and having bones were attributed less to invertebrates than vertebrates, so there was a small (21%) difference of differences: $(\text{Vert}^{bo} - \text{Inv}^{bo}) - (\text{Vert}^{br} - \text{Inv}^{br})$. With increasing age, the difference between vertebrates and invertebrates on having bones becomes increasingly bigger than the difference between vertebrates and invertebrates on breathing. Third, although the interaction in figure 4.1 supports the findings of chapter 3 that there is an increasing differentiation in patterns of attribution of properties as

Table 4.1
Percentage of attribution of breathing and having bones

Age	Property	Animals							Nonanimals				
		People	Dog	Aardvark	Dodo	Bee	Stinkoo	Worm	Flower	Sun	Cloud	Harvester	Garlic press
4	Breathes	100	94	92	82	65	73	69	24	12	6		
	Has bones	100	96	92	90	65	59	31	6			0	6
6	Breathes	100	100	96	90	84	96	86	24	0	0		
	Has bones	100	100	92	94	63	67	33	6			0	0
10	Breathes	100	100	100	98	100	100	90	47	6	0		
	Has bones	100	100	100	100	55	67	14	0			0	0
Adult	Breathes	100	100	100	96	96	94	94	65	6	0		
	Has bones	100	100	98	96	22	22	6	0			0	0

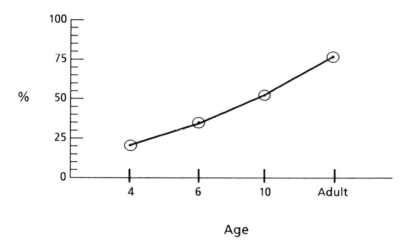

Figure 4.1
Difference of difference score: (Vertebrates^{bones} − Invertebrates^{bones}) − (Vertebrates^{breathes} − Invertebrates^{breathes})

children get older, the ANOVAs show that at no age are the two properties completely undifferentiated.

Although the major findings from chapter 3 receive support here, the present study's 4-year-olds resemble the 6-year-olds in the earlier studies more than they do the earlier 4- and 5-year-olds. There is no large drop in attribution from people to other mammals, and there is, as already noted, some differentiation of the profiles for breathing and having bones. These differences may be due to the fact that many fewer animal properties were probed in the present study than in the studies in chapter 3.

Projection from People
As predicted, when taught that spleens (omenta) are found inside people, subjects at all ages projected the new property to nonhuman animals (fig. 4.2). In all groups attribution decreased regularly from mammals to worms. The concept *animal* constrained all children's projection in that attribution to nonhuman animals was greater than to flowers or inanimate objects ($p < .001$, t-test for correlated means,[1] even for 4-year-olds, the only group with any attribution to inanimate objects).

The goal of this procedure was to establish how similar to a person subjects of each age consider each animal to be. Having these similarity

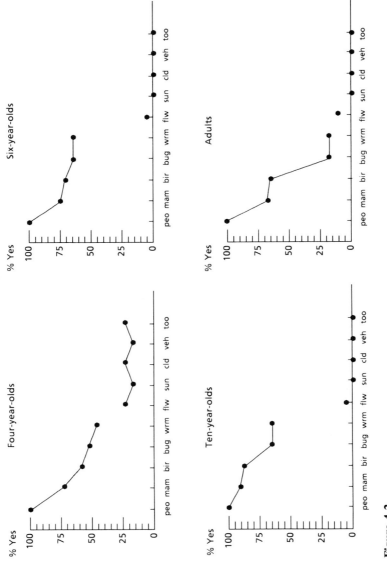

Figure 4.2
Patterns of projection from people. Spleen (4-year-olds, 6-year-olds); omentum (10-year-olds, adults).

measures allows us to assess whether this is the function that describes the attribution profiles of eating, sleeping, having a heart, having bones, etc. The profiles for spleens (omenta) could be related to those for known animal properties in one of four different ways (fig. 4.3). First, they could match. I arbitrarily defined as matching those profiles that deviated from each other in absolute values an average of 10 percentage points or less. Not matching, the two profiles could parallel one another, diverge, or cross. In parallel patterns, the attribution of the property was simply elevated with respect to that of spleens (omenta). Diverging patterns were observed for older subjects in the cases of universal animal properties, such as eating. Since attribution of having a spleen (omentum) fell off from people, but the attribution of eating was 100% for all animals, the differences between the two curves diverged. I arbitrarily set as a criterion for diverging curves that the difference between the curves at bugs and worms had to be at least twice the difference at mammals. Finally, the two curves could cross, as generally happened for having bones. In crossing profiles, the property began being more widely attributed than having a spleen (omentum) and ended by being much less widely attributed. To classify as crossing, two profiles had to exhibit a total swing of at least 35 percentage points.

Table 4.2 presents the comparison between the projection patterns for spleen (omentum) and the attribution patterns for the animal properties. A positive entry indicates that the property was attributed more to the animal than was having a spleen (omentum); a negative entry indicates that the property was attributed less than was having a spleen (omentum). For the comparison with the data from chapter 2, the level of attribution of each property was calculated from all children who were asked about it. The entry for mammals having a heart, for example, was averaged from 4 groups of 4- and 5-year-olds—the 4-year-olds and the 5-year-olds in Experiment 1 of chapter 2 and the two groups of 4-year-olds in Experiment 2 of chapter 2. The attribution of spleens to mammals by the 4-year-olds in the present study was then subtracted from the resulting average and the difference (-2%) entered in table 4.2.

In six of the eight cases, the profiles from the 4- and 5-year-olds in chapter 2 matched the profile for attribution of spleens (table 4.2). This strongly suggests that comparisons to people determined the child's judgments of these animal properties, just as it did in the case of having a spleen. Parallel profiles also suggest a major role for comparison-to-

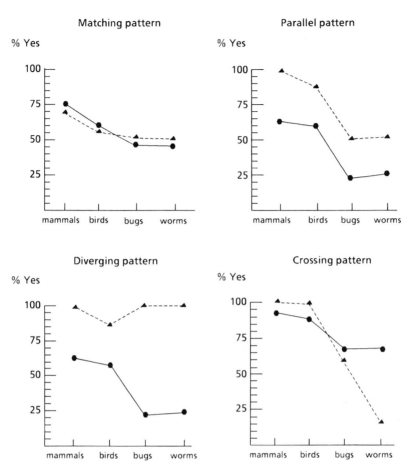

Figure 4.3
Four possible relations between profiles for projection for spleen (omentum)
and profiles of attribution of known properties. Matching: 4-year-olds,
chapter 3, has a heart. Parallel: adults, chapter 3, has a heart. Diverging:
adults, chapter 3, eats. Crossing: 10-year-olds, present study, has bones.
●——● spleen, omentum; ▲---▲ known property.

Table 4.2
Deviation from spleen (omentum)

Age	Source of data	Property	Animal				Average (absolute)	Pattern
			Mammal	Bird	Bug	Worm		
4–5	From chapter 2	Has bones	1		0	−2	1	match
		Has a heart	−2	−3	3	3	3	match
		Has babies	−4		15	3	7	match
		Breathes	10	19	6	−3	10	match
		Can get hurt	−7	8	6		7	match
		Thinks	−12	8	−8		8	match
		Eats	12	30	19	28	22	diverge
		Sleeps	16	22	19	35	23	diverge
	From present study	Has bones	20	31	12	−16	20	cross
		Breathes	19	23	19	22	21	parallel
6–7	From chapter 2	Has bones	23		2	−25	17	cross
		Has a heart	8	18	23	−2	13	?
		Has babies	23		28	15	22	parallel
		Breathes	23	29	27	13	23	parallel
		Thinks	3	7	−8	−3	5	match
		Eats	23		38	30	30	diverge
		Sleeps	23	29	33	19	26	parallel
	From present study	Has bones	19	23	3	−22	17	cross
		Breathes	21	19	28	21	22	parallel

10	From chapter 2	Has bones	9		-35	-30	25	cross
		Has a heart	-1		15	5	7	match
		Has babies	9		30	5	15	?
		Thinks	-6		-5	-10	7	match
		Eats	9		30	25	21	diverge
		Sleeps	9		10	-10	10	match
	From present study	Has bones	9	12	-6	-51	20	cross
		Breathes	9	10	35	35	22	diverge
Adult	From chapter 2	Has bones	38		-1	-14	18	cross
		Has a heart	38	30	39	29	34	parallel
		Has babies	38		79	65	61	diverge
		Breathes	38	41	79	65	56	diverge
		Can get hurt	38	30	79	65	53	diverge
		Thinks	18	30	37	18	26	parallel
		Eats	38	30	79	76	56	diverge
		Sleeps	38	41	74	71	56	diverge
	From present study	Has bones	37	37	1	-18	23	cross
		Breathes	38	40	69	70	54	diverge

exemplar reasoning. The similarity metric producing the matching profiles is in evidence, but other factors contribute to the data. Consider attribution of breathing in the case of the 4-year-olds in the present study. There is a steady 20% difference between attribution of breathing and attribution of having a spleen (table 4.2). The difference between the two profiles is due to the fact that three (18%) of the children attributed having a spleen to people alone, whereas none did so for breathing. Removing these three from the analysis, the patterns become identical. In contrast, the remaining three profiles from the 4- and 5-year-olds are clearly influenced by other factors than comparison to people. Attributions of eating and sleeping diverge from attribution of having a spleen, and attribution of having bones by the 51 4-year-olds in the present study crosses attribution of having a spleen. However, even in these cases the divergence or crossover is not fully evident until worms: the curves are parallel through the bug.

In sum, it is clear that factors other than comparisons to people play a role in the judgments of some of even the youngest children. Nonetheless, the profiles of judgments of eating, breathing, sleeping, having babies, having a heart, having bones, and thinking match or parallel those for having a spleen to a great extent. Model Type I or Model Type II reasoning cannot underlie the attribution of having a spleen. Therefore, to the degree of the match, it is likely that neither played much role in the attribution of the other animal properties. These data also militate against the guessing model. Attribution of having a spleen fell off regularly from mammals to worms, matching the whole functions. The approximately 50% levels of judgment that bugs and worms have hearts, have babies, think, etc., must reflect the same generative process that produces the 77% attribution for aardvarks or the 60% attribution for dodos. The best candidate is the child's estimate of similarity to people, similarity in terms of the same features in both cases.

The adults' attribution profiles for the various properties differed markedly from one another. Therefore, it would be impossible for many of these profiles to match those for having an omentum. And indeed they do not; the profiles for most (6 out of 8) of the known animal properties either diverge from or cross the profiles for having an omentum (table 4.2). None matches. The profiles for two properties, thinking and having a heart, parallel that of having an omentum. Plausibly, some adults may attribute these properties to animals on the basis of similarity to people. A heart, being an internal organ like the omentum, might be projected beyond mammals mainly on the basis of similarity to people (or mammals). For 10-year-olds, attribution of thinking and having a heart actually matches their respective profiles for having an omentum. Thus, in the absence of specifically relevant biological knowledge that would support Model Type I or II reasoning, even 10-year-olds and adults may call upon Model Type III reasoning.

The data from the 6-year-olds are ambiguous, because projection of having a spleen did not vary much from the mammals (77%) to the bug and worm (62% and 65%). Whereas the profile for having bones clearly crosses that for having a spleen, and the profile for eating clearly diverges, the rest seem roughly parallel.

Conclusions: Processes Underlying Attribution of Animal Properties
Four-year-olds projected having a spleen from people to new animals in exactly the same pattern as they attributed six of the eight animal properties probed in chapter 3. This suggests that the process underlying the judgments about those properties was also an inductive projection from the knowledge that people have them. The conclusion of chapter 3 is thus supported. Preschool children appear to decide whether a given object eats, breathes, sleeps, has babies, has a heart, or has bones by comparing that object to people. As expected, with increasing age attribution profiles for all animal properties became differentiated from the projection pattern for having a spleen (omentum). Ten-year-olds and adults, by and large, do not generate their judgments in this way.

Why do 4-year-olds rely heavily on comparison-to-people reasoning, whereas adults use it rarely, if at all? Adults clearly *can* employ comparison-to-exemplar reasoning, as they did in the case of projecting omenta from people. And 4-year-olds *can* employ deductive inferences from category membership and can reason from definitions, as they frequently do in their justifications. The shift we are seeing is not in overall reasoning strategies available to subjects at different ages.

Older children and adults employ comparison-to-exemplar reasoning in situations such as this one, or Rips's, when they have no other information to go on. Being given no inkling of what omenta are or do, they cannot reason on the basis of a definition, and being told only that people have them, they cannot reason on the basis of category membership. Ten-year-olds (and some adults) may be in just this state of knowledge for the properties of having a heart and thinking. And 4- and 5-year-olds (and some 6-year-olds) are in this state of knowledge for most animal properties of people. Preschool children know what breathing and sleeping and thinking are; that is, they know what it is for a person to breathe and sleep and think. And they know what bones are (the hard things in their fingers) and some know what a heart is (the thing that beats hard inside them when they run fast). But in the absence of understanding how these processes and organs function together in supporting life, such knowledge does not support inferences that other animals must breathe and think and have hearts. In sum, 4- and 5-year-olds' reliance on comparison-to-people reasoning is yet another reflection of their impoverished biological knowledge.

As figure 4.2 shows, 6-year-olds and 10-year-olds are more likely to attribute spleens (omenta) to nonhuman animals than are 4-year-olds. This reflects increasing understanding that animals share solutions to biological problems. There is still much to learn about which biological functions are universal, and how subgroups of animals differ from each other. Such learning is reflected in the adults' projection of omenta more to aardvarks and dodos than to stinkoos and worms (fig. 4.2).

People as Prototypical Owners of Animal Properties
As we have just seen, when taught that a person is one thing that has a spleen (or an omentum), subjects of all ages behaved as Rips's adult subjects did: they projected having a spleen or an omentum to other animals on the basis of similarity to people. Analysis of the other teaching conditions (being taught on dogs or on bees) will allow us to evaluate the ways in which people are prototypical animals. In the presentation that follows, the results from each group are first discussed separately, and then the age trends, backed with ANOVAs, are summarized.

Age 4. People as Strong Prototype   When 4-year-olds were taught on people, they attributed spleens to other animals to a much greater extent than when taught on dogs or bees (fig. 4.4). Indeed, when taught on dogs or on bees, they projected to the four animals no more than to the four inanimate objects (dog group, $t = 1.57$, n.s.; bee group, $t = 1.69$, n.s.). Only when taught on people did 4-year-olds project spleens to other animals more than to inanimate objects ($t = 4.36$, $p < .001$). This is a counterintuitive result. When 4-year-olds are taught that a person is one thing that has a green, round thing inside it, they assume that other animals also have green, round things inside them. Not so when they are taught that dogs or bees are things that have green, round things inside them.

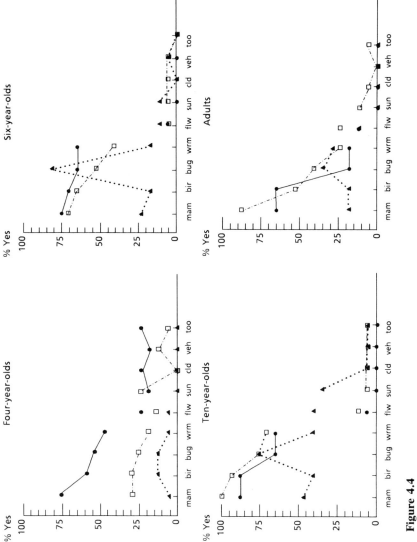

Figure 4.4
Patterns of projection from people, dogs, and bees. Spleen (4-year-olds, 6-year-olds); omentum (10-year-olds, adults). ● taught on people; □⋯⋯□ taught on dogs; ▲⋯⋯▲ taught on bees.

Two further analyses underscore the degree to which people are the 4-year-olds' prototypical owner of animal properties. First, projection from people to dogs (71%) was enormously greater than from dogs to people (18%, $p < .02$, χ^2, 1-tailed, see fig. 4.5). A parallel asymmetry is observed in the comparison of bees and people: projection from people to bees (47%) was significantly greater than from bees to people (0%, $p < .001$ Fisher exact test, 1-tailed). This asymmetry is similar to the prototypicality effect reported by Rips, but it is much greater. The second analysis pits prototypicality against similarity, and asks which contributes more to the child's judgments. The animals probed included a second mammal (aardvarks) and a second insect (stinkoo). Projection from people to aardvarks (76%) was greater than from dogs to aardvarks (29%, $p < .02$, χ^2 test, 1-tailed; see fig. 4.6). Similarly, projection from people to stinkoos (52%) was greater than from bees to stinkoos (12%, $p < .05$, χ^2 test, 1-tailed). The prototypicality of people plays a much larger role in determining 4-year-olds' projection of having a spleen than does similarity among animals, a reversal of the results Rips found with adults.

Further insight into the differences among the three groups is gained from an analysis of how individuals attributed having a spleen. There were four possible patterns: having a spleen could be credited *only* to the exemplar used in teaching, or spleens could be credited to some additional animals, to all additional animals, or even to some nonanimals as well. When children were taught on bees, they almost never projected spleens to anything else at all (table 4.3). This was not true of children taught on people ($p < .001$, χ^2 test, 1-tailed). Thus, the asymmetries between these two groups were due to the tendency of the children taught on bees to restrict attribution to bees alone. The bee group also differed from the dog group in this respect ($p < .05$, χ^2 test, 1-tailed).

The differences between the children taught on people and those taught on dogs have another source. Children in both groups projected spleens to new objects, although those taught on dogs did so somewhat less. Some in both groups projected spleens to inanimate objects. The difference is that those taught on people were more likely to project spleens to animals and only animals (53%) than were those taught on dogs (29%), although this difference was not significant. Those taught on bees attributed spleens only to bees; those taught on dogs did not know what to do.

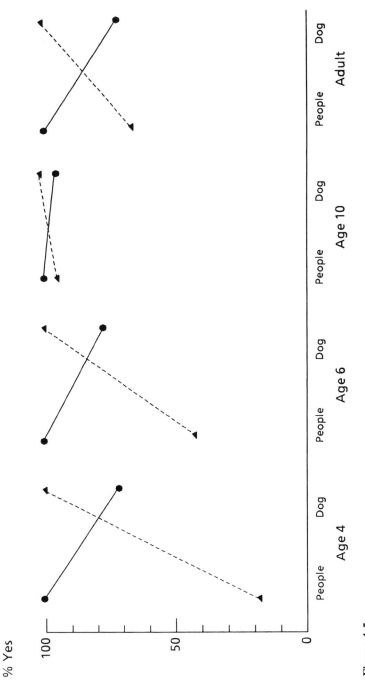

Figure 4.5
Projection from people to dogs compared to projection from dogs to people. ●——● taught on people; ▲- - -▲ taught on dogs.

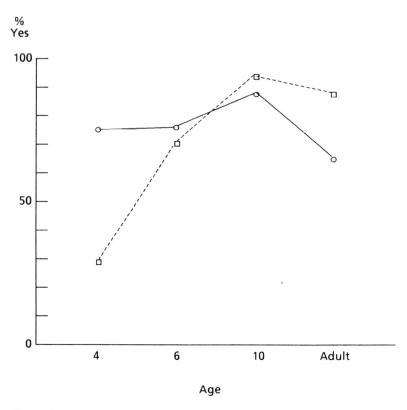

Figure 4.6
Projection of spleens (omenta) to aardvarks. ○────○ taught on people;
□ - - -□ taught on dogs.

Most surprising in these data is the degree of prototypicality of people relative to dogs—familiar, central exemplars of mammals. The
most important conclusion to be drawn is that people play the role of
standard in 4-year-olds' Type III inferences about animal properties for
reasons beyond the fact that people are the most accessible owner of
these properties. When dogs (or bees) are the most accessible owner of
such a property, 4-year-olds do not attribute it to other animals any
more than to inanimate objects.

Age 6. In Transition   Unlike the 4-year-olds, the 6-year-olds did not
require that a spleen be exemplified on people in order to project it to
other animals more than to inanimate objects (fig. 4.4). Further, attribution clearly reflected similarity, as witnessed by the markedly dif-

Table 4.3
Patterns of projection

Age	Projection pattern		Taught on people	Taught on dog	Taught on bee
4	Taught on animal only		3	7	14
	Only living things	Some animals	6	4	3
		All animals	3	1	0
	Some inanimate objects		5	5	0
6	Taught on animal only		3	3	3
	Only living things	Some animals	5	9	10
		All animals	9	3	1
	Some inanimate objects		0	2	3
10	Taught on animal only		1	0	1
	Only living things	Some animals	8	7	7
		All animals	8	8	2
	Some inanimate objects		0	2	7
Adult	Taught on animal only		3	2	11
	Only living things	Some animals	13	11	3
		All animals	1	2	3
	Some inanimate objects		0	2	0

ferent profile for the bee group (most projection to stinkoo) in relation to either the dog group or the people group. Nonetheless, there were several reflections of the prototypicality of people compared to dogs, just as for the 4-year-olds. Children taught on people attributed spleens to nonhuman animals to a greater degree (69%) than did those taught on dogs (54%). Also, there was an asymmetry in projection from people to dogs (76%) and projection from dogs to people (41%, $p < .1$, χ^2 test, 1-tailed; see fig. 4.5). Similarly, projection was greater from people to bees (59%) than from bees to people (12%, $p < .05$, Fisher exact test, 1-tailed). Finally, projection was greater from people to a four-footed mammal (aardvarks, 76%) than from dogs to the same four-footed mammal (71%; fig. 4.6). At age 6 as well as at age 4, the prototypicality of people relative to dogs outweighs the greater similarity between dogs and aardvarks than between people and aardvarks, although not significantly.

Table 4.3 presents the individual patterns. There was little attribution of spleens to inanimate objects by children in any of the three groups, and few children restricted spleens only to the animal taught on. The three groups did not differ in either regard. Rather, when children projected spleens to new animals, those taught on people were more likely to judge that all animals have spleens than were those taught on dogs ($p < .05$, Fisher exact test, 1-tailed) or bees ($p < .01$, Fisher exact test, 1-tailed).

The 6-year-olds are in transition. For them, knowledge of people still plays a privileged role, relative to knowledge of dogs, in the projection of a new animal property. However, unlike the 4-year-olds, the 6-year-olds will project a property to new animals even if it is not taught on people.

Age 10. People Not More Prototypical Than Dogs   By age 10 there is no suggestion that people are more central than dogs. Projection from dogs is even slightly greater than from people (figure 4.4), presumably because dogs are seen as more similar to other nonhuman animals than are people. The distributions of individual patterns in the people group and in the dog group are virtually identical (table 4.3).

The peripherality of bees with respect to both people and dogs is apparent. Projection from people to bees (65%) is greater than from bees to people (29%, $p < .1$, χ^2 test, 1-tailed). Similarly, the projection from dogs to bees (94%) is greater than that from bees to dogs (35%, $p < .05$, Fisher exact test, 1-tailed). One curious finding is that many 10-year-olds taught on bees credited inanimate objects, especially the sun, with omenta (fig. 4.4, table 4.3). Few 6-year-olds did so. This may be due to the differences between how the 6-year-olds conceptualized spleens and how the 10-year-olds conceptualized omenta. The effect of the property taught will be explored in chapter 5.

In sum, by age 10 results parallel to those of Rips are observed. If taught that an omentum is found in some animal's body, children of this age project omenta to other animals primarily on the basis of their similarity to the exemplar on which they were taught. People and dogs are approximately equally good examples of animals with respect to having animal properties, both being better than bees.

Adults. A Different Difference   Adults did not differ from 10-year-olds with respect to centrality effects and the relative importance of similarity in determining projection. Adults taught that dogs have omenta are hardly distinguishable from those taught that people have omenta. There is slightly more projection from dogs than from people (fig. 4.4). Projection from dog to aardvark (88%) is greater than from people to aardvark (65%, fig. 4.6).

The centrality of dogs and people with respect to bees is less apparent for adults than for 10-year-olds. Projection from bees to people (18%) is equal to that from people to bees (18%). Projection from dogs to bees (41%) is greater than from bees to dogs (18%), but not significantly. The peripherality of bees shows up only in the distribution of individual patterns of attribution (table 4.3). Adults were more likely to restrict their attribution of omenta to bees alone when taught on bees than to dogs alone when taught on dogs ($p < .1$, Fisher exact test, 1-tailed) or to people alone when taught on people ($p < .1$, Fisher exact test, 1-tailed).

Thus, the data from the adults exemplify those Rips found when the new property taught was having a disease. The main determinant of projection was the similarity between the animal taught on and other animals, as seen by the different profiles of attribution when taught on bees, on the one hand, and dogs or people, on the other, and by the greater projection to aardvarks from dogs than from people. And as Rips found, there was a small effect of peripherality—there was less projection from bees than from dogs or people.

Adults differed from the 10-year-olds in being more conservative in projection of omenta to new animals. They also honored the vertebrate-invertebrate distinction more strictly (see fig. 4.2 for a clear demonstration). Thus, although similarity was the main determinant of the adults' responses, the similarity metric underlying their judgments was more sharply focused, more finely tuned, than that of any of the groups of children.

The Whole Developmental Picture   The most important comparison, for our purposes, is between the profiles of projection from dogs and the profiles of projection from people. Both are highly familiar animals. One might expect dogs, good examples of mammals, to typify the animal kingdom more than do people, rather special examples of mammals. In the analyses just presented of the different ages, it seemed that this expectation was met for 10-year-olds and adults, but not for the two youngest groups of children. However, for such a comparison to be legitimate, we must show, statistically, that the patterns at different ages are truly different.

An analysis of variance with age (4, 6, 10, and adult) and animal taught on (dog, people) as between-subject variables and animal probed (aardvark, dodo, bug, and worm) as a within-subject variable revealed two main effects, for age and for animal probed, and one interaction, between age and animal taught on. The effect of age was due to 4-year-olds' (38%) and adults' (46%) making the least attributions to new animals, both differing from the 6-year-olds (63%), who in turn differed from the 10-year-olds (81%). The effect of property was the result of projection to the aardvarks (73%) being greater than projection to the dodo (63%), which was in turn greater than projection to the stinkoo (48%) and the worm (43%). The most important result was the interaction between age and animal taught on. Six-year-olds, like 4-year-olds, projected spleens more from people than from dogs, whereas 10-year-olds and adults projected slightly more from dogs (projection from people minus projection from dogs: age 4, 43%; age 6, 12%; age 10, -8%; adults, -12%; age-by-animal-taught-on interaction, $p < .006$).

Figure 4.5 shows the whole developmental picture with regard to the asymmetry of projection from people to dogs compared with projection from dogs to people. An ANOVA examined the effects of age ($n = 4$) and animal taught on (people, dogs) on the level of attribution to one animal (dogs, in the taught-on-people case; people in the taught-on-dogs case). There was a highly significant interaction between age and animal taught on ($p < .001$). At age 4, the asymmetry of projection was 53%; at age 6, 35%; and at ages 10 and adulthood, 0% and 6%.

Finally, projection to aardvarks was analyzed (fig. 4.6). Again, the interaction of age and animal taught on was highly significant ($p < .001$). For 4-year-olds, having a spleen was projected to aardvarks more from people than from dogs (by 47%), whereas the reverse was true for adults (by 23%). The crossover point was between ages 6 and 10.

These analyses reveal the interactions that legitimize the comparisons among ages that were made when each age was discussed separately. Projection of spleens and omenta from one animal to other things reflects the similarity of the object probed to the animal taught on, and the relative prototypicality of the animals taught on. At age 4, the prototypicality of people swamps almost all other effects. By age 10, there is no longer any reflection of the prototypicality of people compared to dogs. With increasing age, similarity accounts for most of the variance in projection.

The developmental story with regard to projection from bees can be simply summarized. At age 4 there is no significant projection from bees, but this is a side effect of the extreme centrality of people. At ages 6 and 10 there are strong indications, and among adults there are weak indications, of the peripherality of bees with respect to both people and dogs. Thus, for all subjects over age 4 results like those of Rips were found: both similarity and relative peripherality influenced projection from bees.

Conclusions

The induction paradigm of this chapter provides new insights into the differences in biological knowledge between young children and adults. To a great extent preschool children's attribution patterns for animal properties like breathing, having babies, having a heart, and thinking match their projection patterns from people of the newly taught property of having a spleen. This result suggests that projection from people underlies the preschooler's attribution of these animal properties as well. In the case of having a spleen, all children know is that a spleen is something found inside a person's body. Apparently, they know little else about most animal properties that can help them decide what creatures or things exhibit them.

Though older children and adults use this kind of reasoning when they have no knowledge that supports other forms of inference, by age 10 attribution patterns for most animal properties either diverge from or cross those for having an omentum. Six-year-olds fall in between. Profiles for most animal properties did not match the projection profile for having a spleen, indicating reliance on some other process of decision. But most profiles paralleled the one for having a spleen, indicating that comparison to people still plays a large role in the 6-year-old's attributions.

The tentative conclusions of chapter 3 were supported: there is a developmental progression in the child's judgments from comparison-to-exemplar reasoning and toward the use of definitions and category membership. Developmental changes in the way judgments are generated could have two sources: changes in the types of reasoning available to the child, or changes in the nature and organization of the knowledge entering into the judgments. In this case, the latter seems the correct choice.

That biological knowledge is restructured during these years is confirmed by the new findings of this experiment. Four-year-olds projected spleens sensibly to new animals only if taught on people, not if taught on dogs or bees. The asymmetry of projection between people and dogs was still present at age 6, but was totally absent by age 10. The remaining discussion considers the explanation of the asymmetry and the significance of the developmental change.

I have repeatedly compared the present results to those of Rips (1975) from a similar induction paradigm. He too found projection asymmetries. For example, when taught that all of the robins on an island had a disease, subjects estimated that 30% of the ducks would have the disease as well. In contrast, projection from ducks to robins was only 18%. On the assumption that this induction task involves computation of similarity between the object probed and the exemplar taught on, these asymmetries can be assimilated to the more general case of asymmetries in similarity judgments discussed by Tversky (1977). Tversky showed that in a variety of tasks, using a variety of stimulus domains, subjects treat peripheral, less salient members of the domain as more similar to central, salient members than vice versa.

Tversky proposed a set-theoretical model of similarity that would account for such asymmetries. On this model, the two items being judged for similarity (A and B) are each represented in terms of a set of features. The asymmetry is explained in terms of two parameters—a weighting resulting from the directionality of the comparison ("How similar is A to B?" compared to "How similar is B to A?") and the relative salience of the two difference sets (features of A not shared by B and features of B not shared by A). Tversky's model applies to the present case. The comparison is directional—the object taught on serves as the standard to which probed objects are compared. And for young children it seems plausible that the weighted feature set $f(P - A)$ would be greater than $f(A - P)$, where P stands for the features of people, and A stands for the features of any other animal, and f is the function that provides salience weighting for the features. That is, it seems plausible that young children would be aware of many more salient features of people not shared by other animals than salient features of animals not shared by people.

Although Tversky's model applies here, and predicts the direction of the asymmetries of projection, it provides only a partial framework for viewing the present results. The model is intended to provide a very abstract conception of psychological similarity. It contrasts with the spatial models underlying factor analysis and multidimensional scaling. As such, it is silent on the choice of features, or their weighting for salience, in any particular similarity judgment. Within Tversky's framework, one could view the developmental changes as being due to changes in the features used in the comparisons, or as being due to changes in the weightings of the features.

The choice and weighting of features in any similarity comparison is subject to context effects of many types. Tversky (1977) discussed context effects due to the other stimuli in the comparison set. For example, Spain is judged more similar to Portugal in the context of France than in the context of Argentina. The contrasts set up by other items in the set cause different features (geographical and linguistic in this example) to be weighted differently. Inductive projection establishes context effects as well, albeit of a quite different kind from those set up by item contrasts. The property being projected determines both the features used in the similarity comparisons underlying projection and the weightings of these features. This can be seen by contrasting the projection of spleens (omenta) from people in the projection study with the similarity judgments between people and other objects reported in chapter 3. The two studies were the same as far as item context effects were concerned. Both required pairwise comparisons to people, and in both cases the items compared to people and the orders in which the comparisons were made were identical. In the similarity judgment case, subjects were simply asked to assess degree of similarity. In the projection case, similarity was computed as part of the process of deciding whether the objects in question would have a spleen (omentum), given that people do. The two profiles of similarity to people differed markedly (table 4.4). Spleens and omenta were denied all inanimate objects, but both children and adults assigned substantial similarity between the inanimate objects and people. Also, both groups judged the plants to be just as similar to people as some nonhuman animals, whereas projection of spleens (omenta) respected the animal-plant distinction. Clearly, the projection of spleens (omenta) sets up an entirely different context for comparisons between people and other objects than does the simple request for similarity judgments.

In terms of Tversky's framework, the developmental changes in patterns of projection should be seen in terms of differences in these internal context effects. But although Tversky's framework allows us to locate the developmental changes, it does not explain them. The adult (and the 10-year-old) data are easy to understand. With respect to the context set up by the requirement of projecting an internal organ, the two weighted difference sets (between the properties of people and those of dogs and vice versa) do not differ in magnitude and are probably very small. In other words, with respect to a biological property such as having some internal organ, both dogs and people are much alike, and the differences between the two of them (such as the fact that

Table 4.4
Comparison of patterns of projection of spleens (omenta) from people to other objects (% yes) and estimates of similarity between people and other objects (1 to 10 scale, 10 most similar)

	Age 6		Adult	
	Projection pattern	Similarity estimates	Projection pattern	Similarity estimates
Dog	71	2.4	71	6.8
Aardvark	76	2.0	65	6.4
Dodo	71	2.4	65	4.5
Stinkoo	65	3.2	18	5.8
Bee	65	2.8	18	6.2
Worm	65	2.3	18	4.0
Flower	6	2.4	12	4.3
Sun	0	1.8	0	3.2
Cloud	0	2.1	0	2.2
Harvester	0	1.8	0	2.8
Garlic press	0	1.5	0	1.4

one is a primate and one a canine) are symmetrical. This is why there is no asymmetry of projection from people to dogs and vice versa. Also, dogs are more similar to other nonhuman animals than are people, both because the overlap of biologically relevant features is greater and because the difference set between features of dogs and other animals is smaller than the difference set between people and other animals. This is why projection from dogs to other animals is greater than from humans to other animals.

The problem comes in accounting for the young child's, especially the 4-year-old's, data. For the young child, no less than the adult, the distinction between people and nonhuman animals is extremely salient. The young child restricts the extension of the word "animal" to exclude people and will vehemently deny that people are animals. Why, then, does the context of projecting an internal organ mitigate the sharp distinctions between people and other animals, leading to greater similarity between animals and people than between animals and dogs? And we still have the puzzle we cannot even state within Tversky's framework: why will the 4-year-old not project spleens to other animals from dogs or bees at all?

The answer, I believe, must be stated first in terms of what 4- to 6-year-olds do not have, and then in terms of what they have in its place. They do not have an autonomous domain of biological knowledge that flags these properties as biological properties and flags what features of people, dogs, and other objects are relevant to the comparisons. For the 10-year-old, knowledge of the interrelations among the various biological functions and internal organs renders people just one mammal among many, in the context of biological properties like having particular internal organs. For the young child, on the other hand, knowledge of these functions is instead integrated into schemata for human activity.

Suppose I am right that a complete reorganization of knowledge of functions like eating and sleeping and organs like stomachs and hearts results as the domain of biological knowledge becomes differentiated from the domain of knowledge of human activities. By what mechanism are we to explain the young child's responses? Why will young children project from people but not from dogs or bees, even granting that the representations of biological properties of people do not constitute a separate domain from the representations of psychological knowledge of people? One possible mechanism is Gricean implicature. Given that all of the general animal properties the child knows about are seen in terms of human activity and are known to be true of people and other animals, the child may assume (unconsciously) that a property described as true of dogs or bees must be true only of dogs or bees, or of some haphazard class of things. If it were a general human property, why would the adult teacher not mention people as the thing that has that property?

If this Gricean mechanism explains the 4-year-old's responses, we must now explain why the 10-year-old or the adult is not subject to the same implicatures. But we have already done so. Having an autonomous domain of biological knowledge, called into play by a property that is clearly an internal organ, mitigates the implicature effect.

Inductive projection should be one of the central phenomena in a theory of similarity; such conceptual productivity must be one of the primary uses to which people put similarity comparisons. Pursuing this line of thought further is one of the goals of the studies reported in chapter 5. For now, let me conclude by highlighting the use to which I have put this methodology here. Since inductive projection must be constrained by the content and organization of the knowledge the subject represents, its study provides insight into both. The differences between 4-year-olds, on the one hand, and 10-year-olds, on the other, suggest a major reorganization of knowledge about animals between those ages.

Chapter 5
Projection of Properties of Two Objects

The most direct access the psychologist has to children's concepts is through their words. Often the first step in studying a particular concept among children is to probe their meaning for the word that adults map onto that concept. Thus Piaget studied the child's concept *life* by probing how the child uses the word "alive." As we have seen, this very sensible first step is not without problems. There is always the possibility that the differences that emerge between subjects of different ages reflect semantic factors, not deep conceptual factors. For example, children under 7 have not mapped the word "animal" onto the biological concept that encompasses all animals, for they exclude people from its extension. Chapters 3 and 4 have shown the exclusion of people from the extension of "animal" to be partly a semantic fact. The biological concept *animal* serves as an inductive base for children ages 4 to 7, constraining inductive inferences from the knowledge that people have spleens. The source of the semantic difference is not mysterious; in the adult lexicon "animal" is sometimes used in contrast to "people." That contrast is picked up by young children and incorporated in their first lexical entry for "animal."

The methods of chapters 3 and 4 were designed to provide evidence about the child's concept *animal* apart from the meaning assigned to the word "animal." We found that a concept with the same extension as the adult biological concept constrains inductive projection of eating, breathing, having babies, sleeping, having bones, having a heart, thinking, having a spleen, and having an omentum. However, this does not mean that the child represents a concept with the same intension as the adult's. Indeed, several reflections of the organization of the child's knowledge and of the child's reasoning suggest quite a different concept. The young child relies on similarity to people when the adult relies on considerations of biological functioning applicable to all animals. And the asymmetries of projection found in chapter 4 show that for 4- to 7-year-olds, people are not merely one animal among many, even with respect to such properties as internal organs.

In this chapter I probe further the reasoning underlying inductive projection of newly learned properties of animals and living things. Suppose that instead of telling you that one of the things in the world that has an omentum inside it is a dog, I tell you that two of the things in the world that have omenta inside them are dogs and bees. Knowing, as you do, that certain biological problems are common to all animals, and that certain solutions, such as nervous systems and digestive systems, are shared by all animals at least as complex as insects and molluscs, you might conclude that all animals, or all complex animals, are likely to have omenta. However, since young children know little of the biological problems common to all animals, or of universal solutions to these problems, a young child taught that dogs and bees have spleens might not be expected to conclude that all animals have spleens. Rather, such a child might have no way at all of combining these pieces of information. In Experiment 1 two models for utilizing the information that both dogs and bees have spleens (omenta) are contrasted:

Two-stage model. A two-stage process could underlie the judgment. First, the subject retrieves the known spleen (omentum) owner most similar to the object being probed. In the case of people or aardvarks, for example, it would be dogs; in the case of stinkbugs, it would be bees. Then the subject decides whether the object being probed has a spleen (omentum) on the basis of its similarity to the retrieved exemplar. Such a process would yield a curve that is the intersection of the projection patterns from dogs alone and from bees alone. In this model, the concept *animal* constrains projection in the weakest possible sense. The similarity metric respects the animal-nonanimal boundary, just as it did in the case of projection from dogs alone and from bees alone.

Conceptual combination model. At the other extreme, the subject may reason that if two such disparate animals as dogs and bees have spleens (omenta), all complex animals must. Such reasoning would lead to patterns of projection in which all, and only, animals are judged to have spleens (omenta).

Experiment 1 concerns how subjects rationalize the knowledge that two disparate animals share an unknown property. The data are analyzed for two purposes—to diagnose the models underlying projection of spleens (omenta) from two animals, and to provide further information about children's and adults' concepts of animals. Experiment 1 also allows a further test of the asymmetry documented in chapter 4. When taught that both dogs and bees have spleens, are young children still reluctant to project spleens to people? In Experiment 2 projection patterns from two objects (dogs and flowers) are analyzed to probe the concept *living thing*, as subjects are taught that dogs and flowers share a property (having golgi).

Experiment 1: Projection of Spleens (Omenta) from Dogs and Bees

The subjects were 20 adults and 25 6-year-olds from the same populations as those who participated in the experiments of chapter 4. Subjects were taught about spleens and omenta exactly as in chapter 4, except that they were told, "Here are *two* of the things in the world that have spleens (omenta), dogs and bees." Spleens (omenta) were then drawn inside the dog's body and inside the bee's body. After testing the first 8 6-year-olds, we found it necessary to change the procedure. Five of these children restricted spleens to the animals taught on, a percentage much higher than in any previous sample. When asked why they denied a spleen to some animal (e.g., the aardvark), all five replied, "You said only dogs and bees have spleens." Apparently, they thought the teaching required them to remember just the animals they had been taught on. Further work would be needed to understand why just this group understood the teaching in this way. Since this question was not the focus of the experiment, the teaching session was changed for the remaining 17 subjects, by adding one new sentence after "Here are two of the things in the world that have spleens (a dog and a bee)," namely, "There are other things in the world that have spleens as well." The data from the first 8 subjects were discarded; the data from the next 17 subjects were retained and analyzed.

Results
Patterns of Attribution   Figure 5.1 shows the data from the 6-year-olds. Projection from dogs and bees is almost perfectly predicted by the intersection of the projection patterns from dogs alone and from bees alone, taken from chapter 4. Over all five new animals (people, aardvark, dodo, stinkoo, and worm), projection from dogs and bees was 55%. The maximum of projection from dogs alone or from bees alone to those five animals averages to 54%. When taught that both dogs and

% Yes

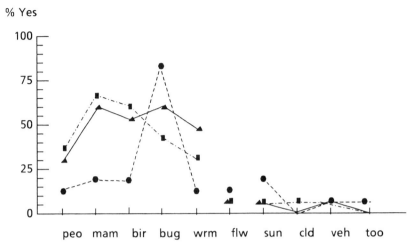

Figure 5.1
Patterns of projection of spleen (6-year-olds). ●---● taught on bees;
■····■ taught on dogs; ▲——▲ taught on dogs and bees.

bees have spleens, children attribute spleens to people, aardvarks, and
dodos no more than children taught only that dogs have spleens. This
part of the projection pattern from both dogs and bees matches exactly
the pattern from dogs alone. And when taught that both dogs and bees
have spleens, 6-year-olds project spleens to stinkoos no more than
when they are taught only that bees have spleens. Only in the case of
judgments about whether worms have spleens is there any hint that
being taught that both dogs and bees have spleens leads to more projection than does being taught on dogs alone or bees alone. This may be
because worms are not perceived as particularly similar to either dogs
or bees.

Analysis of individual patterns (table 5.1) shows that being taught
that both dogs and bees are among the things in the world that have
spleens, even with the explicit statement that other things do as well,
led to no more attribution of spleens to all animals or to all living things
than did being taught on dogs alone or bees alone. In sum, this experiment provided no evidence that the concept *animal* constrains the
young child's induction in any but the weakest sense. Being taught that
two disparate animals have spleens does not lead 6-year-olds to infer
that all complex animals must. Rather, their judgments seem to be
based on similarity to the nearest object known to have a spleen.

Table 5.1
Distribution of projection patterns (percentages)

Age	Organ	Object(s) projected to	Animal(s) taught on		
			Dogs	Bees	Dogs and bees
6	Spleen	All animals or all living things	18	6	12
		Some animals or some living things	53	59	71
		Includes some inanimates	12	18	12
		Taught-on animal(s) only	18	18	6
Adult	Omentum	All animals or all living things	12	18	50
		Some animals or some living things	65	29	30
		Includes some inanimates	12	0	5
		Taught-on animal(s) only	12	53	15

Adults present a mixed picture. As can be seen from table 5.1, being taught that both dogs and bees have omenta led to a higher proportion of "all animal" or "all living thing" patterns than did being taught on dogs alone ($p < .03$, χ^2, corrected for continuity, 1-tailed) or on bees alone ($p < .05$, χ^2, corrected for continuity, 1-tailed). In contrast to the 6-year-olds, then, adults were influenced by the knowledge that two disparate animals both have omenta. Nonetheless, being taught on both dogs and bees did not lead to greater projection to other vertebrates than being taught on dogs alone (fig. 5.2). This may seem counterintuitive. If I tell you that dogs have omenta, there is a 65% chance that you will decide people do too. If I tell you that dogs and bees have omenta, the chance that you will decide people do too is also 65% (fig. 5.2). Regarding projection to other vertebrates, then, the adults' results do not differ from the 6-year-olds'. The difference lies in projection to invertebrates. Here projection from dogs and bees *is* much greater than from either dogs alone or bees alone.

A further analysis of individual patterns of judgments resolves the puzzle of why the curves in figure 5.2 overlap in the area of new mammals. As far as projecting omenta is concerned, adults taught on dogs alone saw dogs as exemplars of superordinate categories of animals that included all mammals or all vertebrates. That is, even when taught on dogs alone, adults considered that dogs have omenta by virtue of being mammals, vertebrates, complex animals, or animals. Of all patterns where there was some projection to new objects, 60% were

% Yes

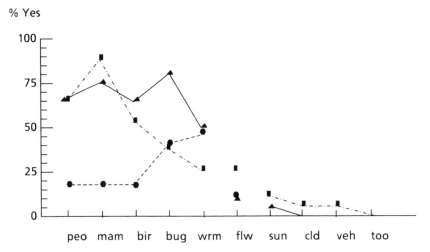

Figure 5.2
Patterns of projection of omentum (adults). ●‑‑‑● taught on bees; ■‑‑‑‑■
taught on dogs; ▲——▲ taught on dogs and bees.

one of the following: all living things, all animals, all complex animals
(excluding the worm), all vertebrates, and all mammals. Therefore,
telling adults that both dogs and bees have omenta did not increase
projection to new mammals (relative to being taught on dogs alone). It
did increase the proportion of "all animal" patterns (table 5.1).

Projection to People   Being taught that both dogs and bees are among
the spleen owners of the world did not ameliorate the phenomenon
noted in chapter 4: markedly less projection from dogs to people than
from dogs to aardvarks (fig. 5.1). Six-year-olds taught that dogs and
bees have spleens judged people to have spleens 29% of the time and
aardvarks to have spleens 71% of the time. Adults taught that dogs and
bees have omenta projected them to people 65% of the time and to
aardvarks 75% of the time. Being taught on two animals did not increase the likelihood that 6-year-olds would project a new property to
people. Adults, in contrast, treated aardvarks and people as equivalent
mammals with respect to having omenta.

Conclusions
Animal as an Inductive Base   The last object probed was the mechanical monkey. No subject, adult or child, attributed a spleen or an

omentum to the mechanical monkey. As we saw in chapter 3, when subjects of these ages are asked to simply judge similarity, they rate the mechanical monkey as highly similar to other animals. The fact that they deny this object a spleen (omentum) emphasizes that their projection is constrained by the biological concept *animal,* at least in the weak sense that spleens (omenta) are attributed only to animals.

Only adults were influenced by learning that both dogs and bees have omenta to conclude that all animals do. Half of the adult subjects judged all animals to have omenta, and another 15% judged all complex animals (that is, all animals but the earthworm) to have omenta. Over three-quarters of all adult patterns that included some projection were of these two types. Adults did reason as expected: if two such disparate animals as dogs and bees have omenta, then all animals (or all complex animals) will probably have omenta. Very notably, 6-year-olds did not do so. Only 13% of their patterns that included some projection were of these types—no more than the percentage when taught on dogs alone or on bees alone.

In sum, the concept *animal* constrained both adults' and children's inductive projection of a newly encountered internal organ. The information that spleens (omenta) are found inside dogs' and bees' bodies influenced both groups to attribute them only to other animals. They clearly interpreted spleens and omenta as biological properties of animals. However, the concept played different roles in the two cases. The developmental difference can be most precisely stated in terms of the different models underlying the attribution of spleens by 6-year-olds and omenta by adults.

Models of Projection from Two Animals The 6-year-olds' projection pattern from dogs and bees was the intersection of the projection pattern from dogs alone and from bees alone. The simplest model that would account for this result is a two-step decision process: first, find the known spleen owner most similar to the object probed, and second, decide whether the object has a spleen on the basis of its similarity to the retrieved exemplar. In this model there is no integration of the information that there are *two* known exemplars of objects that have spleens. When 6-year-olds were told that dogs are one of the things in the world that have spleens, the similarity metric underlying their generalization of spleens to other objects respected the animal-nonanimal boundary. So did their inductive generalization from bees alone. When they were taught on both dogs and bees, the concept *animal* played no further role.

As described above, adults did not integrate the information that both dogs and bees have omenta. Their knowledge of biology led them to reason that an internal organ shared by a mammal and an insect would likely be shared by all animals with at least the complexity of insects.

The contrast between the models underlying the projection of 6-year-olds, on the one hand, and adults, on the other, extends the analyses of chapters 3 and 4. In those chapters, 4- to 7-year-olds were seen to rely heavily on similarity to people in their attribution of breathing, eating, thinking, sleeping, and so on. This was shown by the match between patterns of attribution of those known properties and patterns of projection of spleens from people. Ten-year-olds and adults, in contrast, did not rely on similarity to people in attributing known biological properties, since the patterns of projection of omenta from people differed from the patterns of attribution of most properties probed. In making their decisions, older children and adults relied upon category membership and detailed knowledge of biological properties. In the present study children again relied solely upon similarity, in a very striking way. True, the similarity metric is influenced by the property projected, but it is completely uninfluenced by the knowledge that more than one animal has that property. In contrast, adults' projection of omenta is articulated by biological categories—all animals (or all complex animals) are likely to share an internal organ shared by dogs and bees.

The differences between the models underlying adults' projection of omenta and children's projection of spleens can be understood in terms of the two groups' biological knowledge. Adults understand that internal organs have evolved to solve biological problems. Even in the absence of knowing *what* function an unknown internal organ serves, the knowledge that a mammal and an insect have evolved that organ suggests that, like blood vessels and nerves, it must have very wide generality in the animal kingdom. In contrast, young children, do not understand the biological functions of most internal organs (chapter 2). They certainly do not have an articulated idea of what general biological problems must be solved by all animals, and what common solutions nature has evolved. Six-year-old children know that certain properties, including having internal organs, are *animal* properties, and that similar animals would be more likely to share some biological property than would dissimilar animals. To know this is already to know quite a bit about animals. But this knowledge does not give children the wherewithal for the inference that adults make from the knowledge that dogs and bees share a particular internal organ. Whereas the concept *animal* plays a definite role in the inferential apparatus of 6-year-olds, it plays a quite different role in the inductive generalizations of adults. Young children's concepts of animals differ from those of adults in ways that can be understood in terms of the emergence of biology as a separate domain of intuitive theorizing.

In chapter 1 we saw that there is a semantic component to the young child's responses to questions about what is alive and what is not. Some young children map the contrast "alive–not alive" onto the contrast living-dead, some onto the contrast exists–does not exist, some onto real-unreal, and some onto real-representation. These interpretations of "alive" are not mysterious; each is supported by contexts in which adults use the word "alive." What we do not know is whether other techniques may reveal that children do indeed represent the biological contrast living–not living and that it does play some role in their conceptual system. The data from chapters 2, 3, and 4 make this unlikely. Biological theory, including the life cycle, the composition of organisms, and the role of metabolism in growth and activity, is the domain in which the concept *alive* does some work. Given 4- to 7-year-olds' paucity of biological knowledge, they are unlikely to be able to see why animals and plants are alike, and why they in turn differ from all inanimate objects. In Experiment 2 I begin to explore some ways in which *living thing* might play a role in young children's conceptual systems, apart from what meaning they assign the word "alive." It is unlikely that the concept *living thing* serves as an inductive base in even the weak sense. Indeed, the biological concept *living thing* is likely to be absent from their conceptual repertoires altogether.

Suppose that 6-year-olds are taught a new property (say, having golgi) in a manner comparable to the teaching about spleens and omenta in Experiment 1 except that the two objects indicated to have golgi are a dog and a flower. If they do not have the concept *living thing* available to constrain projection, they should attribute golgi to inanimate objects. Indeed, these children should be in exactly the same position as those who know that animals and plants are alive, but who cannot rationalize the inclusion of animals and plants in a single class and so conclude that other things must also be alive. If it is possible to mimic the phenomenon of animistic projection merely by teaching children that animals and plants share some property, then the analysis of childhood animism in chapter 1 receives support.

A control group is needed to ensure that the subjects do not project golgi to inanimate objects merely because there were two exemplars of objects with golgi, rather than one. Another group of 6-year-olds must be taught that the two animals—say, dogs and bees—have golgi. Since the concept *animal* does constrain projection at age 6, those taught that dogs and bees have golgi should not attribute golgi to inanimate objects. The main prediction from this experiment, then, is that there will be more projection of golgi from dogs and flowers to inanimate objects than from dogs and bees.

A third group would also be of interest: those taught on flowers alone. If the concept *living thing* does not constrain 6-year-olds' projection of golgi at all, these subjects should project golgi to inanimate objects as much as to animals.

Suppose that the child taught that dogs and bees have golgi restricts attribution of golgi to living things. It is possible that the concept *living thing* constrains projection of golgi at this age, but it is equally possible that the concepts *animal* and *plant* are independently constraining projection. Similarity might be computed in a two-step process: first find which of the objects taught on is most similar to the object in question, then compute similarity modulo plant (if flower is picked) or modulo animal (if dog is picked). If, in contrast, golgi are attributed to all living things, rather than merely only living things, we could be more certain that *living thing* serves as an inductive base. Evidence that the information that dogs and flowers both have golgi is being integrated via the hypothesis that all living things have golgi would provide unequivocal evidence that the child represents the concept *living thing*.

Experiment 2: Projection of Golgi from Animals and Plants

This study was carried out in collaboration with Richard Carter, who has generously allowed me to present it in this monograph.

Subjects were 59 6-year-olds from a private school in Cambridge, Massachusetts. Twenty were taught on dogs and bees, 18 on dogs and flowers, and 21 on flowers alone. Sixty adults (20 in each of the three conditions) also participated.

The teaching event was modeled on that for spleens and omenta (Experiment 1). Groups of about 5 children at a time were introduced to golgi as follows: "Have you ever heard of golgi? Golgi are tiny, curly

Table 5.2
Projection of golgi to inanimate objects

Age	Object(s) taught on	Results	
		Percentage of inanimate objects attributed golgi	Percentage of subjects making at least one attribution to an inanimate object
6	Dogs and flowers	38	44
	Flowers	11 [a], b	19 [c], d
	Dogs and bees	4	15
Adult	Dogs and flowers	16	20
	Flowers	16	30
	Dogs and bees	1	5

[a] $p < .10$ t-test, 1-tailed
[b] $p < .10$ t-test, 1-tailed
[c] $p < .10$ χ^2, corrected for continuity, 1-tailed
[d] $p < .05$ χ^2, corrected for continuity, 1-tailed
All differences among adult groups nonsignificant ($p > .1$)

things, so small that you can't even see them without a microscope. Here are pictures of two (one) of the things in the world that have golgi—a dog and a flower (or a dog and a bee, or a flower). Golgi are found all through dogs and flowers (or dogs and bees, or flowers)." At this point the experimenter drew tiny squiggly lines all over the pictures. The children (but not the adults) were encouraged to do the same. In addition, they used the word "golgi" several times while drawing golgi all through the objects on which they were taught.

The projection trials were administered to the children in two sittings, within a week of the introducing event. Adults were tested immediately after teaching, working from booklets. The items probed and the questions asked were the same as those in Experiment 1. This had the unfortunate consequence that no new plant was included.

Results

Attribution of Golgi to Inanimate Objects   As predicted, children taught on dogs and flowers attributed golgi to inanimate objects more than those taught on dogs and bees (table 5.2). Indeed, when taught that dogs and flowers have golgi, 6-year-olds attributed golgi to inanimate objects on 38% of the occasions they were asked. When taught that dogs and bees have golgi, children attributed them to inanimate objects only 4% of the time ($p < .1$, t-test for correlated means, 1-tailed). Three times as many children taught on dogs and flowers made at least one animistic attribution (44%) as did children taught on dogs and bees (15%, table 5.2, $p < .05$, χ^2 test, corrected for continuity, 1-tailed). Projection to inanimate objects depended upon being taught on both dogs and flowers. Those taught on flowers alone fell between the other two groups, but differed more from the dogs and flowers group. Thus, as predicted, 6-year-olds have difficulty justifying the inclusion of animals and plants in a single category of objects possessing golgi.

The adults also sometimes projected golgi to inanimate objects (table 5.2). Some adults attributed golgi to objects in contact with the object known to have golgi (e.g., bees, for the subjects taught on flowers). Some children may have used this strategy as well. In contrast, other cases of adult projection reflected a quite different phenomenon than did the children's. Unlike the children, adults were no more likely to judge inanimate objects to have golgi when taught on dogs and flowers than were taught on flowers alone or when taught on dogs and bees (table 5.2; no differences are significant).

The teaching about golgi left ambiguous whether golgi are an aspect of cellular structure or molecular structure. If the latter, then all material objects would have golgi. Several adults explicitly said that they thought golgi must be subatomic particles. Six-year-olds know little or nothing about atomic structure (Piaget and Inhelder 1941). They are also shaky on the concept *material object,* as contrasted with nonmaterial things such as shadows, holes, ideas, and laughter (Keil 1979, Smith, Carey, and Wiser (in press)). I can provide an informal demonstration of the lack of availability of the concept *material object* as a source of constraint for 6-year-olds' inductive projection. I taught four first graders that molecules are tiny things, so small that they can't be seen with an ordinary microscope. I told them that three of the things in the world that have molecules all through them are people, flowers, and rocks. I also used the locution "made completely out of molecules." I told each of the children that there are many, many other things in the world made out of molecules, and asked if they had any idea what these things might be. None of the four offered any spontaneous guess. I then asked about several animals, plants, and inanimate objects (both solid and liquid), plus several nonmaterial things (such as shadows, ideas, laughter). None of the children thought any of the nonmaterial things were made out of molecules, but none came close to judging all of the material things to be made out of molecules either. For example, one child denied that cars, buildings, tables, grass, rivers, or worms were made out of molecules. Indeed, the only new inanimate object credited

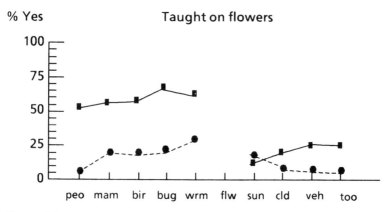

Figure 5.3
Patterns of projection of golgi. Taught on flowers. ■——■ adults; ●---●
6-year-olds.

with being composed of molecules was a pebble. Thus, it is extremely
unlikely that the 6-year-olds who attribute golgi to inanimate objects
are interpreting the teaching in the same way as are the adults who
do so.

The major prediction of Experiment 2 was confirmed. Six-year-olds
projected golgi to inanimate objects to a substantial degree when taught
on dogs and flowers, more so than when taught on dogs and bees or
flowers alone. The phenomenon of childhood animism—attribution of
life to inanimate objects—can be mimicked by teaching the young
child a new property of animals and plants. However, this analysis does
not show that the concept *living thing* is completely unavailable as a
source of constraint on the 6-year-old's inductive projection. A more
detailed analysis of the data from each group is required to address that
question.

Flower Group: 6-Year-Olds The children were conservative in their
projection of golgi from flowers (fig. 5.3). Unfortunately, no other plant
was included in the set of items probed, and 6-year-olds were not
inclined to consider either animals or inanimate objects relevantly
similar to flowers. Of course, one may still ask what role, if any, the
concept *living thing* played in the inductive generalizations they *did*
make. Minimal evidence that the concept of life was constraining their
induction would be greater attribution of golgi to animals than to inanimate objects. This was found: overall, golgi were attributed to ani-

Table 5.3
Distribution of attribution patterns of golgi (percentages)

		Age	
Object(s) taught on	Objects judged to have golgi	6	Adult
Flowers	Taught-on only	57	20
	Only living things		
	Some	24	20
	All	0	30
	Attribution to inanimate objects		
	Some	14	20
	All	5	10
Dogs and flowers	Taught-on only	11	20
	Only living things		
	Some	39	20
	All	6	40
	Attribution to inanimate objects		
	Some	22	5
	All	22	15
Dogs and bees	Taught-on only	25	35
	Only living things		
	Some	45	30
	All	15	30
	Attribution to inanimate objects		
	Some	15	5
	All	0	0

mals 18% of the time and to inanimate objects 10% of the time, a small difference that nonetheless reaches significance ($p < .05$, t-test for correlated means, 1-tailed).

The individual patterns tell the same story (table 5.3). Over half of the children did not project golgi to anything. About one-fourth respected the living-inanimate boundary; about one-fourth did not. Five children projected golgi from flowers to animals alone; none projected golgi from flowers to inanimate objects alone. In sum, the concept *living thing* may have constrained the projection of golgi of slightly fewer than one-fourth of the subjects, in the weak sense that golgi were projected only to other living things.

The pattern of projection in which golgi are attributed to all living things would provide much better evidence that the concept *living thing* was playing a role in the child's judgments. After all, any property shared by a flower and any particular animal is likely to be shared by all living things. Thus, we might expect that any child who attributed golgi to animals alone would have attributed them to all animals. This expectation was not remotely met. Of the five children who projected golgi from flowers to an animal, four favored only one animal (the worm, the stinkoo, the dog, and the aardvark, respectively). Even the remaining child did not judge all of the animals to have golgi, since she omitted people.

In sum, the projection patterns from flowers provide no evidence that *living thing* plays a role in the 6-year-old's conceptual system.

Flower Group: Adults The 6-year-olds' responses are all the more striking when contrasted to those of the adults (fig. 5.3). Apparently, adults considered animals quite similar to flowers in whatever respects are relevant to having golgi, and they considered inanimate objects markedly less so. An ANOVA carried out on these data showed the interaction between age and item type (animals, inanimate objects) to be significant ($F = 6.56$, d.f. $= 1$, $p < .02$).

The inductive projection of 50% of the adults was constrained by the concept *living thing* at least in the weak sense. That is, half of the adults made some inductive projection and also restricted it to new living things. The comparable proportion for the children was 24% (table 5.3). More than half of these adults (30% of the total sample) showed the all-and-only-living-things pattern, indicating constraint by the concept *living thing* in the strong sense, whereas none of the children did so ($p < .05$, Fisher exact test, 1-tailed).

The adults who were taught that flowers have golgi, then, provide unequivocal evidence that the concept *living thing* serves as an inductive base. By no means, however, did they *always* attribute golgi to all and only living things, the pattern that shows the concept determining inductive projection. Twenty percent of the subjects restricted attribution to living things, but did not judge all animals to have golgi. Some were judging objects in contact with flowers to have golgi. Others seemed genuinely to believe it likely that some, but not all, animals might share a biological property with flowers.

In sum, the concept *living thing* influenced 6-year-olds' inductive projection of golgi from flowers little or not at all. The adults provided markedly more evidence that the biological concept of life constrained projection of golgi, but the evidence from adults was far short of what it might have been. Apparently, being taught that flowers have golgi leaves open all sorts of possibilities for adults, only one of which is that all living things are likely to have golgi. But this particular possibility never occurred to any 6-year-old.

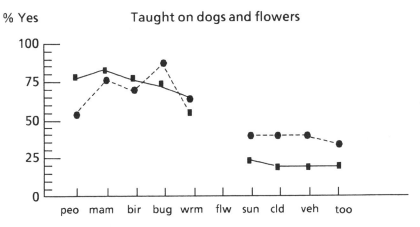

Figure 5.4
Patterns of projection of golgi. Taught on dogs and flowers. ■——■ adults;
●---● 6-year-olds.

Dog and Flower Group: 6-Year-Olds The 6-year-old children taught
that dogs and flowers have golgi widely attributed golgi to inanimate
objects (table 5.2). For at least some, then, *living thing* did not constrain induction. However, there was substantially more projection to
new animals than to inanimate objects (fig. 5.4, $p < .05$, t-test for
correlated means, 1-tailed). Half of the children who made any inductive projection at all attributed golgi only to new animals, whereas half
attributed golgi to at least one inanimate object (table 5.2). The former
group *may* have been constrained by the concept *living thing,* since
their projection respects the animate-inanimate boundary. Equally
likely, their projection was constrained separately by the concepts
animal and *plant.* Again, projection to all living things, rather than only
to living things, would strengthen the inference that the child represents the concept. At issue is whether those children who restricted
attribution to living things included *all* animals among the objects that
have golgi. They did not. Only 1 of the 8 children who respected the
animate-inanimate boundary attributed golgi to all animals. Interest-
ingly, 7 of the 8 who attributed golgi to inanimate objects judged all
animals to have golgi (difference between the two groups, $p < .005$,
Fisher exact test, 2-tailed). Those subjects who attempted to encompass all animals and plants in a category of things that have golgi also
included inanimate objects. For these the concept *living thing* did not
constrain projection. Those for whom it might have done so judged

only a few animals to have golgi. In sum, just as in the case of the 6-year-olds taught on flowers, the children taught on dogs and flowers gave no indication that the concept *living thing* played any role in their projection of golgi.

Dog and Flower Group: Adults   The contrast between adults and children is not as obvious in the data from the dog and flower group (fig. 5.4) as it was in the case of projection from flowers alone. Both groups showed substantially more projection to animals than to inanimate objects. The interaction between age and item type was not significant. Within the animals, attribution falls off regularly from dog to worm. This indicates that some adults projected golgi to new objects on the basis of similarity to dogs separately from similarity to flowers. Indeed, the puzzle in figure 5.4 is why the children's curve does not have that shape. I have no explanation for why the 6-year-olds attributed golgi most to the stinkoo.

The difference between adults and 6-year-olds emerges in the analysis of the patterns of attribution (table 5.3). Two-thirds of the adults who restricted golgi to living things judged all animals to have golgi, compared to one-eighth of the 6-year-olds ($p < .025$, Fisher exact test, 2-tailed). The concept *living thing* determined the inductive projection of adults substantially more than the projection of 6-year-olds.

The lesson from the subjects taught on dogs and flowers is exactly the same as the lesson from those taught on flowers alone. Though the concept *living thing* played little or no role in the 6-year-olds' patterns of judgments, it did influence the adults' projection of golgi to new animals. However, adults also sometimes interpreted golgi to be aspects of molecular structure, and sometimes thought only some new animals would have golgi.

Dog and Bee Group: 6-Year-Olds   The subjects taught on dogs and bees could restrict attribution of golgi to just new animals, could attribute golgi to new animals and the flower (i.e., to living things), or could judge inanimate objects to have golgi as well. Data from these subjects bear both on how the concept *living thing* plays a role in projection and also on just how the concept *animal* constrains induction. Let us consider the role of the concept *living thing* first, and then return to the role of the concept *animal*.

Projection from dogs and bees to the flower, but not to inanimate objects, would suggest that the concept *living thing* served as an induc-

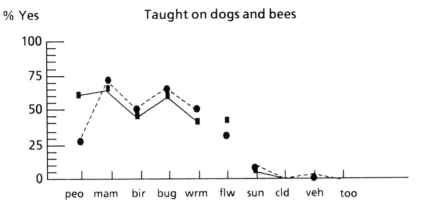

Figure 5.5
Patterns of projection of golgi. Taught on dogs and bees. ■———■ adults;
●---● 6-year-olds.

tive base. Figure 5.5 shows the projection of golgi from dogs and bees.
There was certainly some (25%) attribution to the flower. Although
projection to new animals was greater than to the flower ($p < .05$, t-test
for correlated means, 2-tailed), projection to the flower was markedly
greater than to inanimate objects ($p < .01$, t-test for correlated means,
2-tailed).

That the concept *living thing* may be playing a role in the projection
of golgi is confirmed by analysis of individual patterns. Twelve (of 20)
subjects projected golgi to some new animal or plant and to no inanimate object. Seven projected golgi to new animals alone and 5 projected golgi to new animals and to the flower. Not only did the latter
group's projection respect the living-nonliving boundary; for some
subjects, *living thing* in fact determined the attribution pattern. Three
of the 5 attributed golgi to all of the animals as well as to the flower.
These data, then, provide the first evidence that the concept *living
thing* is available to at least some 6-year-olds.

Dog and Bee Group: Adults   Projection of golgi by adults who have
been taught that dogs and bees have golgi is virtually identical to their
projection by 6-year-olds. Adults too projected more to new animals
than to the flower, and more to the flower than to inanimate objects.
Indeed, projection patterns of the 6-year-olds and adults are practically
superimposable (fig. 5.5). The same proportion (60%) of adults as children restricted attribution of golgi to living things (table 5.3). Twice

Table 5.4
Percentage of subjects whose inductive projections respected the living-inanimate boundary who judged all living things to have golgi

Object(s) taught on	Age	
	6	Adult
Flowers	0 ($n = 5$)	60 ($n = 10$)
Dogs and flowers	13 ($n = 8$)	67 ($n = 12$)
Dogs and bees	25 ($n = 12$)	50 ($n = 12$)
	16 ($n = 25$)	59 ($n = 34$)

n = number of candidate subjects in each group. Candidates attributed golgi to at least one new object and did not attribute golgi to any inanimate object.

as many adults (6 of 20) as children (3 of 20) projected golgi to all of the new animals and the flower, a nonsignificant difference. Thus, the data from the dog and bee group provide evidence for *living thing* as an inductive base for 6-year-olds, and at the same time reveal that the concept plays only a slightly greater role in constraining adults' projection.

Conclusions

Living Thing **as an Inductive Base**   Subjects taught that having golgi is a property of one or two living things could show one of three main patterns of projection. They could restrict attribution to the object taught on. They could project golgi to inanimate as well as living things. Or they could restrict their attribution to new living things. Only the last case provides evidence that *living thing* plays a role in inductive projection. Table 5.4 summarizes the data from subjects who respected the living-inanimate boundary in their projection. Note first that there are fewer such subjects among the children (25 of 59 subjects, 43%) than among the adults (34 of 60 subjects, 57%). Much more important, though, is that the role of the concept *living thing* was much more obvious in the case of adults. Adults in this group judged *all* living things to have golgi more than did 6-year-olds. Overall, this difference was significant ($p < .001$, χ^2 test, 1-tailed), as it was within both the flower group and the dog and flower group. It did not reach significance for the dog and bee group.

As predicted, 6-year-olds had great difficulty rationalizing the inclusion of an animal and a plant into a single category of things that have golgi. When taught that dogs and flowers have golgi, almost half judged

Table 5.5
Comparison of projection of golgi to aardvarks with projection of golgi to people

| Age | Object(s) taught on | Percentage attribution | | Difference |
		Aardvarks	People	
6	Flowers	19	5	14
	Dogs and flowers	78	55	23
	Dogs and bees	75	30	45
				x̄ = 27
Adult	Flowers	65	60	5
	Dogs and flowers	80	75	5
	Dogs and bees	55	50	5
				x̄ = 5

at least one inanimate object to have golgi, a higher rate of attribution than when they were taught that just flowers have golgi or that dogs and bees do. Adults also sometimes judged inanimate objects to have golgi, but adults who did so interpreted golgi as an aspect of molecular structure and were not influenced by the objects on which they were taught. Not only did many 6-year-olds generalize from dogs and flowers to inanimate objects; in fact, few in any of the three groups (4 of 59) attributed golgi to all and only living things. Adults were five times as likely (20 of 60) to produce this pattern. The concept *living thing* is certainly markedly less available to 6-year-olds as an inductive base than it is to adults.

Projection to People   Inspection of figures 5.3–5.5 (especially figure 5.5) shows one striking developmental difference in the patterns of attribution of golgi to new animals. Adults projected golgi to the two new mammals, people and aardvarks, equally. Six-year-olds, in contrast, projected golgi less to people than to aardvarks. Table 5.5 shows this to be the case for all three teaching conditions. This result is a manifestation of the same asymmetry of projection that we saw in Experiment 1 and in chapter 4: less projection from other animals to people than vice versa.

The Effect of the Property Taught   In Experiment 1 subjects were taught that dogs and bees are among the objects in the world that have spleens. In one condition of Experiment 2 subjects were taught that dogs and bees are among the objects in the world that have golgi. If the animals given as examples completely determined the responses, then the patterns of projection in the two cases should be identical. They matched considerably (figures 5.1, 5.2, and 5.5), but differed in the degree of projection to flowers. Fewer than 10% of the subjects attributed a spleen (omentum) to flowers, whereas about 40% of both the 6-year-olds and the adults attributed golgi to flowers. The information provided about the spleen (omentum) suggested that it is an internal organ, or part of an internal organ, and subjects of both ages did not consider it likely that flowers, dogs, and bees would all have a similar internal organ. The information provided about golgi suggested to the adults either cellular structure or molecular structure, both levels of description unknown to 6-year-olds. Some 6-year-olds (and adults) thought of golgi as a dust-like material found on the surface of objects, and some thought of golgi as germ-like things. How subjects interpreted the property influenced attribution of the property.

Conclusions

The experiments in this chapter show that the concepts *animal* and *living thing* play quite different roles in the inductive reasoning of 6-year-olds and adults. Deep conceptual differences underlie the different meanings children and adults attach to the words "animal" and "living thing."

The diagnosis of biological knowledge that emerged from chapters 1 through 4 predicts that 6-year-olds would have no basis for rationalizing the inclusion of animals and plants in a single category. When taught that both dogs and flowers have golgi running through them, almost half of the children attributed golgi to inanimate objects. And when they restricted golgi to just living things, they virtually never judged all living things to have them. What they were told about golgi provided 6-year-olds with no basis for judging that dogs and flowers have golgi because they are alive. Adults often (but not always) made this inference.

Though the conclusions from Experiment 2 were expected, Experiment 1 might well have gone either way. We already knew that young children's inductive projection is constrained by the biological concept *animal,* and it was certainly possible that they would reason that if two disparate animals share an internal organ, all complex animals do. However, unlike adults, 6-year-olds do not reason this way. They do not even infer that if dogs and bees both have spleens, people are likely to have spleens as well. The 6-year-olds in Experiment 1 employed a two-step reasoning process—first finding the known possessor of the organ most similar to the object being probed, and then estimating the likelihood that the latter object has the organ on the basis of its similarity to the former. The concept *animal* played a very weak role in this process, influencing the similarity metric on the basis of which the comparison was made. Most (but not all) adults reasoned very differently. They used considerations of the universal solutions to common biological problems to infer that all animals, or at least all complex animals, share this unknown internal organ. The concept *animal* organizes adult inferential processes in a way not seen in 6-year-olds.

These experiments warrant two conclusions. First, patterns of inductive inference provide evidence of conceptual organization. Therefore, developmental differences in such patterns are one source of evidence about conceptual reorganization during development. Second, the conceptual reorganization documented in this chapter involves both the concept *animal* and the concept *living thing,* and is interpretable in terms of the emergence of a domain of knowledge in which both superordinate concepts come to play a central organizing role—an intuitive biology.

Chapter 6
Matters of Ontology

Some concepts play a more important role in our mental lives than others. Two types of concepts are especially important: ontologically basic concepts and natural kind concepts. *Animal* and *living thing* are among the ontologically basic concepts, and individual species such as *tiger, squirrel, lemon* are examples of natural kind concepts. In this chapter I briefly discuss the special characteristics of these two types of concepts. I ask at what ages children's concepts of *animal* and *living thing* become ontologically important concepts and at what ages children's concepts of individual species become natural kind concepts. I argue that both of these developments result from (or better, are part of) the conceptual change documented in the previous chapters. Throughout the discussion I draw on studies of ontologically important concepts by Frank Keil (1983a,b) and studies of natural kind concepts by Gelman and Markman (1984) and by Keil (in press).

Ontologically Basic Categories

Ontology is the study of what exists. Since the time of Aristotle, philosophers have argued that our conceptual system is articulated by a core of ontologically basic categories, such as *physical object* and *event*. Within the category of physical objects, *living thing* is such a category, as are *animal* and *plant* within the category of living things.

Our conceptual system includes hundreds of thousands of concepts. Intuitively, it is easy to see that there are not hundreds of thousands of *fundamentally* different kinds of things. A car is the same kind of thing as a truck, and even the same kind of thing as a house, at least as compared to a thunderstorm, a war, or a baseball game. The first group is made up of human artifacts and the second of events, both of which are ontologically basic concepts.

Philosophers have noted a linguistic test that can at least roughly reveal the ontologically basic categories. Some predicates cannot be sensibly applied to some terms, as for example in "The thunderstorm is broken" or "The house is an hour long." Such predicate-term combinations are called *category mistakes*. "Category mistake" is difficult to define precisely; the best feel for what category mistakes are comes from examples such as the ones just given. Category mistakes are wrong in a stronger sense than merely being false. If "The thunderstorm is broken" were merely false of some particular storm, then the sentence "The thunderstorm is unbroken" would be true; but this sentence is also nonsensical. It is inconceivable that thunderstorms could be fixed with a screwdriver, a computer, or anything else. They are not the kinds of things that get broken. When a predicate can be applied sensibly to a term, whether or not it applies truly, it is said to "span" the term. "About a princess" spans "movie," in that a movie could be about a princess, even though most particular movies, such as *Deliverance* and *Bambi,* are not. "About a princess" does not span "sofa." "The sofa is about a princess" is a category mistake.

Patterns of spanning relations diagnose ontologically basic concepts. Very large numbers of predicates span the very same terms—for example, predicates such as "is tall, is heavy, is red, is hard, is in San Francisco" all span terms such as "table, chair, mountain, Ronald Reagan." These clusters of predicates and terms pick out ontologically basic categories—in this case, the category *physical object.* Note that our conceptual system contains vastly many more concepts than it does ontologically basic concepts. For example, we distinguish among all kinds of animals, yet only the concept *animal* is diagnosed as an ontologically basic category by the test of category mistakes. This is shown by the fact that properties unique to any animal can be predicated of other animals without generating such an error. Only bees make honey, but "Sharks make honey" and "Beavers make honey" are merely false, not category mistakes. (The one exception is the concept *person,* which is revealed by this test to be ontologically basic.)

The ontologically basic concepts, being few in number, are the backbone of our conceptual system. They constrain induction in various ways (Keil 1983b, Carey 1985). For example, since ideas and princesses are such different kinds of things, it is unlikely that a single word "plotzkel" would ever mean *idea or princess.* Similarly, if we learn that plotzkels weigh an average of 10 tons each, we know that they are physical objects, since only physical objects have weight.

In his early work, Keil stressed a putative structural constraint on ontologically basic categories (Keil 1979). Following the philosopher Fred Sommers (1963), Keil claimed that ontologically basic categories form a strict hierarchy and that predicates in natural language do not apply to ontological types on different branches of the tree without generating category errors. These two claims are equivalent to Sommer's *M-constraint* on ontological concepts. If these theses were true, ontological categories would be very much more constrained than are our concepts in general, and they could thereby be a source of strong constraints on induction. Unfortunately, neither of the two claims seems to be correct (Carey 1985, Gerard and Mandler 1983). What is important here, however, is that even if the M-constraint does not hold, the special status of the ontologically basic concepts is not diminished. The distinction between category error and falsehood remains, and patterns of category errors still diagnose a central set of concepts that represent the truly different kinds of things we are committed to.

Developmental Findings
In the studies reported in chapters 3, 4, and 5 subjects were warned that some of the questions they would be asked would be silly, and that some would be difficult, but that most would be easy. The warning about silliness was included for two reasons. Obviously silly questions, such as whether harvesting machines are kept in refrigerators, were designed to keep the children mildly amused and paying attention. More important, some of the questions involved category errors, and many children thought these just as funny as those we designed to be amusing. For example, when asked if clouds have hearts, one 7-year-old laughed and said, "That's silly, clouds don't have blood or anything; they couldn't have a heart." Asked if worms have hearts, the same child said, "I don't know. No—do they?" She seemed to think it a category mistake to predicate hearts of clouds and merely probably false to predicate hearts of worms. She certainly considered it possible that worms could have hearts. Our procedure, probing simply for yes/no responses, could not distinguish between category mistakes and mere falsehoods. Keil (1979) developed a procedure that could do so, and he has carried out a series of studies probing the development of ontological distinctions (Keil 1979, 1983a).

In Keil's procedure, children are asked to say whether sentences like "The table is happy" are silly or not. Keil had two ways of checking whether children were using "silly" to indicate false statements or category mistakes. First, he probed with antonyms. That is, children were also given "The table is unhappy." If they judged both to be silly, Keil credited them with the view that neither "happy" nor "unhappy" spans "table," because if a predicate-term combination is false, that predicate's opposite will be true of the term, whereas the opposite of a predicate that does not span a term also does not span that term. Second, Keil followed up all judgments with short interviews to clarify the child's beliefs. Examples are given below (from Keil 1979:88–90):

1. Five-year-old
E. The fight is skinny.
C. That's OK.
E. How could a fight be skinny?
C. Mm, not sure.
E. Well, how could you tell if a fight was skinny?
C. Oh, if the boys were skinny.
E. Is it the boys that are skinny, or the fight, or both?
C. Both.
E. Why not just the boys, or just the fight?
C. Because they're both skinny. It's the same thing.

2. Seven-year-old
E. The fight is skinny.
C. That's silly.
E. Why can't a fight be skinny?
C. Because it just can't. That's impossible.
E. What if you didn't feed a fight, could it then be skinny?
C. No, fights just happen. You can feed people, but you can't even touch a fight.

The first child does not consider "The fight is skinny" a category mistake; the second clearly does.

Keil's work on the development of ontological categories has yielded fascinating and counterintuitive results. As can be seen from the examples above, it is possible to obtain reliable judgments of category errors from children as young as age 5. The main finding that has emerged from Keil's studies is that young children do not make many of the ontological distinctions that adults do. The fragment of a 5-year-old's protocol given above illustrates Keil's data—the child was not easily able to conceive of events apart from the entities participating in them, since he thought that a fight could be skinny. Keil (1979, 1983a) has probed with several different predicate-term pairs concerned with this distinction, all of which are judged category mistakes by adults, and all of which are deemed acceptable, even after probing, by young children. Similar results are found for many other basic ontological distinctions, such as the distinction between events and abstract objects: an event such as a fight can have a physical location, can take time, etc., whereas an abstract object such as an idea or love cannot. Young children do not honor this distinction in their patterns of judgments of category errors (Keil 1979).

The child's developing distinctions among animals, plants, and inanimate objects present quite a different developmental pattern (Keil 1983a). This is the only case to date in which Keil has found children to be systematically *more* restrictive in their application of predicates than are adults.

Judgments of Category Errors: Biological Predicates

Keil (1983a) presented subjects with all predicate-term combinations from the tree fragment in figure 6.1. That is, the subjects were asked whether "The man is heavy" makes sense, whether "The bird is sick" makes sense, whether "The weed is asleep" makes sense, etc. Each judgment was followed up with questions as described above, and the subjects were also probed with opposites ("The man is light," "The bird is healthy," "The weed is awake," etc.).

The tree fragment in figure 6.1 represents the intuitions of 11 of the 16 adult subjects probed. The remaining 5 differed only in their placement of the predicate "hungry." These considered "hungry" to span plants as well as animals. Conventions for reading the tree are as follows: Predicates are in upper-case letters, terms in lower-case letters. Predication without category error results whenever a predicate is applied to a term it dominates in the tree. Thus, "heavy" spans all of the terms in the tree; "alive" spans the animals and plants, but not "rock" and "chair"; and "asleep" spans only the animals.

Two important results emerged. The first concerned the youngest children (5-year-olds), who tended to restrict only to animals the predicates that adults apply to all living things. That is, 38% of the 5-year-olds thought it a category mistake to say that plants, flowers, weeds, or trees are alive. Moreover, 75% thought it a category mistake to predicate being sick or starving of plants (table 6.1). This pattern is rarely seen among 8-year-olds and never seen among 9½-year-olds or adults. Not surprisingly, since predicates that for adults span living things were

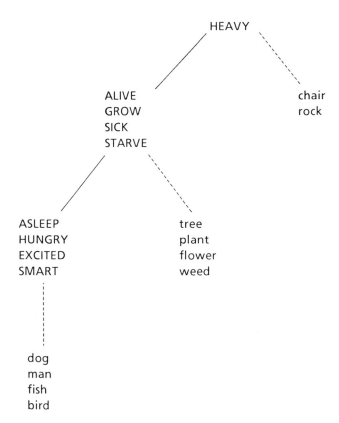

Figure 6.1
Predicates and terms probed in Keil's (1983a) study of children's judgments
of category errors

Table 6.1
Percentage of subjects who restricted
predicates of living things to just animals
(Keil 1983a)

Predicate	Age			
	5½	8	9½	Adult
Alive	38	13	0	0
Sick	75	0	0	0
Starving	75	13	0	0

Table 6.2
Percentage of subjects who judged predicates
of animals to span plants as well (Keil 1983a)

Predicate	Age			
	5½	8	9½	Adult
Hungry	25	88	88	31
Excited	0	13	13	0
Smart	0	0	13	0
Asleep	13	13	25	0

restricted by the 5-year-olds to animals, so were predicates that adults restrict to animals (table 6.1). As Keil puts it, children of this age know full well what sorts of things animals are and what properties they can conceivably have. Plants are a distinct class of things that do not have these properties. What the 5-year-old lacks, relative to the adult, is the superordinate concept *living thing*.

The second finding concerns the two oldest groups. They had a tendency to agree that what are purely animal predicates for adults ("hungry," "excited," "smart," "asleep") could apply to the four plants (table 6.2). This was most striking in the case of "hungry." Although some adults (31%) thought that "hungry" could be predicated of plants, 88% of the 8- and 9½-year-olds did so. Apparently, as the children become aware that plants have some of the properties of animals, they are not sure which ones remain solely properties of animals.

Keil's data confirm, in yet a new way, that very young children lack the superordinate concept *living thing*. They find "The weed is healthy" more than false; they find it a category error. Keil interprets his data as a reflection of the abstractness of the properties that living things share with each other. However, the results reviewed in the previous chapters of this monograph allow a more precise interpretation of his data. The properties that animals and plants share are physiological and must be understood in their physiological sense before they can motivate the superordinate concept. Five-year-olds have not yet achieved this. The overextension of intentional predicates like "excited," "hungry," and "asleep" to plants in the years from 8 through 10 shows that youngsters still do not have a firm grasp of the distinction between the biological function of eating and the psychological function of alleviating hunger.

Conclusions

In his writings on the development of ontologically basic concepts, Keil stresses the structural constraint known as the M-constraint. As evidence that the M-constraint actually serves as a constraint on the acquisition of knowledge, he offers the fact that at all ages subjects' judgments honor it. No matter how unadult a young child's judgments of category errors, they define a hierarchy (Keil 1979, 1983a). Because Keil has focused on the putative structural constraint, so have his critics (e.g., Carey 1985, Davis 1979, Gerard and Mandler 1983). Carey (1985) argues that the M-constraint does not hold and (more crucially) that even if it did, it would not provide an important source of constraint on young children's concepts. The main reason for this is the young child's radically collapsed set of ontological distinctions. However, we must not throw out the phenomena when we deny one of their possible interpretations. Children *do* make reliable judgments of category errors, and their judgments differ markedly and systematically from those of adults. How are these differences to be explained?

An individual's ontological commitments and intuitive theories are closely intertwined. Where nature is at issue, as it is with concepts such as *physical object, living thing, animal, plant,* and *person,* nothing tells us about its basic entities except our theories of the world. It follows that insofar as conceptual development involves theory change, developmental changes in ontological commitments are to be expected. The reverse is also likely true. Any developmental changes in ontological commitments detected with studies such as Keil's are probably best interpreted in terms of theory change. I have tried to show that this is the case for Keil's data that show *living thing* becoming an ontologically basic category around age 10. We should also be able to interpret other deviations from adult judgments of category errors in this way.

One other example will suffice. The child's concepts of *size, weight,* and *density* have been the focus of many studies, the most well known being Piaget and Inhelder's (1941). Carol Smith, Marianne Wiser, and I have undertaken another case study of these concepts, focusing on the issue of differentiation. We asked whether there is ever a moment when children do not differentiate *size* and *weight* (answer, no), and whether there is ever a moment when they do not differentiate *weight* and *density* (answer, yes). As part of our case study, we probed further Piaget and Inhelder's question of the relation between the development of these concepts, on the one hand, and children's conception of matter, on the other. We have evidence that young children do not distinguish between material and nonmaterial objects (that is, they think that tables and shadows are each made of some kind of stuff, in just the same sense of "kind of stuff"). Relatedly, they do not know what weight is a property of, and they happily maintain that it is possible for a piece of styrofoam to weigh nothing at all. "Kind of stuff" does not refer to *kind of matter* for the child, and "made of" does not refer to *constituted from*. Between the ages of 4 and 10 the child articulates a concept of matter out of which physical objects are constituted. The concepts of *weight* and *density* become differentiated in the course of this theoretical development. This conceptual reorganization has profound implications for the ontologically basic concept *physical object*. Two of the predicates that Keil uses in his probing of the distinctions between objects and events are *heavy* and *light*. The work cited above on the concept *heavy*, even as applied to physical objects, corroborates Keil's conclusions that the child's predicates do not span the same terms as the adult's. It goes beyond Keil's important findings in offering a framework for interpreting them, namely, in the context of the emergence of an intuitive theory in which the distinction between material and nonmaterial objects comes to have important ontological status for the child.

In sum, Keil has shown that the child draws different ontological distinctions than does the adult. In the case of biological predicates and terms, the young child distinguishes between animals and inanimate objects, but has not yet coalesced the concepts *animal* and *plant* into a single ontological type, *living thing*. Although Keil's data in support of these claims are fragmentary,[1] the claims are most probably true, and they can be interpreted in terms of the argument developed in chapters 1 through 5 of this monograph. Keil's most important contribution to the argument is to highlight the distinction between the ontologically important concepts that provide the backbone of our conceptual system, on the one hand, and the thousands of other concepts we represent, on the other. Keil argues, and I concur, that judgments of category errors contribute to the diagnosis of the ontologically basic categories, and therefore that developmental changes in judgments of category errors contribute to the description of ontological development. Finally, I suggest that our deepest ontological commitments are to be analyzed in terms of our theories of the world. It follows that ontological development cannot be separated from theory development. The interconnection between the two has been clearly shown in the case of the development of the concept *living thing*.

Animal and Plant Species as Natural Kinds

A 4-year-old in one of the studies in chapter 3 was shown the pictures of earthworms and told they depicted annelids. He was then asked whether he thought that annelids breathe. He replied, "I don't know—what kind of thing is an annelid—is it a piece of rope or a kind of worm?" One cannot tell simply by looking at something what its properties are; one must know what kind of thing it is. The child's puzzle was at the level of ontologically basic categories (animal vs. human artifact), but the same principle applies within a single ontological type. One cannot know whether a flying animal suckles its young unless one knows whether it is a bat or a bird. Sharks resemble dolphins much more than they resemble angelfish, yet the common classification as fish predicts warm- or cold-bloodedness. Gelman and Markman (1984) asked whether 4-year-olds would override appearance and use membership in a biological kind as a basis for inductive projection. They argued that doing so is one reflection of treating the term for the kind as a natural kind term.

At least since the time of John Locke, philosophers have distinguished between natural kind terms, such as *tiger, gold, water, proton, star, gene,* and non–natural kind terms, such as *box, thing, table.* Though the distinction is easy to appreciate, it is not easy to state precisely, partly because many competing analyses have been offered in the philosophical literature. One characteristic of natural kind terms is that they refer to entities that scientific disciplines evolve to study. The properties of natural kinds are myriad, and typically are not readily apparent.

Gelman and Markman's Study
Gelman and Markman wanted to know whether 4-year-olds already appreciate that being classified as a "fish" predicts properties like

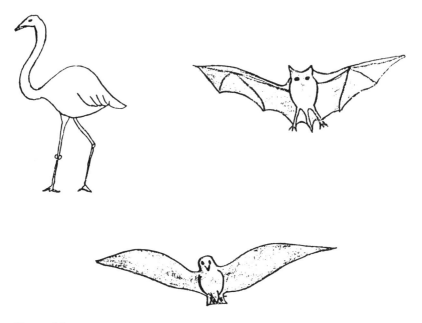

Figure 6.2
Examples of stimuli used by Gelman and Markman (1984)

whether an animal breathes above or below the water better than does surface physical resemblance. Figure 6.2 is an example of their materials. Children were told mutually exclusive properties of the top two objects: "This bird gives its baby mashed up food" and "This bat gives its baby milk." They were then shown the third picture, closely resembling the bat but labeled the same as the bird, and were asked, "What does this bird do—feed its baby milk or give its baby mashed up food?" In other words, Gelman and Markman pitted appearance against membership in a biological category as bases for inductive projection of a new property.

When appearance and classification coincided, children were correct 89% of the time. When the two conflicted, as in the above example, category determined inductive projection 67% of the time. This is significantly better than chance, and significantly better than a control condition in which children were asked about the property without having been told anything about the first two objects. There were a total of 20 items, 10 involving biological categories and 10 involving materials such as diamonds and glass. Thirty-seven percent of the subjects based at least 15 of the 20 judgments on common category label

(15 of 20 is better than chance, $p < .05$, sign test). In contrast, no child consistently projected the two properties on the basis of appearance.

Gelman and Markman stress that their results belie the characterization of preschool children as "perceptually bound." In this task, at least, 4-year-olds are able to override misleading perceptual cues, expecting the *kind* of thing something is, as signaled by its being called "fish," "lizard," "squirrel," "bird," etc., to predict such properties as what it eats (4 items), how it breathes (2 items), and its constitution (4 items; whether it has warm or cold blood, whether it has eggs or seeds inside it, the nature of its eyelids and feet). In a crucial control, they found that children of this age did not expect the animal's kind to predict such properties as how much it weighs, how fast it can move, whether it is visible at night, etc. Children's projections of the latter properties were not systematic, based neither on appearance nor on category.

Gelman and Markman rightly emphasize their 4-year-old subjects' reliance on category, which was, overall, better than chance. However, performance was nothing like that of adults on a comparable task requiring projection of unknown properties. Only slightly over a third of the children consistently projected the new property on the basis of category, whereas all of the adults did. For biological kinds alone, in two separate experiments the girls as a group were at chance; only boys exceeded chance. Four-year-old children's failure to use biological category to project such properties would not be surprising, in light of their scant biological knowledge. What is surprising, in this light, is that they did as well as they did.

Children know animals are different from each other. They look different; they behave differently; they have different capabilities and different interactions with human beings. We have seen that the 4-year-old does not understand the biological functions of eating and breathing (chapter 2), nor even that all animals must do so (chapter 3). Nonetheless, children of this age apparently can grasp that different kinds of animals may well eat different kinds of things, have different kinds of teeth and feet, and breathe in different ways. Different kinds of animals have begun to be natural kinds in the sense that they have properties not readily apparent. They are not yet firmly biological natural kinds, but they are kinds in some intuitive theory children hold, presumably their intuitive theory of behavior (or what I have been calling a naive psychology). Another study by F. Keil (in press), which examines at what age children realize that individual species have biological essences, emphasizes how much further the 4-year-old has to go.

One thread running through the literature on natural kinds since the time of Locke is that natural kind terms refer to kinds that have essences that it is the proper business of science to discover. The essence of a natural kind is the property that kind must have in order to *be* that kind. The essence of water is being H_2O; the essence of gold is being the element with atomic number 79; the essence of tigers is presumably to be stated in terms of genetic theory. We can believe that some kind is a natural kind, and therefore that its members have an essence, without yet knowing the essence. Such is the case for tigers. We do know which science, if any, will discover the essence of tigers, namely biology, but we can only guess at the nature of that essence. We can see, then, that the specification of natural kinds is closely tied to our theories of the world. A rough and ready test for non–natural kinds is that they play no role in scientific theories. There is no essence of a box or a table ever to be discovered; neither of these is likely to play an important role in any present or future scientific theory.

When people treat a term as a natural kind term, they are willing to grant that those properties they know of things to which the term applies do not actually determine category membership. That is, although they may have a prototype of members of the kind, they are ready to defer to experts or to their own theory building to discover that this prototype may be misleading as far as actual category membership is concerned. Suppose I show you a piece of fruit with nubbly skin that has the size, shape, color, and taste of an orange, but tell you that it grew on a lemon tree and has the genetic structure of a lemon. You would probably be happy to conclude that this piece of fruit is a funny-looking lemon, even though it perfectly matches your prototype of an orange. Our current theories of biological kinds, being tied to genetics as they are, lead us to weight parentage very heavily. If something that looked exactly like a cactus nevertheless had the genetic structure of a grapefruit and could breed with grapefruits, we would be surprised, but we would accept that it was a very weird grapefruit. Keil (in press) probed at what age children have the adult intuitions in such cases.

Two considerations determine whether a term is a natural kind term or not: facts about the world (*is* there a kind in nature picked out by the term?) and facts about the user's knowledge (does the user realize that the kind referred to has an underlying essence?). The second consideration is important, for it makes it possible that two people may share a vocabulary item that functions as a natural kind term for only one of them. Putnam (1962) provides an historical example. The word "atom" was not a natural kind term until enough physics and chemistry were known for it to actually refer to atoms. Before that time, in the nineteenth century, it meant "smallest indivisible particle of matter" and did not refer to any kind in nature. Similarly, the word "atom" may function as a natural kind term for me, but not for my 6-year-old daughter, for whom it means "little bit of stuff, too small to see." For adults, species names like "tiger," "pin oak," and "human being" are natural kind terms. Although many have attempted to provide the definition of "human being" by linguistic analysis (e.g., "rational animal," "featherless biped"), most would agree that discovering the essence of the kind "people" will be the work of the sciences of biology, psychology, and anthropology.

Keil used two converging methods to assess at what age words like "raccoon" and "lemon" begin to function as natural kind terms in the child's lexicon. The idea behind both methods was the same: if a term such as "raccoon" is a natural kind term, then the child should be willing to entertain the possibility that something could lack *all* of the characteristic features of raccoons and yet still be a raccoon. In one method Keil pitted his best guess of what the child might consider an individual species' essence against what the child might consider merely characteristic features. The other method left entirely open what the child might consider the essence.

Keil's Study: Method 1
In the first of Keil's studies (Keil (in press)) the child was shown a picture of an animal, say a skunk as in figure 6.3, and told various things about the behavior of that animal, such as that it is active at night, squirts smelly stuff when it is attacked or frightened, and so on. (Keil used actual photographs and emphasized that he was talking about a particular animal, the one pictured.) In other words, both its appearance and its behavior fit the prototypical skunk. The subjects (ages 5 and 9) were asked what they thought it was a picture of, and of course they ventured that it was a skunk. They were then told that scientists had studied this particular animal in great detail and had discovered that its parents had been raccoons, that its babies were raccoons, and that its heart, brain, and blood were like the heart, brain, and blood of raccoons. They were then asked again what they thought the animal

Figure 6.3
Pictures of skunk and skunk transformed into raccoon, as in Keil (in press)

was—a raccoon or a skunk. The younger children insisted that the picture depicted a skunk; 9-year-olds said it was a raccoon that merely looked like a skunk.

By age 9, then, the authority of experts, plus matters of parentage and internal organs, together can override all of the characteristic features of an individual animal the child is likely to know. Five-year-olds, in contrast, are not swayed by such considerations. If a given animal looks and acts like a skunk, it is a skunk, no matter what its internal organs and other family members. Of course, this result is open to the objection that Keil failed to guess what a 5-year-old might consider the essence of a skunk, and that had he pitted the characteristic features against some *other* candidate essential features, he would have obtained data like those from the 9-year-olds. Although this is unlikely—I myself cannot imagine a plausible alternative candidate for the child's notion of an animal's or plant's essence—Keil's second method (in press) depended upon no such guess.

Keil's Study: Method 2

As in the first study, the children were shown a picture such as the first one in figure 6.3, and asked what they thought it was—skunk again being the answer. They were then told that some doctors and scientists had taken that animal, shaved off all its fur and replaced it with black and brown fur, made it much fatter, removed its tail and replaced it with another, removed its smell glands, made a mask for its eyes, and so on, until the result looked like the second animal in the figure. The question was what the second drawing depicted. Five-year-olds were adamant that it was a raccoon; 9-year-olds were equally sure that it was

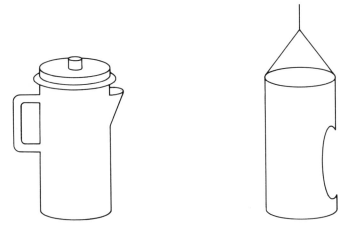

Figure 6.4
Pictures of coffeepot and coffeepot transformed into bird feeder, as in Keil
(in press)

a skunk that merely looked exactly like a raccoon. Nine-year-olds
know that all of those characteristic features that actually provide the
basis for classification of a given animal as one kind or another are not
essential to its being that kind. Not so for 5-year-olds. If it looks like a
raccoon, it is one, no matter what its origin or how it came to have the
appearance it does.

Before these data may be interpreted, we must know whether a
similar kind of shift occurs for terms that are not natural kind terms.
Keil carried out parallel controls for the two methods; I will describe
those for the second one only. The children were shown a picture such
as the first one in figure 6.4, and all agreed it was a coffeepot. A
transformation was described, whereby various parts were rearranged,
excised, and added until the final result looked like the second object
shown in figure 6.4. The children were then asked what they thought
the object was—a coffeepot or a bird feeder. In this case children of
both ages agreed that it was a bird feeder. There is no general tendency
for 9-year-olds to conserve kind across transformations such as these
when the objects are artifacts, only when they are members of biological species.

Even 5-year-olds would not accept transformations that crossed
boundaries of basic ontological categories. A porcupine transformed
into what looks identical to a cactus is still a porcupine; a squirrel

transformed into what looks identical to moss is still a squirrel. Similarly, a stuffed dog transformed into a real dog remains a toy. By age 5, *animal, plant,* and *artifact* are already basic ontological categories. The development between ages 5 and 9 occurred in those cases where an animal (or plant) was transformed into an animal (or plant) of another similar species.

Keil used many different examples, taken from the plant as well as the animal kingdom and from various types of non–natural kinds. He saw his data as reflecting a shift, between the ages of 5 and 9, in the nature of all the biological species terms the child knows. For 5-year-olds, species terms such as "raccoon" function like artifact terms such as "coffeepot," whereas by age 9 they are natural kind terms.

For some, Keil's description of his data in terms of natural kind terms, in terms of essences, may seem unnecessarily tendentious. There is another way of describing the shift that is perhaps more familiar to developmental psychologists and that supports the argument I wish to make from the data equally well: the 9-year-olds make a distinction between appearance and reality that the 5-year-olds do not. These two ways of describing the shift (in terms of a shift to natural kind terms and in terms of a distinction between appearance and reality) are in fact closely related. Essences are the deep, hidden, real natures of things. It is the business of science both to discover essences and to discover deeper realities underlying surface appearances. The 9-year-old's distinction between appearance and reality is supported by the acquisition of biological knowledge, just as the 5-year-old's failure to make the distinction is explained by the lack of that knowledge.

Keil also looked at a different class of natural kind terms—those for kinds of stuff such as "gold" and "water." He found parallel results: 5-year-olds did not treat them as natural kind terms, whereas most 9-year-olds did. In spite of the similarity of the developmental trends in the two cases, Keil does not argue for a general shift between these ages such that all terms that refer to natural kinds by adulthood begin to function this way around age 9. Keil suggests that many terms undergo that shift during adulthood, and many may have done so in the preschool years (this is yet unknown, of course). Similarly, there is no general emergence of the appearance-reality distinction around age 9. Children as young as age 3 command the distinction in some contexts (Flavell, Flavell, and Green 1983). After then, grasp of the distinction develops in two respects: the child comes to appreciate it on a meta-conceptual level (Flavell, Flavell, and Green 1983) and comes to know, through domain-specific conceptual change, more and more cases where surface appearances do not accord with deeper reality (Carey 1983). It is likely that the latter sort of development underlies Keil's phenomenon.

Conclusions

There *are* kinds in nature picked out by names for species (Mayr 1982).[2] So the first requirement for these terms being natural kind terms is met. The second is that the subject have sufficient knowledge to believe that these terms refer to objects with an underlying essence. This, in turn, requires adequate knowledge of the scientific domain in which the terms are embedded. Of course, in the case of names for biological species, the requisite domain is biology. In earlier chapters I have argued that biology does not become an independent domain of knowledge until the end of the first decade of life. That 5-year-olds can have no notion of the biological essences of biological species is therefore to be expected. Thus, in broad terms it is clear how Keil's results fit into my argument. But can we do better? Can we understand the details of Keil's data in terms of the detailed information we have gleaned so far about the acquisition and reorganization of biological knowledge in the years between 4 and 10?

Let us take the results from the two different methods in turn. In the first, family membership and internal organs were pitted against the characteristic features of animals and plants. As we saw in chapters 2, 3, and 4, the former are not embedded in an autonomous intuitive biology for 5-year-olds. Rather, children's knowledge of them is embedded in their knowledge of human activities and society. If having blood is fundamentally a property of people, then the notion Keil wished to convey with the locution "the blood of a skunk" (namely, blood with unique properties of skunk blood) is not available to the 5-year-old. If having a mother or having babies is primarily a social matter, then there is no reason why a skunk could not have raccoons for parents and children. By age 9, in contrast, knowledge of internal organs and their functions structures the child's knowledge of growth, death, and reproduction. Each animal has properties determined by its own unique solution to common biological problems, and properties of parents are passed on to children. One would have no way, a priori, of knowing how much biological knowledge is required for a person to have the notion of a biological essence; Keil's data show us that the 9-year-old's is enough.

The second method trades on the information about *how* the transformation is achieved—a person intervenes and adds fat, changes the color and length of fur, changes the shape of the tail, and so on. If subjects have any notion of biological essence, they will know that these kinds of transformations, being nonbiological in their mechanism, cannot affect this essence. Five-year-olds have no notion of biological essence, not having differentiated the domain of biology from the domain of psychology. Therefore, their concepts of fruits, plants, and animals must be exhausted by their knowledge of the characteristics by which they are recognized, and by their behavior as it affects people (e.g., the smell of a skunk, the taste of a lemon). To change these is to fundamentally change the object.

Keil's data dramatically embellish the picture drawn in chapters 1 through 5. Let us accept Keil's conclusion that the very kind of word that "tiger" is differs for a 5-year-old and a 9-year-old, the latter using it like an adult. This shift, while interpretable in terms of the framework developed in the earlier chapters, was not predictable from that framework. Species names become biological natural kind terms in the years just before age 10. The shift Keil has described is yet another reflection of the emergence of biology as a separate domain of intuitive theorizing.

Chapter 7
Conclusions

By age 10, children have made remarkable strides in many conceptual domains. Knowledge of animals and living things is no exception. In this concluding chapter I briefly summarize the findings presented in chapters 1 through 6 and consider what type of restructuring (weak or strong) is involved in the changes between ages 4 and 10. I then discuss the lessons of this case study for the description of cognitive development, for the understanding of constraints on induction, and for the characterization of human concepts.

Summary of Results

I have attempted to trace several concepts through early childhood: *living thing, animal, person, plant,* the concept of a particular species, such as *raccoon,* and concepts of various internal body parts and bodily processes. In each case children's and adults' concepts may be compared with respect to three questions:

1. Does the child represent a concept with the same extension as does the adult?
2. What word does the child use to denote the concept? That is, has the child mapped the word the adult uses onto the same concept?
3. Does the child's concept differ from the adult's, and if so, in what respects?

There are many dimensions along which even concepts that carve the world at the same joints may differ. For example, they may function differently in thought or they may have different ontological cores.

Results: *Living Thing*

If it can be shown that the child represents a concept with the same extension as the adult's, but has not mapped the adult word onto that concept, then the developmental difference is said to have a semantic component. There is a semantic component to the acquisition of the meaning of the word "alive." For young children, the salient contrast is not between *alive* and *inanimate,* but between *alive* and *dead.* However, since these children do not yet understand death as the cessation of bodily functions, they conflate this contrast with others, such as the contrasts between *real* and *imaginary, existent* and *nonexistent,* and *functional* and *broken.* This is shown both by young children's patterns of judgments and justifications (as when they say that a button is alive because it can fasten a blouse, or that a table is alive because you can see it) and by what they list when asked to name some things that are not alive (George Washington, ghosts, dinosaurs; see chapter 1).

Several results confirmed that the differences between young children and adults are not merely semantic. The young child does not represent any concept with the same extension as the adult concept *living thing,* subsuming animals and plants in a single category. First, no 4- to 7-year-old judged all animals and plants, but no inanimate objects, to be alive. Those children who denied life to inanimate objects also denied that plants are alive (chapter 1). Second, from being told that dogs and flowers both have golgi all through them, 6-year-olds never inferred that all and only living things have golgi (chapter 5). Third, not only do young children consider plants not to be alive, they consider it a category mistake to attribute certain basic biological states to them, such as being sick or starving (chapter 6). That is, they judge "The flower is starving" to be nonsense, just like "The idea weighs 15 pounds." In the terminology of chapter 6, the distinction between animals and plants has ontological status for young children, and the two ontologically basic categories *animal* and *plant* have not yet been merged into a single ontological type, *living thing.*

By age 10 children display the adult patterns of responses. They judge animals and plants, but not inanimate objects, to be alive, and they judge many predicates to span both animals and plants without generating category errors. Thus, by age 10 children represent a concept with the same extension as the adult's concept *living thing;* they have mapped the same word, "alive," onto it; and it seems to function in the same way in the 10-year-old's conceptual system as it does in the adult's.

Results: *Animal*

Although young children map a different concept onto the word "animal" than do adults, there is no doubt that a concept *animal* with the same extension as the adult's plays an important role in their thought. Even the judgments of 3- and 4-year-olds reflect the distinction between animals, as a class, and nonanimals. Young children attribute animal properties of various sorts only to animals, and not to inanimate objects much like animals (e.g., dolls and stuffed animals; chapter 3). Further, inductive projection of newly taught internal organs is constrained by the distinction between animals and nonanimals, in the sense that only animals are credited with having the organ (chapters 4 and 5).

Nonetheless, *animal* functions in the thought of 10-year-olds and adults differently than it functions in the thought of young children. Unlike 10-year-olds and adults, young children do not realize that all animals eat, breathe, and reproduce (chapter 3). Further, from the knowledge that dogs and bees both have some internal organ, young children do not infer that all animals (or all complex animals) probably share that organ (chapter 5).

That the young child's concept *animal* differs from the adult's is understandable in light of the young child's different conceptions of the bodily processes that all animals share (see below). I characterize this change by claiming that the young child sees animals as behaving beings, whereas the 10-year-old and the adult see them as biological beings as well.

Results: *Person*

Though the child's concept of a person has not been the focus of this book, the phenomena reviewed leave no doubt that this concept plays a central role in even the 4-year-old's ontology. Young children represent a concept with the same extension as the adult's and have mapped the words "person" and "people" onto this concept. This is indicated by the vast amount of knowledge that young children command about people. Young children know people to have all of the properties probed in this monograph, from being alive (chapter 1) to thinking, having hearts, having bones, and breathing (chapters 2 through 6). Further, preschool children have an elaborate theory of mind (chapter 2).

Nonetheless, the data reviewed in this monograph show changes in the concept between ages 4 and 10. The relations between young children's concepts of people and animals are exceedingly complex, and a certain tension is evident—people are the prototypical animal for young children and at the same time are not animals at all, certainly not merely one animal among many. This tension was reflected in many results. Although 4-year-olds always attributed the investigated animal properties to people, they did not even always attribute them to other mammals, let alone to more peripheral animals (chapter 3). If taught on people, a newly taught internal organ was credited to other animals according to their similarity to people; but, if taught on dogs or bees, it was not projected to people (chapter 4). Even when 6-year-olds were taught that dogs and bees share an internal organ, they failed to project that organ to people as much as they did to another mammal (chapter 5).

By age 10, children *do* see people as just one mammal among many; 10-year-olds resemble adults in every respect probed in this monograph. These results are also understandable in terms of the changes between ages 4 and 10 in children's conceptions of bodily functions (see below).

Results: Concepts of Individual Animals and Plants
Young children think that a skunk submitted to cosmetic changes can become a raccoon. By age 9, children see this as impossible, and even allow that a particular animal that looks and behaves exactly like a skunk could in fact be discovered to be a raccoon, if it is found that its parents and children are raccoons and that its internal organs are those of a raccoon (chapter 6). Keil (in press) found parallel results for many transformations from one animal to another and from one plant to another. Five-year-olds think that category membership is determined by appearance and behavior; 9-year-olds think it is determined by deeper biological considerations. I have argued that these results too can be understood in terms of changes in children's conceptualization of bodily processes.

Results: Conceptions of Bodily Processes
As reviewed in chapter 2, young children are largely ignorant of the organs found inside the human body. Insofar as they know internal organs, they assign functions to them on the principle "One organ— one function": the stomach is for eating; the heart is for making blood; the brain is for thinking; etc. These children conceptualize processes such as death, growth, reproduction, and ingestion in terms of the

behavior of the whole person and not in terms of the functioning of internal body parts.

All this has changed by age 10. Ten-year-olds know of many internal organs and have constructed a model of how the integrated functioning of these organs supports life, growth, and reproduction. The first model (achieved by age 9 or so) represents substances—air, food, blood—being passed around and used by the body. Different organs contain or conduct these substances along the way. Only later does the child understand how the body breaks down and transforms substances. Even the first model, however, allows for understanding death as the cessation of internal bodily processes.

I have argued that this conceptualization of the body as a machine supporting life allows the child to see all animals as fundamentally alike and to conceive of plants as being like animals. It also allows the formulation of the general biological problems to which each animal is a solution, and therefore enables the child to see that the real nature of each animal is to be found in its unique solution to these problems.

Results: Information-processing Models of Inductive Projection

The inductive inferences of young children differ from those of 10-year-olds and adults in three respects. First, to a very large extent young children decide what things in the world have certain properties, such as breathing or thinking, by inductive projection from the knowledge that people have them. This results in nearly identical patterns of attribution for all properties probed in chapters 3 and 4, including the newly taught property of having a spleen. Ten-year-olds and adults rely little on this method for attributing biological properties. Instead, they reason from category membership and knowledge of biological function, producing patterns of attribution that vary from property to property (chapter 3). Second, in the inductive projection of newly taught properties, young children show a marked asymmetry between being taught on people, on the one hand, and being taught on other animals, on the other. In the case of 4-year-olds, this asymmetry is total—projection to new animals occurs only when the new property is taught on people. There is no hint of this asymmetry among 10-year-olds and adults (chapters 4 and 5). Third, when projecting properties taught on two animals or living things, adults integrate the information and infer some superordinate category that includes the two objects, whereas a different process underlies the judgments of 6-year-olds. The children make their decision in two steps—first finding the object known to have the property that is most similar to the object probed, and then computing the similarity between the two (chapter 5).

Restructuring in What Sense?

Clearly, a great deal of knowledge about living things is acquired in the years before age 10. But do the results just reviewed indicate that the child's knowledge is *restructured?* If so, which kind of restructuring occurs—the weaker kind claimed by Chi, Glaser, and Rees (1982) to characterize the novice-expert shift or the stronger kind claimed by historians of science to characterize theory change?

Two successive conceptual systems are structurally different in the weaker sense if the later one represents different relations among concepts than the earlier one does, and if patterns of these relations motivate superordinate concepts in the later system that are not represented in the earlier one. The novice-expert shift in chess provides a paradigm example. Two successive conceptual systems are structurally different in the stronger sense if the transition between the two involves conceptual change; the presence versus absence of conceptual change is the essential difference between the two kinds of restructuring. The change from Aristotelian to Galilean mechanics provides a paradigm example of strong restructuring (see introduction).

Between ages 4 and 10, knowledge of animals is restructured in at least the weaker sense. The 10-year-old represents relations among such processes as eating, breathing, growing, dying, and having babies that the 4-year-old does not. For 10-year-olds, the relations among these basic biological functions provide a framework for inferential processes and motivate the superordinate concepts *animal* and *living thing*.

The discovery of qualitatively different processes underlying different solutions to the same problem is evidence for knowledge restructuring. The information-processing models discussed in this monograph are models of inductive projection. Although inductive projection is not typical of the kind of problem solving usually studied in the literature on the novice-expert shift (where the problems are typically quantitative problems in physics, chemistry, geometry, algebra, and so forth), deciding when an inductive projection is warranted and when not is certainly a ubiquitous problem faced in scientific reasoning.

As in the case of the literature on the novice-expert shift, the three differences in information-processing models reviewed above are interpretable in terms of the restructuring of knowledge that characterizes the shift. First, when the functions of eating, breathing, and reproduction are understood in terms of the life cycle and in terms of maintaining life, children infer that all animals must eat, breathe, and reproduce, and they no longer attribute such properties on the basis of similarity to people. Second, people become just one mammal among many with respect to internal body structure, and the asymmetries of projection from people and from other animals therefore disappear. Finally, reliance on the two-step process of projection from two animals disappears as subjects come to realize that some aspects of the bodily mechanisms for maintaining life are widely shared.

We have seen how the superordinate concept *living thing* comes to be represented in the course of acquiring biological knowledge between age 4 and age 10. We have also seen that the superordinate concept *animal* organizes inferences differently for adults and 6-year-olds. Both of these superordinate concepts, *living thing* and *animal,* emerge from the patterns of relations among biological functions described above.

That 4- to 10-year-olds undergo a novice-expert shift does not, of course, imply that 10-year-olds, or normal adults for that matter, are experts in biology. Patently, they are not. My point is that the *kind* of conceptual reorganization children experience during these years is at least as radical as the conceptual reorganization adults experience when gaining expertise in some fields. Apparently, expertise is a relative matter; there is room for many novice-expert shifts in the course of mastering each domain of natural science.

Now, does the acquisition of knowledge about animals and living things between ages 4 and 10 involve restructuring in the stronger sense? Does this case of knowledge reorganization have the properties of theory change: changes in the domain of phenomena to be accounted for by the theory, changes in explanatory mechanisms, and (most importantly) changes in individual concepts? To show that restructuring in the stronger sense has occurred, it is necessary to show all three types of change. It must be shown that it is misleading to characterize the differences between the 4-year-old's and the 10-year-old's knowledge in terms of different relations among the same concepts.

In earlier chapters I have claimed that the years from 4 to 10 witness the emergence of biology as an autonomous domain of theorizing. In cases of theory emergence, there must be overlap between the domain of the new theory and the domain of the older theory from which it emerged, and there must be true theory change in this region of overlap. The claim that the conceptual reorganization described in this monograph is the emergence of an intuitive biology is equivalent to the claim that the stronger sense of restructuring is needed to fully describe the change.

The theory from which an intuitive biology emerges is an intuitive theory of behavior. I call it a "naive psychology" because it mainly concerns human behavior, and because it explains behavior in terms of wants and beliefs. Though based on human behavior, it also concerns animal behavior, since animals are also seen as behaving beings. Many phenomena fall under both a theory of behavior and a theory of biology—that is, the two domains overlap. The concepts *person* and *animal* are central to both domains, and most of the phenomena studied in this monograph properly belong to both. That is, eating, breathing, sleeping, dying, growing, being male or female, and having babies are part of the domain of human activities. For the young child this is their only locus. They are phenomena of the same sort as playing, bathing, and talking. Important facts about eating include when one is allowed to eat candy, the difference between breakfast, lunch, and dinner, whether one is allowed to eat spaghetti with one's fingers, that eating well keeps people healthy, that if people eat too much they will get fat, etc. In spite of generalizations such as the last two, there is yet no autonomous domain of biological facts about eating. Eating is one of the things people (and animals) do, and the child understands eating in terms of the consequences of the act for the whole being. Similarly, important facts about breathing include whether one can hold one's breath while putting one's head under water, that one can see one's breath on a cold day, that breath can smell bad if teeth are not brushed, etc. Important facts about sleeping include what bed-time rituals one observes, whether one has nightmares, whether one is allowed to give up naps, etc. The young child's knowledge about parts of the body is integrated into these same concerns—the child knows that one eats with one's mouth, that one's stomach gets full, sometimes to the point of aching, etc. These activities and facts about people constitute a theoretical domain, because the child has an explanatory framework that accounts for them.

The explanatory structure in which these phenomena are embedded is social and psychological. The whys and wherefores of these matters, as the child understands them, include individual motivation (hunger, tiredness, avoiding pain, seeking pleasure) and social conventions. Asked why people eat, 4-year-olds answer, "Because they are hungry" or "Because it is dinner time." They might also say, "Otherwise they would die" or "To keep healthy," but these are not yet biological explanations because the child knows no biological mechanisms by which eating has these consequences. The child is merely expressing the desirable consequences of eating. Biological explanation, though sometimes also teleological, is not intentional. Supporting life is a bottom-line goal; biological functions and organs are explained in terms of their role in supporting life. The aspects of eating, breathing, internal organs, and so on, that are explained in terms of biological considerations in the 10-year-old's conceptual system are different from the aspects explained in terms of psychological considerations in the 4-year-old's conceptual system. Thus, the changes in both domain and explanatory structure characteristic of theory change are exemplified in this case study.

I believe it is misleading to describe the 10-year-old merely as having represented different relations than the 4-year-old among the same set of concepts. That is, conceptual change is involved in the transition. True, the 10-year-old knows some relations between eating, breathing, growing, and dying (for example) or between being male and having babies (for another example) that the 4-year-old does not know. But it is not the same concepts of eating and dying, or of being male and having babies, that are involved in the two conceptual systems. Learning the role of eating in maintaining the functioning of the body is part of coming to distinguish *dead* from *inanimate*. Learning the role of the body in reproduction is part of coming to see being male as more than a matter of clothing, hairstyle, and behavior patterns.

At least two important kinds of conceptual change that are found in theory changes are found in this case. Both differentiations and coalescences must be achieved (such as the differentiation of two senses of *not alive* and the coalescence of *animal* and *plant*). The coalescence of *animal* and *plant* into a single category involves much more than forming the simple disjunction *animal or plant*. By age 10 the two are seen as fundamentally alike in a way that involves having reconceptualized both. The emergence of the new ontologically basic category *living thing* has implications not only for the concepts *animal* and *plant* but also for the concepts *person, raccoon,* and *cactus* (indeed, all individual animals and plants).

In sum, the child's knowledge of animals and living things is restructured over the years from 4 to 10. The kind of restructuring involved is at least of the weaker sort needed to characterize novice-expert shifts that do not involve theory change and most probably is of the stronger sort needed to characterize theory changes that involve conceptual change.

Implications for the Description of Cognitive Development

Piaget's approach to the description and explanation of cognitive development is often called "structural," referring to the logico-mathematical structures of concrete and formal operations. The structural approach is often contrasted with various learning approaches in which cognitive development is seen in terms of the accumulation of knowledge. Current research on knowledge acquisition, including the present case study, makes it clear that the contrast between structural development and the accumulation of knowledge conflates two different distinctions. The first distinction is between knowledge accumulation that involves restructuring and knowledge accumulation that does not. Examples of the former include theory changes and novice-expert shifts. Examples of the latter might include learning the multiplication tables, learning the capitals of the 50 states, and even learning much of the scientific knowledge that is taught in schools. The second distinction is between domain-general change and domain-specific change. Theory changes, and novice-expert shifts as well, involve restructuring, but only of the concepts and explanatory principles of the domains of knowledge undergoing development. Such changes are domain specific. In contrast, the putative shifts from preoperational thought to concrete operational thought, or from concrete operations to formal operations, are independent of particular content domains. Attaining concrete operations is thought to affect the child's ability to learn mathematical concepts, spatial concepts, concepts in physical science (such as *weight* and *density*), moral concepts, social concepts, etc. Indeed, because concrete and formal operations are the inferential schema putatively available to the child, changes at the operational level necessarily affect the organization of knowledge in all specific domains.

In some of their work, Piaget and his colleagues were very careful to keep separate domain-specific change and operational change. For example, each chapter in *The Child's Conception of Physical Quantities* (Piaget and Inhelder 1941) receives two theoretical summaries. First, the children's concepts of *weight, volume,* and *density,* as well as their understanding of such phenomena as the dissolving of sugar in water and the popping of popcorn, are diagnosed relative to successive models of matter. The construction of an atomistic model of matter is domain-specific conceptual change. Second, the children's emerging conceptions of matter are diagnosed relative to the achievement of concrete operations and formal operations. Piaget and Inhelder argue that limitations in operational thought place upper limits on the theory building the child is capable of, and thus constrain the course of the developing conception of matter.

This is not the place for a detailed critique of Piaget's theory of operational development (see Gelman and Baillargeon 1983 for a balanced treatment). Two kinds of criticisms have been most telling. First, it is impossible to see the consistency across myriad tasks that the theory demands (Gelman and Baillargeon 1983). Second, phenomena offered in support of particular claims about the differences in the thinking of children at different ages have other interpretations that do not implicate differences in operational level (Gelman and Baillargeon 1983, Carey 1983). I believe that a third very general point can be made as well: in much of their research, Piaget and his colleagues confounded the child's problems with domain-specific scientific concepts, on the one hand, and domain-general inferential abilities, metaconceptual notions, or foundational concepts, on the other. For example, in the work on the concepts of *weight* and *density* cited above, the interpretations in terms of the child's developing theory of matter are sufficient to explain the phenomena in the book; no appeal to concrete or formal operations is necessary. (See also chapter 2, where I argue that appeals to concrete and formal operations are superfluous in interpreting the child's developing concepts of reproduction, digestion, death, etc.) More damaging, in the work on logical thinking (Inhelder and Piaget 1958, 1964), the tasks that were used to diagnose formal operations required mastery of particular scientific concepts not in the young child's repertoire. For example, the studies on the separation of variables required the child to have differentiated the concepts of weight, length, and material—perhaps the difficulty lies in *those variables* rather than in the principle that conclusive evidence about the relevance of one variable requires holding other ones constant (see Carey 1983 for elaboration of this point).

It is extremely difficult to improve performance on most Piagetian tasks through teaching. This phenomenon—resistance to training—is often cited in support of Piaget's interpretation that changes in the kinds of responses on his tasks reflect changes in underlying logical operations (see Smedslund 1961, for example). However, resistance to training has an alternative explanation in terms of domain-specific change. If conceptual change in childhood involves theory changes, or even novice-expert shifts, then failed training attempts are to be expected. Indeed, it is the failure of whole semesters of physics teaching to make a dent in the student's intuitive theory of mechanics that motivated the work on the novice-expert shift in science in the first place. These shifts require restructuring, albeit domain-specific restructuring, and this is not accomplished by a few hours, or even many hours, of instruction.

I am not arguing that there are no domain-general changes in the developing child's conceptual system (see Carey 1983 for distinctions among four different kinds of domain-general conceptual change and a critical look at the evidence for each). Rather, I am arguing that much of the evidence that has been taken to support such changes actually reflects domain-specific structural reorganizations. These can, and should, be studied in their own right, for only after they are understood will we be able to sort out the issue of the nature of domain-general constraints on the child's cognitive structures.

Two applications of this point of view from the present case study will clarify my argument.

Operativity

Four- and 6-year-olds rely on computations of similarity where 10-year-olds and adults rely on deductive inferences from category membership (chapters 3, 4, and 5). Could this be because 4- and 6-year-olds are incapable of making deductive inferences, or do not represent true categories? Both of these, after all, are putative characteristics of preoperational thought. Is the developmental change described in this monograph just another manifestation of the transition from preoperational to concrete operational reasoning? I think not. First of all, the evidence that children below age 6 represent concepts differently from adults or are not capable of deductive inferences is flawed (see Carey 1983 or Gelman and Baillargeon 1983 for reviews). Directly relevant to the present point, Smith (1979) showed that 4-year-olds can make deductive inferences from category membership. When Smith told them, "A pug is a kind of dog, but not a poodle," and asked, "Is a pug an animal?", even 4-year-olds answered, "Of course, you told me it was a dog." And in one condition of the study described in chapter 4 (not reported), one group of children was told that all animals, including people, dogs, and bees, have spleens. Both 4- and 6-year-olds attributed spleens to all and only animals in these circumstances. It is not that young children are incapable of deductive inferences from category membership; it is just that their knowledge of biological properties does not make it clear to them that such inferences are warranted. Conversely, adults also make inferences by computing similarity, as in Rips's (1975) study, or when taught that dogs (or people or bees) have omenta, as in the present study. Both adults and children make both types of inferences. Which they make on any particular occasion depends upon the knowledge they bring to bear on the inferential task, and not upon general inferential capabilities.

There is a moral to this story. It is very tempting to interpret differences between younger and older children in the most general way possible. Succumbing to this temptation might have led us to conclude that 4-year-olds are incapable of inferences of a particular form. However, what level of description actually captures any observed developmental difference is a difficult empirical problem.

Causality

Piaget's work on animism preceded his work on operational thinking and therefore was not placed in the context of the attainment of concrete operations. Rather, the development of the concept of life was seen in the context of the child's growing appreciation of causality. As described in chapter 1, Piaget held that young children have no concept of mechanical causation. According to Piaget, the only schema for causal explanation available to the child is human intentional causality, so that when called upon to explain physical phenomena, the child attributes intentionality, and life, to the causal agents in the event being explained. Thus, a rock rolling down a hill is alive, whereas a rock at rest is not, for a rolling rock is active and a potential agent in some event.

If there is a process in children's development whereby they come to appreciate physical causality, this process would certainly be a domain-general change. This change would affect theory building in a wide variety of domains, including intuitive mechanics, intuitive theories of heat and cold, intuitive astronomy, intuitive understanding of electricity, intuitive chemistry, and so on. In Carey 1983 concepts such as causality and the appearance-reality distinction are termed *foundational concepts,* since they are at the foundation of theory building in diverse domains. All theories, intuitive or otherwise, build explanatory frameworks that seek to explain surface phenomena in terms of under-

lying reality. Lacking the concept of causality or the distinction between appearance and reality would certainly limit the conceptual
structures available to the child.

There is now some consensus that, contrary to Piaget's claims, the
preschool child appreciates both mechanical causality (Bullock, Gelman, and Baillargeon 1982, Shultz 1982) and the appearance-reality
distinction (Flavell, Flavell, and Green 1983). Indeed, infants seem to
appreciate mechanical causality (Baillargeon and Spelke (in press),
Leslie 1982). The evidence now available suggests that there is no
developmental change in the foundational notions that underlie all theory building. Human beings are theory builders; from the beginning we
construct explanatory structures that help us find the deeper reality
underlying surface chaos.

The above discussion does not imply that there is no development of
causal notions. Such a claim is patently false—children below age 10,
for example, cannot explain phenomena in terms of the particulate
theory of matter, and most adults do not grasp the structure of explanation in modern physics. If I am correct in my analysis, the restructuring of the child's knowledge of living things in the years before age
10 crucially involves changes in causal explanation. The 4- to 7-year-
old interprets what for adults are biological phenomena in terms of
psychological causal notions; by age 10 the child has constructed a
system of biological explanation as well. The point is this: the developments of explanatory frameworks that can be documented are part
and parcel of theory changes—they are not domain general. Kuhn
(1977a) makes this point about the development of causality in the
history of science. It is not the structure of causal explanation that has
changed historically; rather, our ideas about particular causal mechanisms have changed, as the theories themselves changed.

If causal notions are analyzed relative to theories, then theory
changes that occur during development will implicate changes in the
child's concepts of causality. What is being denied here is the claim that
immature notions of causality, in general, place any domain-indepen-
dent constraints on the conceptual structures of children of young ages.

Constraints on Induction

The inductive inferences studied in chapters 3, 4, and 5 depended upon
computations of similarity between the known possessor of some biological property and the object in question. Thus, Tversky's (1977)

contrast model of similarity can provide a framework for viewing the subjects' inductive projection. His model accounts for asymmetries of similarity, depending upon which object is focused on, and thus accounts for the symmetries between adults' and 10-year-olds' projection from people and dogs, on one hand, and projection from bees, on the other. Also, Tversky presents studies of how context affects the weightings of the features that enter into the similarity computation. In the present studies we have seen that different metrics underlie the degree of perceived similarity between various objects and people when simple similarity judgments are required and when projection of spleens or omenta is required (chapters 2, 3, and 4). My argument in this monograph exploits age differences in projection functions as evidence about developmental changes in the underlying features and in their organization.

At one point Tversky's framework helped us not at all—namely, in providing a way of thinking about the utter failure of 4-year-olds to project spleens to animals similar to dogs, when taught on dogs, or to animals similar to bees, when taught on bees (chapter 4). We need to look elsewhere for an account of these failures of the induction task to engage similarity computations at all. The account I offered is tentative, and appeals to the central place of people in the organization of the young child's knowledge of properties such as eating, breathing, sleeping, having internal organs, etc. Whatever the right account, we see the importance of the theoretical framework in which knowledge is placed in determining the details of inductive projection.

However, Tversky's framework, and our use of it here, barely scratches the surface of the classical problem of constraints on inductive inference. Goodman's new riddle of induction (Goodman 1955) raises the problem in its extreme form. Suppose you have examined an indefinitely large number of emeralds, and each so far has been green. What licenses the inductive inference "All emeralds are green," more than "All emeralds are grue," where *grue* means *green if examined before* A.D. *2000, otherwise blue?* After all, the data available so far are equally consistent with both inferences. In general, there are always an infinite number of inferences consistent with any evidence to date. Or to put the problem in terms of similarity judgments, there is always an infinity of features in terms of which two objects may be compared and, more relevant to the case at hand, there is always an infinity of features of any group of objects one has seen (e.g., emeralds) that one can use to formulate hypotheses about objects yet to be discovered. What makes *green* a projectable predicate while *grue* is not?

Goodman considers at length the possibility of stating a structural constraint that would rule out the class of nonprojectable predicates that contains *grue*. (A structural constraint is one that applies irrespective of the particular concepts involved.) A first suggestion that comes to mind is that *grue* is more complex than *green;* perhaps there are simplicity constraints. A second immediate suggestion is that *grue* contains a proper name in its definition (A.D. *2000*); perhaps projectable predicates cannot be defined in terms of specific individuals (call this the deictic constraint). Goodman constructed the *grue* example precisely to show that such structural constraints as these will not work. In the thirty years since 1955, no one has found a way of specifying complexity on which *grue* comes out more complex than *green;* further, *green* is as much a deictic property as *grue*. For a flavor of Goodman's argument, consider the obvious fact that *grue* and *green* are symmetric with respect to both complexity and deicticality, depending upon the primitives in terms of which the definitions are stated. That is, *green* can be defined as *grue if examined before* A.D. *2000, otherwise bleen,* where *bleen* is a predicate analogous to *grue*. Of course, we want to say why *green* and *blue* are better candidates for primitives in our definitions than are *grue* and *bleen,* but we cannot appeal again to complexity or deicticality. Goodman concludes that there are no structural constraints on predicates that would do the required work. Rather, what makes *green* projectable and *grue* nonprojectable is that *green* is more entrenched in our current theories. That is, the theories we hold to be true are committed to not using predicates like *grue*. Goodman concludes that there is no theory-neutral arbiter of projectability. We must look to our theories, and to nothing else, if we want to understand what licenses inductive projection.

Goodman's arguments about constraints on induction motivate the reanalysis of Keil's work on ontological development (chapter 6) in terms of theory change. Keil's proposal for structural constraints on ontological concepts violates Goodman's principle. The M-constraint is a structural constraint in that it depends upon the location of predicates and terms in an ontological hierarchy; the particular predicates or terms are irrelevant. The constraint is domain independent with respect to particular theories, such as our intuitive theories of the physical, biological, and social worlds. Terms and predicates from all three domains are represented on the tree and are all subject to the M-constraint. If Keil's theory were correct, it would provide an important counterexample to Goodman's pessimistic conclusion, for it would be a case where a structural constraint did rule out a class of nonprojectable predicates. But (although this is not the place to discuss it in detail) Keil's proposal is not correct. Carey (1985), Davis (1979), and Gerard and Mandler (1983) point out that the M-constraint is not true. In addition, Carey (1985) points out two reasons why it could not do the work Keil wants of it even if it were true. First, the young child's ontological tree is so collapsed that the M-constraint could provide almost no source of constraint at just the time when the child's vocabulary is growing explosively. Second, the major result in Keil's studies is that the young child assimilates concepts of nonobjects (events, abstract entities) to the concept *object,* so it is the concept *object* that is providing the main source of constraint, not the structural M-constraint. Close consideration of Keil's proposal (chapter 6 and Carey 1985) leads us right back to Goodman's conclusion: if we want to understand constraints on induction, including constraints on hypotheses about ontologically basic distinctions, we must look to the theories held by the person making the inductive inference.

Conceptual Change

In their descriptions of knowledge acquisition, developmental psychologists and historians of science alike appeal to changes at the level of individual concepts. For example, we are told that before the time of Black, *heat* and *temperature* had not been distinguished from each other (McKie and Heathcote 1935), and that Aristotle did not distinguish *instantaneous velocity* from *average velocity* (Kuhn 1977b). Similarly, we are told that children do not distinguish between *weight* and *size,* or between *weight* and *density* (Piaget and Inhelder 1941, Gibson 1969). When such distinctions are finally made, conceptual differentiation has taken place. Differentiation is not the only kind of conceptual transformation. Coalescence also occurs, as when Galileo collapsed Aristotle's *natural* and *violent motion.* Also, sometimes simple properties are reanalyzed as relations, as when Newton reconceptualized the weight of a body as the force on that body exerted by the earth.

Although historians and psychologists both appeal to differentiations and coalescences in the course of knowledge acquisition, there has been relatively little analysis of just what such changes really amount to. Such an analysis would have to provide the answers to several questions: What is the parentage relation (that is, how do we trace concepts from ancestors to descendents)? In what sense is an ancestor undifferentiated relative to two or more descendents? What evidence bears on diagnosing lack of differentiation? Often evidence for lack of differentiation has been entirely behavioral. However, more than one representational alternative could underlie any observed lack of differentiation. We certainly would want to distinguish lack of differentiation between, say, *weight* and *density* from mere absence of the concept of *density,* even though subjects in either conceptual state may make judgments entirely on the basis of weight.

An obvious first answer to some of these questions, stated in terms of current feature list models of concepts, comes to mind. Descent is partly traced through shared features: descendent concepts have some of the features of the ancestors. An ancestor concept is undifferentiated relative to its descendents if it contains some of the features of both descendents. This is not enough, of course; *tiger* and *lion* share features, but are not related by descent. We must have additional ways of identifying concepts in order to trace descent. There is another problem as well, namely, how we individuate concepts. What prevents us from changing the level of analysis to that of the features themselves? Since undifferentiated concepts, by hypothesis, contain features that will later distinguish their descendents, the differentiated concepts already exist in the guise of these features. On this analysis, conceptual nondifferentiation could not occur.

One solution to the problems of identifying the same concepts over successive conceptual systems and of individuating concepts is to analyze them relative to the theories in which they are embedded. Concepts must be identified by the roles they play in theories. A concept is undifferentiated relative to descendents if it contains features of those descendents, and if the theory states neither any relations among those features nor any separate relations among those features and other concepts. Wiser and Carey (1983) have shown that the concept of *heat* in the thermal theories of the seventeenth-century Academy of Florence met these criteria. The Academy's *heat* had both strength and intensity—that is, aspects of both modern *heat* and modern *temperature*—but the Experimenters (their own self-designation) did not separately quantify heat and temperature and, unlike Black, did not seek to study the relations between the two. Furthermore, they *did* relate a single thermal variable, degree of heat, to mechanical phenomena. Therefore, we can be confident in ascribing an undifferentiated concept that conflated *heat* and *temperature* to these seventeenth-century scientists. Smith, Carey, and Wiser (in press) apply this analysis of differentiation to the developmental case of coming to differentiate *weight* and *density*.

If the above analysis is correct, differentiations must be analyzed relative to the theories in which the differentiating concepts are embedded. The present case study suggests the same to be true of coalescences. Young children represent the concept *animal* and the concept *plant*. They also can form the union *animals and plants* and even know some properties true of animals and plants (e.g., that they grow). Why, then, do we wish to deny them the concept *living thing?* Because as yet they represent no theoretical context in which the concept of living things does any work. The coalescences of *animal* and *plant* into the concept *living thing* occurs as part of the knowledge reorganization documented in this monograph. I have previously argued that coalescences are part of the process of theory change; here I am making the stronger claim that the very diagnosis of whether or not a coalescence has occurred requires analysis of the theoretical context in which the concept is embedded. The same is true for cases of differentiation.

Explanations of Development

This monograph explores how to think about cognitive development. My concern has been to discover in what senses knowledge is restructured in the course of acquisition. I have been noticeably silent about the explanation of that change. At most, I have appealed to learning about the biological functions of eating, breathing, growing, reproduction, etc., such learning presumably being the result of instruction, either formal or informal. One could imagine other routes. Nature programs on television, such as the magnificent BBC series on the diversity of life, drive home the idea that each animal is a unique solution to the problem of finding a life-supporting niche. An important next step in this research program might be to specify and test an instructional sequence that could effect the reorganization. This is no easy task. The burden of the description in this monograph is the far-reaching ramifications of the child's conceptual organization—the concepts affected range from individual species, to superordinates such as *animal, plant,* and *living thing,* to biological functions such as eating, breathing, and growth to matters of reproduction and its relation to gender identity, to the nature and function of internal organs, to the relation between mind and brain. A short instructional sequence would hardly change all that.

Many students of development decry our lack of explicit theories of the mechanisms of change. Although the explanation of change is important, clearly the description of change must come first, or at least proceed in tandem with the search for mechanisms. As this case study illustrates, the proper description of cognitive change is no trivial matter. And unless we know exactly what kinds of changes occur, we do not know what our theories of learning must explain.

Any theory of learning must have at least two components: a specification of the initial state and a specification of the mechanisms in terms of which that initial state is modified. "Initial state" here is specified relative to the particular change under consideration. Both components are necessary for stating the constraints on induction that guarantee that learning is possible. Psychologists who decry the lack of mechanisms of conceptual change focus on only half of the problem. Equally important is the specification of the initial state. This monograph sketches the initial theory from which biology emerges: intuitive psychology. But what is the origin of the intuitive psychology? Where does the child come by an explanatory system in which wants and beliefs account for actions? There is good evidence that such a system is intact by the third year of life (Shatz, Wellman, and Silber 1983), and there are hints of it in infancy (Golinkoff, Harding, Carlson, and Sexton 1984). My own guess is that human infants are endowed with the tools to build an intuitive psychology, just as they are endowed with the tools to build an intuitive mechanics and a human language. That is, my guess is that the "initial state" of human children can be described by saying that they are innately endowed with two theoretical systems: a naive physics and a naive psychology. Whether or not this guess is correct is, of course, an empirical issue. My point here is merely that it is an *important* empirical issue, especially for those who seek explanatory theories of learning. We cannot ignore the problem of the specification of the initial state when we seek explanations for developmental changes.

Theory-like Conceptual Structures

In this monograph I have often appealed to subjects' theories—in order to state constraints on induction, explicate causal notions and ontological commitments, analyze whether terms refer to natural kinds, and specify aspects of the initial state. Further, I have placed conceptual change and knowledge reorganizations in the context of theory changes. The time has come to step back and ask a basic question: just exactly what is meant by "theory"?

As outlined before, a theory is characterized by the phenomena in its domain, its laws and other explanatory mechanisms, and the concepts that articulate the laws and the representations of the phenomena. Explanation is at the core of theories. It is explanatory mechanisms that distinguish theories from other types of conceptual structures, such as restaurant scripts. To see this, consider such questions as "Why do we pay for our food at a restaurant?" or "Why do we order before the food comes?" The answers to these questions are not to be found within the restaurant script itself; the answer to the first lies in the domain of economics, where questions of the exchange of goods and services are explained, and the answer to the second lies in the domain of physics, since it involves the directionality of time.

The distinction between theory-like structures and other types of cognitive structures is one of degree. Probably all conceptual structures provide some fodder for explanation. My conjecture, however, is that there are only a relatively few conceptual structures that embody deep explanatory notions—on the order of a dozen or so in the case of educated nonscientists. These conceptual structures correspond to domains that might be the disciplines in a university: psychology, mechanics, a theory of matter, economics, religion, government, biology, history, etc. On the view of development put forward in this monograph, the child begins with many fewer such domains—perhaps only a naive mechanics and a naive psychology. Conceptual development consists, in part, of the emergence of new theoretical domains from these beginning ones, as in the emergence of biology from psychology described in this monograph. Another example is provided in Smith, Carey, and Wiser (in press): the emergence of a theory of matter from a domain of physics in which objects and the kinds of stuff from which they are made are not fully distinguished.

I have not shown, of course, that theory-like structures are relatively few in number, and that such structures can be distinguished from other conceptual structures along the continuum of explanatory depth. Rather, I have attempted to make these claims at least plausible, so that they may be further explored. Clearly, the ultimate interest of the arguments in this monograph depends upon these two propositions being true.

Appendix

Experiment 1, Chapter 3

The Ordering of the Animals: Analyses of Concordance
I will explain the analysis using the 4-year-olds as an example. In Experiment 1 each was probed about five animal properties for each animal. Suppose one subject attributed all five to people, 4 to the aardvark and the dodo, 3 to the stinkoo, and 1 to the hammerhead. This subject ordered the animals as follows: people (rank 1), aardvark and dodo (rank tied for 2.5), stinkoo (rank 4), and hammerhead (rank 5). Suppose another subject ordered the animals thus: people (rank 1), aardvark (rank 2), dodo (rank 3), hammerhead (rank 4), and stinkoo (rank 5). An analysis of concordance assesses the degree of agreement among subjects in the rank ordering of the animals. Table A1 shows that each of the 4-year-old subjects ranked the 5 animals in the same order, as the

Table A1
Experiment 1: Concordance of ordering of animals by each subject

	Age 4		Age 5		Age 7	Adult
Number of subjects	9		9		9	9
W	.64		.49			
p	< .01		< .01		n.s.	n.s.
Ranking	People	(12.5)[a]	People	(18.5)		
	Aardvark	(22.5)	Aardvark	(28.0)		
	Dodo	(28.0)	Dodo	(28.5)		
	Stinkoo	(32.5)	Stinkoo	(29.0)		
	Hammerhead	(39.5)	Hammerhead	(35.0)		
			Worm	(50.0)		

[a]Numbers in parentheses are sums of ranks.

agreement level differed significantly from chance. This was also true for the 5-year-olds (table A1), but not for the 7-year-olds and the adults.

The concordance in table A1 concerns whether each subject ordered the animals in the same way. We might also ask whether each *property* ordered the animals in the same way. For example, 9 subjects might have attributed breathing to people, 7 to aardvarks, 6 to dodos, 5 to stinkoos, and 3 to hammerheads. Breathing would have then been ordered as follows: people (rank 1), aardvark (rank 2), dodo (rank 3), stinkoo (rank 4), and hammerhead (rank 5). We could analogously ask how attribution of eating ranked the animals, how attribution of getting hurt ranked the animals, etc. Table A2 presents the concordances of these rankings. In the case of all three groups of children, each property probed ordered the animals in the same way: people, aardvark, dodo, stinkoo, hammerhead, worm.

Analysis of Individual Patterns of Attribution
The concordances presented in tables A1 and A2 reflect group data. We also want to know how each child distributed each property over the animals probed. There were three different possibilities. First, the child might attribute the property to people alone. As can be seen from table A3, this option was extremely rare, and no child consistently took it. For example, 4-year-olds showed this pattern a total of five times, and each case was contributed by a different child. Second, the child might attribute the property in question to all animals. This was a frequent pattern, but again there was no consistency with regard to particular children or particular properties distributed in this way. For example, all 9 of the 4-year-olds showed this pattern at least once, and all properties were distributed in this way at least once. Third, the child might attribute the property to only some of the animals. This was the option most commonly taken. Consider breathing as an example. A child who attributed breathing to just some animals might credit people, aardvarks, and dodos with breathing (case 1), or people, aardvarks, and stinkoos (case 2), or people and worms (case 3), or any of myriad other combinations. Each case may or may not be consistent with the overall ordering of the animals reflected in the concordances in tables A1 and A2. Case 1 is consistent; cases 2 and 3 are not. To assess degree of consistency, I enumerated all possible patterns of attribution to just some animals and calculated the ratio of consistent to inconsistent patterns. I then assessed whether the proportion of consistent patterns was greater than would be expected by chance. As table A3 shows, this

Table A2

Experiment 1: Concordance of ordering of animals by each property

	Age 4	Age 5	Age 7	Adult
Number of properties	5	4	4	5
W	.73	.69	.89	
p	< .01	< .01	< .01	n.s.
Ranking	People (5.5)[a]	People (6.0)	People (7.0)	
	Aardvark (13.0)	Aardvark (12.0)	Aardvark (10.0)	
	Dodo (14.5)	Dodo (12.5)	Dodo (11.0)	
	Stinkoo (20.5)	Stinkoo (13.0)	Stinkoo (12.5)	
	Hammerhead (21.5)	Hammerhead (16.5)	Hammerhead (20.0)	
		Worm (24.0)	Worm (23.5)	

[a]Numbers in parentheses are sums of ranks.

Table A3
Experiment 1: Individual pattern analyses

Age	Number of children	Number of properties	Incidence of three different patterns of attribution
4	9	5	People only: 5 (5 different children, 3 different properties)
			All animals: 18 (9 different children, 5 different properties)
			Some animals: 22 (8 different children, 5 different properties)
			Some animals ⎰ consistent: 9 expected ratio 3:11
			⎱ inconsistent: 13 $\chi^2 = 5.0; p < .02$
5	9	4	People only: 3 (2 different children, 2 different properties)
			All animals: 5 (2 different children, 3 different properties)
			Some animals: 28 (9 different children, 4 different properties)
			Some animals ⎰ consistent: 13 expected ratio 2:13
			⎱ inconsistent: 15 $\chi^2 = 26.8; p < .001$
7	9	4	People only: 2 (1 child, 2 different properties)
			All animals: 19 (7 children, 4 different properties)
			Some animals: 15 (7 children, 4 different properties)
			Some animals ⎰ consistent: 11 expected ratio 2:13
			⎱ inconsistent: 4 $\chi^2 = 46.7; p < .001$

was so for all three groups of subjects. Thus, each child tended to respect the ordering of the animals in *each* attribution of *each* property.

Analyses of Variance
Another way of examining ordering of animals is by an analysis of variance. An ANOVA assesses whether some animals were attributed significantly more properties than were others. As table A4 shows, there was a main effect for animal probed at every age. Post hoc analyses (Neuman-Keuls) assess where the significant breaks are. For 4-year-olds, there is one significant break between people and all other animals, and another between the dodo and the other two animals (table A4). For 5-year-olds, there is again a significant break between people and all other animals, and another between the hammerhead and the worm. By age 7, the drop between people and aardvarks is no longer significant.

As mentioned in the text in chapter 3, an analysis of variance simultaneously assesses whether some properties are more widely attributed than others, and whether there is a property-by-animal interaction. The implications of the absence of a main effect for property at age 4, and the absence of a property-by-animal interaction at ages 5 and 7, are also discussed in chapter 3.

Experiment 2, Chapter 3

Analyses of Concordance
As in Experiment 1, subjects agreed in the ordering of animals (table A5). This result was found for 10-year-olds and adults as well as for 4-year-olds and 7-year-olds. Also as in Experiment 1, the attribution of each property respected the overall ordering of the group (table A6).

Table A4
Experiment 1: Analyses of variance within each age group

Age	Analysis	F	p	Neuman-Keuls Analysis
4	Animal	9.17	< .0001	people aardvark dodo stinkoo <u>hammerhead</u>
	Property	.41	n.s.	
	Animal by property	1.32	n.s.	
5	Animal	8.07	< .0001	people aardvark dodo stinkoo hammerhead worm
	Property	4.44	< .02	breathes sleeps <u>has heart thinks</u>
	Animal by property	.87	n.s.	
7	Animal	5.06	< .002	people aardvark dodo stinkoo hammerhead worm
	Property	3.81	< .03	breathes sleeps <u>has</u> heart thinks
	Animal by property	1.06	n.s.	
Adult	Animal	2.90	< .03	people aardvark dodo hammerhead stinkoo worm
	Property	5.18	< .0009	sleeps eats breathes can get hurt <u>has heart thinks</u>
	Animal by property	2.37	< .0005	

Table A5
Experiment 2: Concordance of ordering of animals by each subject

	Age 4	Age 7	Age 10	Adult
	Familiar series			
Number of subjects	10	10	10	
W	.53	.47	.66	
p	< .01	< .05	< .01	
Ranking	People (17.0)[a]	People (18.5)	People (19.0)	
	Dog (24.5)	Dog (26.5)	Dog (20.5)	
	Worm (31.5)	Fish (29.5)	Fish (28.0)	
	Fish (33.5)	Fly (36.0)	Fly (41.0)	
	Fly (43.5)	Worm (39.5)	Worm (41.5)	
	Unfamiliar series			
Number of subjects	10	10	10	
W	.36	.72	.79	
p	< .05	< .01	< .01	
Ranking	People (17.0)		People (18.5)	People (17.0)
	Aardvark (29.5)		Aardvark (22.5)	Aardvark (21.0)
	Hammerhead (31.0)		Hammerhead (25.5)	Hammerhead (26.0)
	Stinkoo (33.5)		Stinkoo (36.5)	Stinkoo (43.0)
	Annelid (39.0)		Annelid (47.0)	Annelid (43.0)

[a]Numbers in parentheses are sums of ranks.

Table A6
Experiment 2: Concordance of ordering of animals by each property

Familiar series

	Age 4	Age 7	Age 10	Adult
Number of properties	6	6	6	
W	.77	.54	.81	
p	< .01	< .05	< .01	
Ranking	People (6.5)[a]	People (9.5)	People (9.5)	
	Dog (14.5)	Dog (14.5)	Dog (11.0)	
	Worm (20.0)	Fish (19.0)	Fish (18.5)	
	Fish (21.0)	Fly (23.0)	Fly (24.0)	
	Fly (28.0)	Worm (24.0)	Worm (27.0)	

Unfamiliar series

	Age 4	Age 7	Age 10	Adult
Number of properties	6	6	6	
W	.54	.76	.57	
p	< .05	< .01	< .05	
Ranking	People (7.5)		People (11.5)	People (11.5)
	Aardvark (17.0)		Aardvark (13.0)	Aardvark (12.5)
	Hammerhead (19.0)		Hammerhead (14.5)	Hammerhead (18.5)
	Stinkoo (21.5)		Stinkoo (21.0)	Stinkoo (22.5)
	Annelid (25.0)		Annelid (30.0)	Annelid (25.0)

[a]Numbers in parentheses are sums of ranks.

Analyses of Variance

Table A7 presents the overall analyses of variance for the familiar series and for the unfamiliar series. Table A8 presents the analyses of variance within each age group.

Table A7
Experiment 2: Analyses of variance,
all ages combined

Analysis	F	p
Familiar series		
Age	5.65	< .009
Animal	23.62	< .0001
Age by animal	2.54	< .02
Property	8.96	< .0001
Age by property	1.41	n.s.
Animal by property	5.20	< .0001
Age by animal by property	1.39	< .10
Unfamiliar series		
Age	.64	n.s.
Animal	29.41	< .0001
Age by animal	2.42	< .02
Property	11.56	< .0001
Age by property	2.34	< .02
Animal by property	7.25	< .0001
Age by animal by property	1.80	< .003

Table A8
Experiment 2: Analyses of variance within each age group

Age	Analysis	F	p	Neuman-Keuls Analysis
Familiar series				
4	Animal	9.78	< .0001	people dog worm fish fly
	Property	4.05	< .004	sleeps eats has babies has bones has heart thinks
	Animal by property	1.27	n.s.	
7	Animal	5.59	< .002	people dog fish fly worm
	Property	2.88	< .03	eats sleeps has babies has heart has bones thinks
	Animal by property	2.79	< .0001	
10	Animal	12.7	< .0001	people dog fish fly worm
	Property	5.2	< .0007	eats has heart has babies sleeps thinks has bones
	Animal by property	4.1	< .0001	
Unfamiliar series				
4	Animal	4.50	< .005	people aardvark hammerhead stinkoo annelid
	Property	2.61	< .05	eats sleeps has bones has heart has babies thinks
	Animal by property	1.39	n.s.	
10	Animal	15.08	< .0001	people aardvark hammerhead stinkoo annelid
	Property	3.97	< .005	has babies eats sleeps has heart thinks has bones
	Animal by property	3.46	< .0001	
Adult	Animal	23.55	< .0001	people aardvark hammerhead stinkoo annelid
	Property	9.08	< .0001	eats has babies sleeps has heart has bones thinks
	Animal by property	8.19	< .0001	

Notes

Introduction

1. See Kuhn (1982) for a defense of the claim that successive theories are not mutually translatable. He shows how this version of the incommensurability doctrine does not entail that successive theories cannot disagree about data. He also discusses how the history of science is possible, in the light of this claim. The gist of his explanation is that although early theories (e.g., Galilean mechanics) cannot be stated in the terms of later theories (e.g., Newtonian mechanics), a modern reader can learn the language of the earlier theory and understand it in its own terms.

Chapter 1

1. I am indebted to Mimi Sinclair for this example.

Chapter 3

1. The sun was not included among the inanimate objects probed. Since the sun is the inanimate object most often judged alive, the data from the children in Experiment 1 of this chapter were not analyzed for comparison with those of chapter 1. This is why only the data on attributions of "alive" from Experiment 2 of this chapter are presented in chapter 1.

2. There were various reasons for the changes in properties. "Can get hurt" is ambiguous between being damaged and feeling pain. Also, it was assumed that older children would know that all animals eat. This first experiment was exploratory, and we did not envisage the problem of analysis that would ensue from having changed the animals and properties probed. These problems were of course rectified in later studies.

Chapter 6

1. Keil speaks of the child representing, or failing to represent, an ontological distinction. What is to count as evidence for such an all-or-none characteriza-

tion? If a child has at least one predicate that spans only and all animals and plants, does that mean he represents the ontological distinction between living and nonliving things? Most of the 5-year-olds in Keil's study would seem to meet this criterion. For half of them, the only such predicate was "grow." They judged that growth could be sensibly predicated of weeds, trees, dogs, men, etc., but that it did not make sense to say that rocks grow. As we saw in chapter 2, 5-year-olds most probably do not interpret "growth" biologically. Keil's data do not establish that "grow" can be sensibly predicated only of animals and plants. They merely establish that children do not think it predicable of rocks and chairs, the only two inanimate objects probed in the study. But what of stuffed animal collections, sand castles, bank accounts, crystals, etc.? Would not 5-year-olds agree that it is sensible to say of each of these that it could grow? Most likely "grow" simply means "get bigger" at this age, and all kinds of things can get bigger, including, of course, animals and plants. Indeed, one fourth grader in the study said that rocks can grow, explaining that they must grow, because he had seen little rocks.

There is a general lesson here. Because of the necessity of probing each predicate-term pair, plus each predicate's opposite-term pair, and because of the necessity of following up each judgment with an extensive probe, only a limited number of predicates and terms can be tested on a single child. Meaningful results can be found, of course, as when several children show the same consistent patterns of judgments of category errors, deviating from the adult pattern in an interpretable way. However, it is certainly possible to overestimate the systematicity in the data because of limited sampling. To give another example, Keil (1979, 1983a) makes much of the relatively little overattribution of animal predicates to inanimate objects, claiming that the ontological distinction between animals and inanimate objects is secure by the preschool years. The study in question (Keil 1983a) included terms for only two inanimate objects, a rock and a chair. As it was, 21% of the children judged that at least one of the predicates for living things could be applied sensibly to either the rock or the chair; 13% of the children judged that *all* of the predicates that apply to plants, or to plants and animals, could be applied to the rock. This is a higher level of attribution of biological properties to such inanimate objects than was found in the studies reported in chapter 2. This is to be expected. In the latter studies children were judging truth; Keil's study probed predicability. Predicability holds more widely than truth. What would have happened if Keil had included terms for objects that elicit childhood animism, such as clouds or the sun? In Keil 1979 only the predicate "alive" was included in the first study, and only "sorry," "asleep," and "alive" in the second. The inanimate objects were houses, chairs, milk, and water (Study 1) and cars (Study 2). Again, only very limited conclusions can be drawn from children's judgments that sentences like "The house is alive" are category mistakes; what if they had been asked to judge whether "The sun is alive" is a category mistake? Since a very high proportion of 5-year-olds judge "The sun is alive" to be true, it is unlikely that they would think this sentence silly.

In sum, we do not know whether the distinction between animals and inanimate objects has the status of an ontological distinction for young children. We know that the distinction between animals and *some* inanimate objects—rocks, chairs, houses, cars, water, and milk—does. There may indeed be properties that the preschool child knows can apply to all and only animals. In addition, there may be no predicates that apply sensibly to all and only living things, that is, animals and plants, below age 6 or 7. Keil's data suggest this to be the case, but he has not yet shown that this state of affairs actually holds. If it does, we would have another reflection of the contrast between the hold young children have on the concept of *animal* and the hold they have on the concept of *living thing*.

2. Although Mayr argues at length for the centrality of the concept *species* to modern biology, he also argues against "essentialism." The essentialism he decries requires that species be immutable. The notion of an essence in the philosophic literature on natural kind terms is not incompatible with Mayr's explication of the modern view of biological species.

References

Anglin, J. *Word, Object, and Conceptual Development*. New York: Norton & Company, 1977.

Anthony, S. *The Child's Discovery of Death*. New York: Harcourt, Brace, 1940.

Armstrong, S. L., Gleitman, L. R., and Gleitman, H. What some concepts might not be. *Cognition*, 1982, *13(3)*, 263–308.

Baillargeon, R., and Spelke, E. Object permanence in the 5-month-old infant. *Cognition*, in press.

Bernstein, A. C., and Cowan, P. A. Children's concepts of how people get babies. *Child Development*, 1975, *46*, 77–91.

Brown, A. L., and DeLoache, J. S. Skills, plans and self-regulation. In R. Siegler, ed., *Children's Thinking: What Develops?* Hillsdale, NJ: Lawrence Erlbaum, 1978.

Bullock, M., Gelman, R., and Baillargeon, R. The development of causal reasoning. In W. J. Friedman, ed., *The Developmental Psychology of Time*. New York: Academic Press, 1982.

Carey, S. Semantic development, state of the art. In E. Wanner and L. R. Gleitman, eds., *Language Acquisition, State of the Art*. New York: Cambridge University Press, 1982.

Carey, S. Cognitive development: The descriptive problem. In M. Gazzaniga, ed., *Handbook for Cognitive Neurology*. Hillsdale, NJ: Lawrence Erlbaum, 1983.

Carey, S. Constraints on semantic development. In J. Mehler and R. Fox, eds., *Neonate Cognition: Beyond the Blooming Buzzing Confusion*. Hillsdale, NJ: Lawrence Erlbaum, 1985.

Case, R. Structures and strictures: Some functional limitations on the course of cognitive growth. *Cognitive Psychology*, 1974, *6*, 544–573.

Chi, M., Glaser, R., and Rees, E. Expertise in problem solving. In R. Sternberg, ed., *Advances in the Psychology of Human Intelligence*. Vol. 1. Hillsdale, NJ: Lawrence Erlbaum, 1982.

Childers, P., and Wimmer, M. The concept of death in early childhood. *Child Development*, 1971, *42*, 1299–1301.

Clement, J. Students' preconceptions in introductory mechanics. *American Journal of Physics*, 1982, *50(1)*, 66–71.

Contento, I. Children's thinking about food and eating: A Piagetian-based study. *Journal of Nutrition Education*, 1981, *13*, 86–90.

Crider, C. Children's conceptions of the body interior. In R. Bibace and M. Walsh, eds., *Children's Conceptions of Health, Illness and Bodily Functions*. San Francisco: Jossey-Bass, 1981.

Damon, W. *The Social World of the Child*. San Francisco: Jossey-Bass, 1977.

Davis, S. *Of Ontology and Mental Representations*. Unpublished Master's thesis, MIT, 1979.

DeVries, R. *Constancy of Genetic Identity in the Years Three to Six*. Monographs of the Society for Research in Child Development 34. Chicago: University of Chicago Press, 1969.

Dolgin, K., and Behrend, D. Children's knowledge about animates and inanimates. *Child Development*, 1984, *55*, 1646–1650.

Emmerich, W. Nonmonotonic developmental trends in social cognition. In S. Strauss, ed., *U-Shaped Behavioral Growth*. New York: Academic Press, 1982.

Feyerabend, P. Explanation, reduction and empiricism. In H. Feigl and G. Maxwell, eds., *Minnesota Studies in Philosophy of Science*. Vol. 3. Minneapolis: University of Minnesota Press, 1962.

Fischer, K. W. A theory of cognitive development: the control and construction of hierarchies of skills. *Psychological Review*, 1980, *87*, 477–531.

Flavell, J. *Cognitive Development*. 2nd edition. Englewood Cliffs, NJ: Prentice-Hall, 1985.

Flavell, J., Flavell, E., and Green, F. Development of the appearance-reality distinction. *Cognitive Psychology*, 1983, *15(1)*, 95–120.

Fodor, J. A., Garrett, M. F., Walker, E. C., and Parkes, C. H. Against definitions. *Cognition*, 1972, *8*, 263–367.

Fraiberg, S. *The Magic Years*. New York: Scribners, 1959.

Gellert, E. Children's conceptions of the content and functions of the human body. *Genetic Psychology Monographs*, 1962, *65*, 291–411.

Gelman, R., and Baillargeon, R. A review of some Piagetian concepts. In J. H. Flavell and E. M. Markman, eds., *Carmichael's Manual of Child Psychology*. Vol. 3. New York: Wiley, 1983.

Gelman, R., Spelke, E., and Meck, E. What preschoolers know about animate and inanimate objects. In D. Rogers and J. Sloboda, eds., *The Acquisition of Symbolic Skills*. New York: Plenum, 1983.

Gelman, S., and Markman, E. Natural kind terms and induction in young children. Ms., 1984.

Gerard, A. B., and Mandler, J. M. Sentence anomaly and ontological knowledge. *Journal of Verbal Learning and Verbal Behavior*, 1983, *22*, 105–120.

Gibson, J. *Perceptual Development*. Boston: Houghton-Mifflin, 1969.

Goldman, R. J., and Goldman, J. D. G. How children perceive the origin of babies and the roles of mothers and fathers in procreation: A cross-national study. *Child Development*, 1982, *53*, 491–504.

Golinkoff, R., Harding, C. G., Carlson, V., and Sexton, M. E. The infant's perception of causal events: The distinction between animate and inanimate objects. In L. P. Lipsitt and C. Royce-Collier, eds., *Advances in Infancy Research*. Vol. 3. Norwood, NJ: Ablex, 1984.

Goodman, N. *Fact, Fiction and Forecast*. Indianapolis: Bobbs-Merrill, 1955.

Guardo, C. J., and Bohan, J. B. Development of self-identity in children. *Child Development*, 1971, *42*, 1909–1921.

Huang, I., and Lee, W. Experimental analysis of child animism. *Journal of Genetic Psychology*, 1945, *66*, 71–121.

Inhelder, B., and Piaget, J. *The Growth of Logical Thinking from Childhood to Adolescence*. New York: Basic Books, 1958.

Inhelder, B., and Piaget, J. *The Early Growth of Logic in the Child*. New York: Norton, 1969.

Johnson, C. N., and Wellman, H. M. Children's developing conceptions of the mind and the brain. *Child Development*, 1982, *53*, 222–234.

Keil, F. C. *Semantic and Conceptual Development: An Ontological Perspective*. Cambridge, MA: Harvard University Press, 1979.

Keil, F. C. On the emergence of semantic and conceptual distinctions. *Journal of Experimental Psychology: General*, 1983a, *112*, 357–385.

Keil, F. C. *Semantic Influences and the Acquisition of Word Meaning*. Berlin: Springer Verlag, 1983b.

Keil, F. C. The acquisition of natural kind and artifact terms. In A. Marrar and W. Demopoulos, eds., *Conceptual Change*. Norwood, NJ: Ablex, in press.

Klayman, J. Judgment and justification in concept development: The case of animism. Paper presented at the meeting of the Society for Research in Child Development, San Francisco, 1979.

Klingberg, G. The distinction between living and not living among 7–10 year old children, with some remarks concerning the so-called animism controversy. *Journal of Genetic Psychology*, 1957, *90*, 227–238.

Klingensmith, S. Child animism: What the child means by "alive." *Child Development*, 1953, *42*, 51–61.

Kohlberg, L. A. A cognitive-developmental analysis of children's sex-role concepts and attitudes. In E. Maccoby, ed., *The Development of Sex Differences*. Stanford, CA: Stanford University Press, 1966.

Koocher, G. P. Talking with children about death. *American Journal of Orthopsychiatria*, 1974, *44*, 404–410.

Kuhn, T. S. *The Structure of Scientific Revolutions*. Chicago: University of Chicago Press, 1962.

Kuhn, T. S. Concepts of cause. In T. S. Kuhn, ed., *The Essential Tension*. Chicago: University of Chicago Press, 1977a.

Kuhn, T. S. A function for thought experiments. In T. S. Kuhn, ed., *The Essential Tension*. Chicago: University of Chicago Press, 1977b.

Kuhn, T. S. Commensurability, comparability, communicability. *PSA1982*. Vol. 2.

Larkin, J. H. Enriching formal knowledge: A model for learning to solve problems in physics. In J. R. Anderson, ed., *Cognitive Skills and Their Acquisition*. Hillsdale, NJ: Lawrence Erlbaum, 1981.

Larkin, J. H. The role of problem representation in physics. In D. Gentner and A. Stevens, eds., *Mental Models*. Hillsdale, NJ: Lawrence Erlbaum, 1983.

Larkin, J. H., McDermott, J., Simon, D. P., and Simon, H. A. Models of competence in solving physics problems. *Cognitive Science*, 1980, *4*, 317–345.

Laurendeau, M., and Pinard, A. *Causal Thinking in the Child: A Genetic and Experimental Approach*. New York: International Universities Press, 1962.

Leslie, A. M. The perception of causality in infants. *Perception*, 1982, *11*, 173–186.

Looft, W. R. Children's judgments of age. *Child Development*, 1971, *42*, 1282–1284.

Looft, W. R., and Bartz, W. H. Animism revisited. *Psychological Bulletin*, 1969, *71*, 1–19.

McCloskey, M. Naive theories of motion. In D. Gentner and A. Stevens, eds., *Mental Models*. Hillsdale, NJ: Lawrence Erlbaum, 1983.

McKie, D., and Heathcote, N. H. V. *The Discovery of Specific and Latent Heats*. London: Edward Arnold, 1935.

Maccoby, E. E. *Social Development*. New York: Harcourt, Brace, Jovanovich, 1980.

Marcus, D. E., and Overton, W. F. The development of cognitive gender constancy and sex role preferences. *Child Development*, 1978, *49*, 434–444.

Mayr, E. *The Growth of Biological Thought*. Cambridge, MA: Harvard University Press, 1982.

Mitchell, M. *The Child's Attitude toward Death*. New York: Schocken Books, 1967.

Nagy, M. H. The child's theories concerning death. *Journal of Genetic Psychology*, 1948, *73*, 3–27.

Nagy, M. H. Children's conceptions of some bodily functions. *Journal of Genetic Psychology*, 1953, *83*, 199–216.

Piaget, J. *The Child's Conception of the World*. London: Routledge and Kegan Paul, 1929.

Piaget, J. *Le développement de la notion de temps chez l'enfant*. Paris: Presses Universitaires de France, 1946.

Piaget, J. *On the Development of Memory and Identity*. Worcester, MA: Clark University Press, 1968.

Piaget, J., and Inhelder, B. *Le développement des quantités chez l'enfant*. Neuchâtel: Delachaux et Niestlé, 1941.

Putnam, H. The analytic and the synthetic. In *Minnesota Studies in the Philosophy of Science*. Vol. 3. Minneapolis: University of Minnesota Press, 1962.

Quine, W. V. Two dogmas of empiricism. *Philosophical Review*, 1951, *60*, 20–43.

Quine, W. V. Natural kinds. In W. V. Quine, *Ontological Relativity and Other Essays*. New York: Columbia University Press, 1969.

Rips, L. J. Induction about natural categories. *Journal of Verbal Learning and Verbal Behavior*, 1975, *14*, 665–681.

Rosch, E. Principles of categorization. In E. Rosch and B. Lloyd, eds., *Cognition and Categorization*. Hillsdale, NJ: Lawrence Erlbaum, 1978.

Russell, R. W., and Dennis, W. Studies in animism: II. Development of animism. *Journal of Genetic Psychology*, 1940, *46*, 353–366.

Safier, G. A study in relationships between the life and death concepts in children. *Journal of Genetic Psychology*, 1964, *105*, 283–294.

Schwartz, S. Natural kind terms. *Cognition*, 1979, *7*, 301–315.

Shatz, M., Wellman, H. M., and Silber, S. The acquisition of mental verbs: A systematic investigation of the first reference to mental state. *Cognition*, 1983, *14*, 301–322.

Shultz, T. R. *Rules of Causal Attribution*. Monographs of the Society for Research in Child Development. Chicago: University of Chicago Press, 1982.

Smedslund, J. The acquisition of conservation of substance and weight in children: III. Extinction of conservation of weight acquired "normally" and by means of empirical controls on a balance. *Scandinavian Journal of Psychology,* 1961, *2,* 85–87.

Smith, C. Children's understanding of natural language hierarchies. *Journal of Experimental Child Psychology,* 1979, *27,* 437–458.

Smith, C., Carey, S., and Wiser, M. On differentiation: A case study of the development of the concepts of size, weight, and density. *Cognition,* in press.

Smith, E. E., and Medin, D. L. *Categories and Concepts.* Cambridge, MA: Harvard University Press, 1981.

Sommers, F. Types and ontology. *Philosophical Review,* 1963, *72,* 327–363.

Suppe, F. *The Structure of Scientific Theories.* Urbana, IL: University of Illinois Press, 1974.

Thompson, S. K. Gender labels and early sex-role development. *Child Development,* 1975, *46,* 339–347.

Thompson, S. K., and Bentler, P. M. The priority of cues in sex discrimination by children and adults. *Developmental Psychology,* 1971, *5,* 181–185.

Toulmin, S. *The Philosophy of Science: An Introduction.* London: Hutchinson, 1953.

Tversky, A. Features and similarity. *Psychological Review,* 1977, *84,* 327–352.

Von Hug-Hellmuth, H. The child's concept of death. *Psychoanalytic Quarterly,* 1964, *34,* 499–516.

Wellman, H. M. A child's theory of mind: The development of conceptions of cognition. In S. R. Yussen, ed., *The Growth of Reflection.* New York: Academic Press, 1985.

Wellman, H. M., and Johnson, C. N. Children's understanding of food and its functions: A preliminary study of the development of concepts of nutrition. *Journal of Applied Developmental Psychology,* 1982, *3,* 135–148.

Wexler, K., and Culicover, P. *Formal Principles of Language Acquisition.* Cambridge, MA: MIT Press, 1980.

White, E., Elsom, B., and Prawat, R. Children's conceptions of death. *Child Development,* 1978, *49,* 307–310.

Wiser, M., and Carey, S. When heat and temperature were one. In D. Gentner and A. Stevens, eds., *Mental Models.* Hillsdale, NJ: Lawrence Erlbaum, 1983.

Wittgenstein, L. *Philosophical Investigations.* New York: Macmillan, 1953.

Index

Alive
  concept of (*see* Living thing)
  constraining inductive projections,
    150–159
  introductory questions, 25–26
  meaning of word "alive," 16–18, 25–26,
    148, 182
Anglin, J., 18, 73, 78
Animal, 72–76, 89, 183, 186–187
  concept of animal constraining inductive
    projection, 104–108, 118, 143–146, 183
  meaning of word "animal," 13, 73, 140,
    183
  as ontologically basic, 166–168
Animism. *See* Childhood animism
Anthony, S., 60
Anthropomorphic traits, 21, 73
Appearance-reality distinction, 11,
    178–179
Application of definition, 75, 85–86,
    98–100
Aristotelian mechanics, 5
Asymmetry of projection, 128, 134,
    135–139, 145, 159, 185, 187, 195
Attribution patterns. *See* Patterns of
    attribution

Babies. *See* Patterns of attribution;
    Reproduction
Baillargeon, R., 13, 16, 191–192, 194
Behrend, D., 18, 74, 78, 107–108
Bernstein, A. C., 54–60
Biological explanation, 41, 72, 188–189,
    194
Biological knowledge, 41, 71, 76–77,
    82–83, 96–98, 109–110, 134, 139, 147,
    160

Biology, intuitive, 72, 161, 188–190
Block, Eliza
  concept of death, 26–27
  concept of growth, personal identity,
    65–68
Blood, 46–48
Bodily organs, 42–51. *See also* Patterns
    of attribution
Bodily processes, 43–51, 54–69, 184
Bohan, J. B., 67
Bulluck, M., 16, 194

Carter, R., 149
Category error, category mistake, 12, 163
  biological predicates, 166–169
  "heavy" and "light," 170
Causation, 15–16, 193–194. *See also*
    Intentional causality; Mechanical
    causality
Characteristic features, 176
Chi, M., 1, 3, 186
Childhood animism, 10, 15–40
Circulatory system, 46–48. *See also*
    Patterns of attribution
Classical view of concepts, 19–20
Clement, J., 1, 7
Clinical interview
  what is alive, 16–17, 20–22, 23–26,
    35
  death, 61–65
  reproduction, 54–60
Coalescence, 5–6, 197
  animal and plant, 189, 199
  natural and violent motion, 5
Comparison to exemplar, comparison to
  people, 75, 86–87, 98–100, 120–125

Conceptual change, 5–6, 189–190, 197–199
coalescence, 5–6, 197, 199 (*see also* Coalescence)
differentiation, 5–6, 197–199 (*see also* Differentiation)
ontological core, 6 (*see also* Ontologically basic categories)
property reanalyzed as a relation, 197
Conceptual combination model, 141
Conscious criterion for life, 35–39
Constraints on induction, 194–195
Container theory, 48
Contento, I., 44
Cowan, P. A., 54–60
Crider, C., 47–48
Crossing patterns, 120–124

Damon, W., 53
Death, 26–28, 60–65
Deductive inference, 75, 83–85, 98–100, 192–193
Defecation, 46
Dennis, W., 28
Density, 169–170, 190–191
Differentiation, 5–6, 197–199
alive-dead and alive-inanimate, 25–29, 189
attribution patterns, animal properties, 79–82, 94–96, 116–118
average velocity and instantaneous velocity, 5
heat and temperature, 198–199
intuitive biology and intuitive psychology, 139, 180
mind and brain, 50
size, weight, and density, 170, 198–199
whole body and internal parts, 47–48
Digestion, 43–46, 47. *See also* Patterns of attribution
Diverging patterns, 120–124
Dolgin, K., 18, 74, 78, 107–108
Domain general change, 190
Domain specific change, 190–191

Emmerich, W., 52
Essence, 174–175
Explanation of development, 199–200

Familiarity, 88
Father, role of, in procreation, 57–60

Flavell, J., 11, 13, 178, 194
Foundational concepts, 193
Fraiberg, S., 42–43

Galilean mechanics, 5
Gelman, R., 13, 14, 16, 74, 78, 107–108, 191–192, 194
Gelman, S., 12, 171–173
Gender, 51–54
Gillert, E., 42–48, 50
Glaser, R., 1, 3, 186
Goldman, R. J., and Goldman, J. D. G., 54–60
Golgi, 148–158
Goodman, N., 195–197
Gricean implicature, 139
Growth, 65–69
Guardo, C. J., 67

Heart, 46–58. *See also* Patterns of attribution
Human behavior, 69. *See also* Psychology
Human body
container theory, 48
insides, 42–48 (*see also* Patterns of attribution)
most important part, 43

Impetus theory, 7
Inductive projection, 8–9, 113–116, 161, 185
from animal and plant, 149, 155–156
constraints on, 195–197
and natural kind terms, 171–173
from single animal or plant, 152–155
from two animals, 141–145, 156–158
Information processing model, 75, 98–102, 108–109, 111–113, 125, 146–147, 185
conceptual combination model, 141
guessing model, 76, 101–104, 111–112, 124
Model Type I, 75 (*see also* Deductive inference)
Model Type II, 75 (*see also* Application of definition)
Model Type III, 75 (*see also* Comparison to exemplar, comparison to people)
Two-stage model, 141